AF413126

Empires and Ancient Civilizations

An Enthralling Journey Through Powerful Societies Across History, from Mesopotamia and Egypt to the Indus Valley, and the Forces That Shaped the World

Free limited time bonus

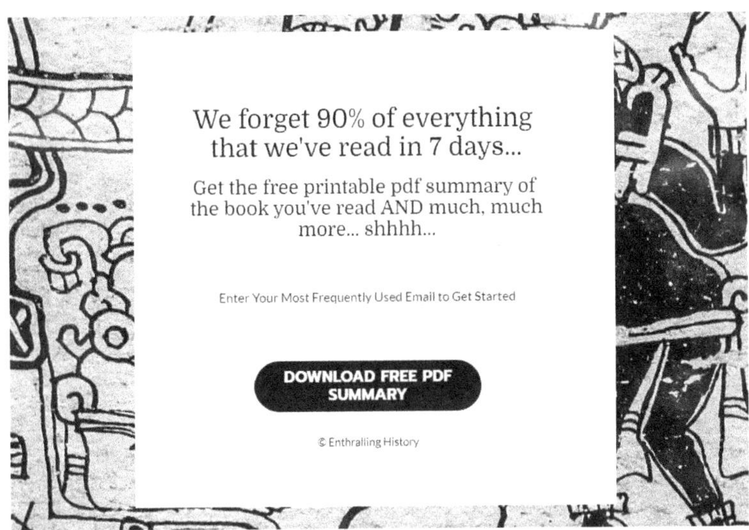

Stop for a moment. We have a free bonus set up for you. The problem is this: we forget 90% of everything that we read after 7 days. Crazy fact, right? Here's the solution: we've created a printable, 1-page pdf summary for this book that you're reading now. All you have to do to get your free pdf summary is to go to the following website:

https://livetolearn.lpages.co/enthrallinghistory/

Or, Scan the QR code!

Once you do, it will be intuitive. Enjoy, and thank you!

Table of Contents

Part 1: History of Empires

An Enthralling Journey through the Rise and Fall of Dominant Powers across the Ages

Introduction

Ur-Zababa, king of Kish, paced back and forth in a rage. "That Sargon! Who is he? Nothing more than the gardener's son! Not even that—he's a foundling! No one knows where he's really from. And now, the goddess Inanna is showering her favor on him. All the gods are against me! That's the thanks I get for making a nobody my cupbearer. Now, I've got to get rid of him before he usurps my throne! What to do?"

Ur-Zababa scowled as he smoothed his long beard. Suddenly, he clapped his hands, his face beaming. "I know! I'll have my metalsmith push him into a statue mold and pour molten bronze over him. Sargon will become my new bronze statue!" Ur-Zababa almost leaped for joy as he rubbed his hands together. "Ha! I'll even build a little temple for my new statue. No one will know it's really Sargon."

Unfortunately for Ur-Zababa, his plot fell through. Sargon survived and went on to establish the world's first empire in what is today's Iraq.

An empire is a group of countries or states governed by one ruler. It usually includes multiple language groups and ethnicities but has a strong central government. Many empires have risen and fallen around the globe since Sargon's Akkadian Empire. This book explores the compelling stories of some of history's most pivotal empires. How did they change the world? Why did they rise to greatness, only to come crashing down? Who were the key figures, and what made them exceptional? How did life-changing events define their trajectory? What were the cultural dynamics and the human stories?

Diving into the histories of our planet's extraordinary empires helps us understand our world today. How did we get where we are now? What were the watershed moments along the way? How did ancient cultures influence our beliefs and worldviews today? What are the inspirational and motivational stories from these empires? Do they warn us of what *not* to do?

This book will not bore you with lists of dates and dry facts. It is full of spellbinding stories of the fascinating men and women who built empires and others who tore them down. It is the tale of winners and losers who changed the world. Some were ingenious role models, others were diabolically destructive, yet they all set the stage for today's world. Unwrapping the histories of these empires around the globe helps us understand today's turbulent political landscape. Let's travel around the world and unlock their legacies.

Chapter 1: Sargon the Great and Mesopotamia

Tales of baby boys in baskets floating down rivers appear in several ancient cultures. The Nile carried the baby Moses along until the pharaoh's daughter rescued him. Romulus and Remus sailed down the Tiber River to be suckled by a she-wolf. Yet long before the founders of Israel and Rome, a baby floated down the Euphrates River in ancient Iraq, according to the *Legend of Sargon of Akkadê*:

> Sargon, the mighty king, king of Agade, am I... My mother conceived me in secret; she gave birth to me in concealment. She set me in a basket of rushes; she sealed my lid with bitumen. She cast me into the river, but it did not rise over me.
>
> The water carried me to Akki, the drawer of water. He lifted me out as he dipped his jar into the river. Akki took me as his son; he raised me and made me his gardener. While I was a gardener, (the goddess) Ishtar granted me her love.[1]

Almost 1,700 years later, the Neo-Assyrians placed Sargon's story, inscribed on clay tablets, in the Library of Ashurbanipal at Nineveh, the capital of their empire. The ancient library held texts the Assyrians collected while raiding other civilizations. Were these tablets copies of

---

[1] *The Legend of Sargon of Akkadê, c. 2300 BCE* (Fordham University, Internet Ancient History Sourcebook, 1999). https://sourcebooks.fordham.edu/ancient/2300sargon1.asp.

what Sargon himself wrote about his origins? No one knows, although most historians think someone else wrote his story much later.

Before Sargon arrived on the scene, what was ancient Iraq's political, social, and cultural landscape? What great civilizations had already left their mark on the region? How did Sargon unite these cultures to form the world's first empire?

Weirdly, although most people have heard of the Babylonian and Assyrian empires that came later, many people are not familiar with Sargon's Akkadian Empire, the first in the world. This chapter aims to correct that!

Why Is Ancient Mesopotamia Called the "Cradle of Civilization"?

The ancient Greeks gave the name "Mesopotamia" to the region that includes today's Iraq and parts of Iran, Kuwait, Saudi Arabia, Syria, and Turkey. Mesopotamia means "between the rivers," as its most important region lay between the Euphrates and Tigris rivers. These two rivers that emptied into the Persian Gulf made Mesopotamia the ancient world's key trade hub.

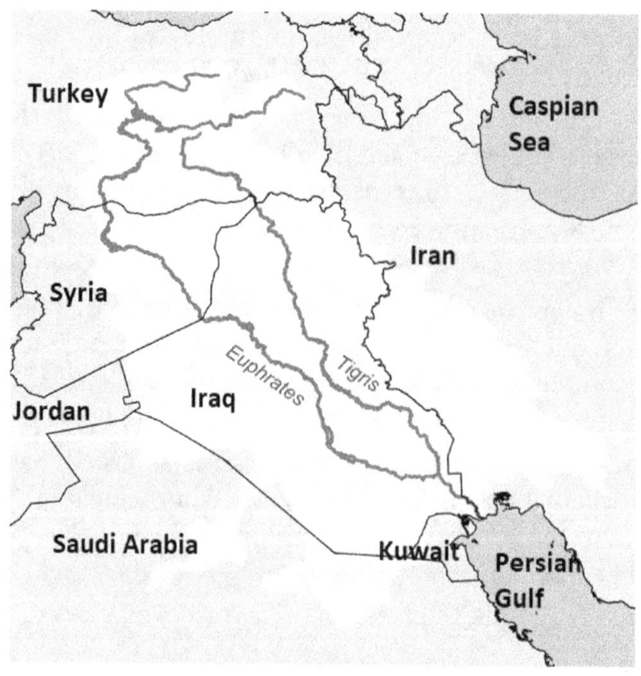

Mesopotamia was the light area on this modern map of the Middle East.[1]

Mesopotamia is called the "cradle of civilization" because its history is an awe-inspiring account of beginnings. The Mesopotamians produced an astounding number of innovations. Around 6000 BCE, the Hassuna, Samarra, Halaf, and Ubaid civilizations emerged in ancient Iraq. They herded cattle, goats, and sheep and built sun-dried brick houses. They began cultivating the land with simple plows to grow barley, flax, emmer wheat, and lentils. Using stone mortars, these ancient people ground the grains into flour to make dough. They baked the dough in clay ovens like the *tannūr* (tandoor) ovens still used today in the Middle East and Indian subcontinent.

The Ubaid people built Eridu around 5400 BCE near the Persian Gulf. The ancient *Sumerian King List* says it was the first city (and it most likely was). Eridu covered twenty-five acres, and its population grew to about four thousand people. It had a temple, infrastructure, a central government, and irrigation canals that watered the farmland around the city. The Ubaid burial grounds had small models of the masted reed sailboats they used to navigate the Persian Gulf.

The Ubaid also built the towns of Ur and Uruk around 5000 BCE. They abandoned Ur and Eridu around 3700 BCE when climate change brought desertification. Uruk was on the Euphrates River, so it survived with a steady water source. The Sumerian people rebuilt Ur and Eridu several centuries later when the climate became more favorable. Ur was the childhood home of the patriarch Abraham during the late Akkadian Empire.

The Sumerians, who called themselves the "black-haired people," may have been a remnant of the Ubaid people or a new civilization that migrated into southern Mesopotamia. They rebuilt the Ubaid cities and made stunning innovations. The Sumerians introduced the world to the first writing system by 3500 BCE. They used reeds to scratch tiny pictures (pictographs) into soft clay that hardened into tablets. Over time, the pictographs became abstract wedge-shaped glyphs in a system known as cuneiform writing. Thankfully, thousands of cuneiform clay tablets survived to the present day, revealing incredible insight into ancient cultures, including the Akkadians, Assyrians, Babylonians, Elamites, and Hittites.

The world's first known wheel was a potter's wheel invented in Iran by 5200 BCE. The Sumerians took it to the next level around 3750 BCE by inventing the axle and building wheeled carts pulled by donkeys. Before long, soldiers rode to war in four-wheeled chariots. The time measurements we use today—the twelve-hour day, the sixty-minute hour, and the sixty-second minute—all came from the Sumerians. By 2600 BCE, the Sumerians developed multiplication, division, cubic and square roots, and simple geometry.

A decorative box crafted around 2600 BCE pictures this early chariot.[2]

By the time Akki, the palace gardener, pulled the baby Sargon from the river, various Sumerian city-states (a large, strong city and its surrounding villages and towns) had become powerful enough to conquer and rule neighboring city-states. These were not true empires because everyone shared the same culture and language.

By 3000 BCE, Semitic-speaking shepherds migrated in from Syria and settled throughout Mesopotamia, mostly in the north. One group was the Akkadians, whose language traces them to Ebla in ancient Syria. Ebla was a trade partner with the city of Kish in Sumer, where Sargon grew up.

The Akkadian language later evolved into the Assyrian and Babylonian dialects. The Akkadians settled Agade (Akkad), which later became Sargon's capital. Agade's location is a mystery. All we know is that it was on the Tigris River. It lies hidden somewhere under the blowing desert sands.

What Are the Legends of Sargon's Origins and Early Life?

The *Sumerian King List*, written in the late third millennium BCE, says that after the Great Flood, the first city to hold "kingship" was Kish, about fifty miles south of today's Baghdad.[2] "Kingship" meant that a city-state dominated other cities. Over the centuries, kingship shifted to Eridu, Ur, Uruk, and other cities. However, Kish retook power several times.

Pictographs from Kish, circa 3500 BCE, that later evolved into cuneiform writing[3]

Sargon's life story picks back up in the badly damaged *Sargon and Ur-Zababa Tablet*.[3] Despite its storied history, Kish fell into ruins until a new king, Ur-Zababa, came on the scene. He rebuilt the irrigation canals and got the pottery and metalworking factories up and running again. During Ur-Zababa's reign, Sargon grew up in Kish as the adopted son of the palace gardener. No one knows what Sargon's real name was. The name Sargon (*Sarru-kin* in Akkadian) was a title meaning "true king."

One night, Sargon brought garden produce to the palace kitchen. King Ur-Zababa was asleep and having an unsettling dream triggered by the high gods Enlil and An. Something in the dream compelled Ur-Zababa to appoint Sargon as his cupbearer when he awakened. A cupbearer's job was to pour the king's wine and taste it to check for poison. Because they

---

[2] *Sumerian King List*, trans. Jean-Vincent Scheil, Stephen Langdon, and Thorkild Jacobsen (Livius, updated 2020), https://www.livius.org/sources/content/anet/266-the-sumerian-king-list/#Translation.

[3] *Sargon and Ur-Zababa*, The Electronic Text Corpus of Sumerian Literature (Oxford: Faculty of Oriental Studies, University of Oxford, 2006), https://etcsl.orinst.ox.ac.uk/cgi-bin/etcsl.cgi?text=t.2.1.4#.

were always nearby, cupbearers tended to be informal advisors to the kings. Becoming the king's cupbearer was a considerable step up for the humble palace gardener.

After about a week, King Ur-Zababa received news so terrifying that he wet himself. Most likely, he heard that Lugal-Zage-Si, king of Uruk, was on his way to attack Kish. Lugal-Zage-Si was a cruel conqueror who had already swept southern Sumer into his mini-empire. Now, Kish was his next target.

That night, Sargon groaned in his sleep, and the palace servants told the king they believed Sargon had had a vision. Ur-Zababa called Sargon to him.

"Tell me about your dream!" he urged.

Sargon paled but reluctantly told him, "Sire, I had a vision of the goddess Inanna. She...well...she was drowning you in a river of blood."

Ur-Zababa dismissed Sargon but chewed his lips in horror. "The dream is a prophecy! Inanna has made Sargon her favorite. She wants him to be king, which means he will kill me. I'll have to strike first!"

Thus, as our introduction story detailed, the king plotted to transform Sargon into a bronze statue. Carrying out his plan, he sent Sargon on an errand to Beliš-Tikal, the metalworker.

However, Inanna intervened. "Don't go inside the house!" she told Sargon.

Sargon met the metalworker at his front gate and survived the murder plot. King Ur-Zababa turned white when Sargon cheerfully walked back into the palace. Now, the king had to find another way to eliminate his rival.

Ur-Zababa sent Sargon to King Lugal-Zage-Si to deliver peace terms. Sargon was aware that his king meant to kill him, so he decided to switch sides and offer his services to Lugal-Zage-Si. He knew Kish inside and out

Inanna (Ishtar) was a chief Mesopotamian goddess. '

and could help the king with the best plan of attack. Lugal-Zage-Si conquered Kish, placing Sargon as his vassal-king over the city around 2334 BCE. Thus, the child found in the river now ruled the great city of Kish.

A bronze sculpture found in Nineveh, probably Sargon the Great [5]

How Did Sargon Conquer and Unify the Sumerian City-States?

After Sargon helped him defeat Kish, Lugal-Zage-Si now controlled Sumer (today's southern Iraq). Sargon unsettled Lugal-Zage-Si when he turned his attention to northern Mesopotamia, uniting the Akkadian-speaking shepherds. The *Sargon and Ur-Zababa* tablet mentions an apparent intrigue between Sargon and Lugal-Zage-Si's wife, which no doubt added fuel to the fire. With his Akkadian army, Sargon marched on Uruk, the capital of his former ally.

Lugal-Zage-Si called up fifty kings of Sumer's city-states to march with him against Sargon. He thought Sargon would yield when he realized he faced such a formidable force. However, the great king soon received such horrifying news that he fell backward on the ground, exclaiming, "Alas! Sargon is not giving up!"

Sargon not only refused to back down but also utterly crushed the Sumerians. He flattened Uruk's walls and forced Lugal-Zage-Si to wear a yoke in shame. On the idol of Enlil, Lugal-Zage-Si's patron god, Sargon inscribed his breathtaking victory.

Of course, the Sumerians in the other cities did not throw open their gates to welcome Sargon. They were happy he got rid of the despot Lugal-Zage-Si, yet they wanted to return to their independent city-state system. Sargon had to march around Sumer, conquering each city in turn. It was a watershed moment when he finally held all of ancient Iraq. The Akkadian people had now replaced the Sumerians as rulers of Mesopotamia. Semitic-speaking people—the Akkadians, Assyrians, and Babylonians—governed ancient Iraq for most of the next 1,800 years until Cyrus the Great invaded from Persia (Iran).

Sargon was just getting started on his massive empire. He marched into ancient Syria, Turkey, Lebanon, and Canaan (today's Israel and Palestine), conquering as far as the Mediterranean Sea. Sargon then turned east, crossed the Zagros Mountains into Elam (Iran), and captured its capital city of Susa.

How did Sargon transform his military into such an indomitable powerhouse? He bragged of winning thirty-four wars and conquered territory stretching from the Mediterranean Sea to Iran's deserts. Before Sargon, no king had a full-time army. The fighting men were farmers, fishermen, craftsmen, and shopkeepers in the off-season. Warfare typically occurred in the summer, between the planting and harvesting of crops. Sargon had the world's first standing army of 5,400 men who could fight in any season. He could march his army five hundred miles to Syria without worrying about getting back in time for harvest.

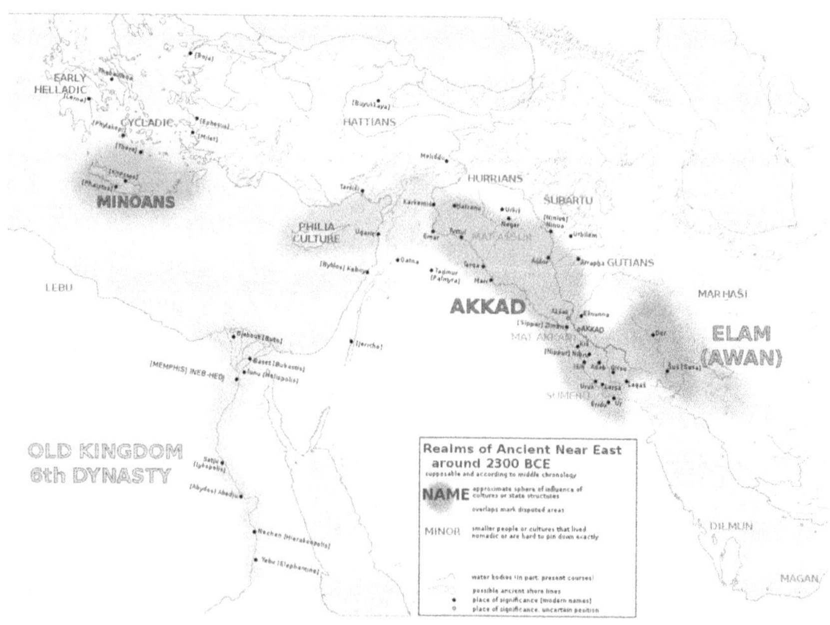

Sargon the Great's Empire [6]

Sargon also had a team of bureaucrats in charge of logistics. They arranged for siege engines to be in the right place at the right time. They ensured the troops had plenty of beer and bread and that the chariot horses and pack animals had water and feed. Cuneiform tablets that have survived to the present day document all the organization involved in maintaining Sargon's war machine.

Carvings show that the Akkadian army used spears, battle axes, bows and arrows, maces, throwing clubs, and slingshots. While the Sumerians used basic bows, the Akkadians were among the first in the world to use the composite bow with bronze arrowheads, revolutionizing warfare. The simple bows used by the Sumerians were a single piece of wood. The composite bows had layers of wood, with animal sinew and horn all glued together. Arrows shot from a composite bow flew two to three times faster and farther than arrows from a simple bow, making them far more lethal. Since they were lighter than regular bows, composite bows could be shot from horseback or chariots.

The cities that Sargon and his successors attacked had high, thick defensive walls surrounding them. As illustrated on an ancient cylinder seal, the Akkadian army had multiple ways to attack these cities.

What was a cylinder seal? The ancient Mesopotamians used these cylinders to sign their names. They were about four inches long with engraved pictures and cuneiform writing. The owner rolled the seal in a piece of damp clay, leaving the imprint of the image and words. The clay hardened to form a small disk. Tens of thousands of these cylinder seals or the disks with their imprints have survived, opening a window into Mesopotamia's ancient culture.

A battle scene from an Akkadian cylinder seal[7]

A seal from an Akkadian city depicts the tower of a city wall with soldiers at the top. Two chariots at the top right and left attack the city. At the bottom left, two soldiers push what looks like a battering ram toward the tower. Two other soldiers use the battering ram as a ramp to run up to the top of the tower. Meanwhile, at the bottom right of the scene, a soldier is pushing a tower-like contraption on wheels with a soldier inside it toward the city tower. This was probably used to protect soldiers while they shot at the city and may also have been a way to climb into the city tower.

What Administrative Systems Did Sargon Use in His Expansive Empire?

Sargon's sweeping empire encompassed multiple nations and ethnicities. He centralized the government, requiring all the lands to pay taxes. The Akkadians maintained meticulous records inscribed on clay tablets. The surviving tablets reveal their marriage arrangements, business deals, taxes, property sales, family archives, and history.

Each region kept its religion and other cultural traditions, but Akkadian was the empire's official language. Although Sumerian and Akkadian belong to different language families, they significantly influenced one another due to continuous interaction. By the end of the Akkadian Empire, Sumerian was mainly used only in temple worship, and Akkadian became the lingua franca.

What Challenges Did Sargon and His Successors Face?

It is one thing to conquer an empire and another to hold it together. The *Legend of Sargon* tells of an uprising in central and northern Mesopotamia:

> In my old age of fifty-five, all the lands revolted against me, and they besieged me in Agade, but the old lion still had teeth and claws. I went forth to battle and defeated them: I knocked them over and destroyed their vast army.[4]

---

[4] *The Legend of Sargon of Akkadê, c. 2300 BCE* (Fordham University, Internet Ancient History Sourcebook, 1999). https://sourcebooks.fordham.edu/ancient/2300sargon1.asp.

Although Sargon thought he was old at fifty-five, he lived about twenty more years. Six Sumerian city-states rebelled within days after his son Rimush took the throne. Sargon had trounced them all five decades earlier, and they dared not rechallenge him. Yet, they may have guessed that Rimush lacked the teeth and claws his father had. It was a deadly misjudgment.

Rimush's revenge was swift and brutal. In his inscriptions, he boasted that he flattened cities, even digging their foundations out of the ground. He massacred 110,000 men in the six cities, sent 29,000 to cut stone in Elam's quarries, and exiled 25,000 Sumerians. He did not destroy two of the now-empty rebel cities—Umma and Lagash. Instead, he handed them over to his Akkadian supporters.

Naram-Sin, grandson of Sargon[8]

Rimush's own officials ambushed and murdered him, making his brother Manishtushu the next king for fifteen years. His son Naram-Sin became the Akkadian Empire's fourth king. Almost immediately, Naram-Sin had to confront the revolt of eighteen Sumerian cities. He defeated them so brilliantly that the citizens of Agade, the empire's capital, asked him to be their city's patron god, equal to Inanna and the other deities. Naram-Sin allowed them to build a temple to him, calling himself "the mighty god of Agade," which brought down heaven's wrath.

His downfall—and the empire's—had begun. The rains stopped. Plagues and famine struck. Gutian tribes from the east invaded and stole livestock. Farmers abandoned their fields and orchards. Without irrigation, the crops and fruit trees died, and the desert reclaimed Agade. The once-mighty empire crumbled, leaving barely a trace.

What Legacy Did the Akkadian Empire Leave Behind?

Sargon and his successors built a road network snaking out from the Euphrates and Tigris rivers. These roads reached every point of the empire. The Akkadians developed the world's first postal system and even used envelopes, although their "letters" were clay tablets. They applied a thin layer of clay over the tablet to provide privacy, which was chipped off when it reached its destination. A common language—Akkadian—unified much of the Middle East. As previously mentioned, Sargon also formed the world's first full-time military. Ultimately, the Akkadian Empire set the framework for the following Babylonian and Assyrian empires.

Chapter 2: The Great Wall and the Qin Dynasty

"He's dead! The emperor is dead!" the chief eunuch, Zhao Gao, whispered to Li Si, the prime minister.

"What? He was in perfect health yesterday!"

"He died during the night." The eunuch wrung his hands. "I...think it might have been what he drank last night. He was certain it would give him immortality."

"You mean that cursed mercury?" Li Si paced back and forth. "You're probably right. He always kept his sword in his lap for fear of assassins. Now, he has accidentally killed himself!"

"What do we do? We're in the middle of nowhere!" asked Zhao Gao, worriedly.

Li Si frowned. "We must keep his death a secret until we return to the palace. Otherwise, they'll put Fusu on the throne before we get there. You and I both know that Fusu is *not* the right person!"

"Well, he's the oldest son...but...are you thinking Ying Huhai?" Zhao Gao asked.

"Exactly! He's young and has no strength of character. You and I will run the empire!"

Zhao Gao smiled. Then his brow furled. "But the emperor...his body will start stinking! It will take weeks to get back to Xianyang."

"Fish! *Chòu yú*—stinky fish! You know how he loved the stuff. We'll fill two wagons in front of and behind his carriage. Everyone will think the foul smell is the fish."

Qin Shi Huang, the first Qin emperor [9]

Thus, China's first emperor came to an ignominious end. But how did his reign begin? How did Qin Shi Huang unify the warring states, implement sweeping reforms, and initiate grand architectural projects that left an indelible mark on China's history? What part did ambition and complex palace intrigue play in China's first, albeit brief, imperial dynasty? Let's explore the answers to these questions through the pages of ancient texts.

The *Shiji* is an ancient comprehensive history of China stretching back to the mythical Yellow Emperor (2697 BCE).[5] The author, Sima Qian, compiled it using older documents and finished it in the early first century BCE.

The *Shiji* and other Chinese histories tell of the Warring States period (475–221 BCE) that spelled the end of the Zhou dynasty (1046–256 BCE), China's longest dynasty. As the Zhou dynasty grew weaker, China's states declared independence, and the seven most powerful states absorbed the smaller ones. Hundreds of wars raged between the seven states in the Warring States era as each attempted to snatch dominance.

Meanwhile, the northern and western states fought the Xiongnu, nomadic horseback-riding tribes who roamed the steppes of today's Mongolia and southeastern Russia. The Xiongnu became such a threat that the Chinese began building miles of walls about thirteen feet high to keep them out.

What Were the Legalist Principles Underpinning the Qin Administration?

In the Warring States period, the highly organized Qin state followed the philosophy of Legalism. It taught that most people let self-interest lead them astray. People are more likely to be corrupt than ethical. Thus, a government must have strict, harshly enforced laws while rewarding those with integrity.

A prominent Qin statesman, Shang Yang (390–338 BCE), promoted Legalism. He believed everyone, regardless of status, should follow the same standard of behavior and be equal before the law. Shang Yang's land reforms upended the ancient aristocratic landowner system and introduced private land ownership.

His Legalist views transformed warfare in China. Before Shang Yang, war followed strict codes of honor. An army on one side waited politely while the other side set up its positions. Winners treated the losers with honor. Most warriors were noblemen. Shang Yang dramatically increased the Qin army by requiring all men to fight and rewarding those who killed the most enemy soldiers. He ranked soldiers based on their brilliance in

---

[5] Sima Qian, *Shiji, Records of the Grand Scribe*, China Knowledge: An Encyclopaedia on Chinese History and Literature, accessed March 13, 2025, http://www.chinaknowledge.de/Literature/Historiography/shiji.html.

battle, not their social status, as in earlier days. Noblemen who refused to go to war lost their grand estates, which were divided up and given to the soldiers who proved themselves. War suddenly became much more lethal and far less polite.

Shang Yang's ideology flew in the face of the suppressed Confucian and Daoist ideologies. Shang Yang punished wrongdoers, whereas Confucianism focused on cultivating morality through patient instruction and social rituals. Confucianism taught respect for the social hierarchy, while Legalism dismantled it. Meanwhile, Daoism taught that harmony grew out of inaction and not getting too involved in the world's affairs. Yet, the ever-pragmatic Shang Yang promoted competition and striving to be the best.

Shang Yang's execution [10]

Shang Yang made enemies, especially among the ruling upper class, who were losing their land. When King Huiwen became the ruler of Qin in 338 BCE, he carried a grudge because Shang Yang had once punished him for a minor crime. Royals were seldom penalized for anything. King Huiwen got his revenge by executing Shang Yang's immediate family. He then killed Shang Yang by attaching ropes tied to his head, arms, and legs to oxcarts and pulling him to pieces. Nevertheless, Shang Yang's philosophy and reforms persevered. He had transformed the Qin military into an indomitable war machine, which led the Qin state to astounding victory.

How Did Ying Zheng Become King at Age Thirteen?

The *Shiji* says that Ying Zheng's father was ostensibly Prince Yiren, who later became King Zhuangxiang of Qin. His mother, Zhao Ji, had been a dancing girl and concubine (sexual partner) of a wealthy merchant named Lu Buwei. When Prince Yiren met Zhao Li, her beauty and charm captivated him. He asked and received permission from Lu Buwei to marry Zhao Ji. However, the whispers began when Zhao Li gave birth to a son in 259 BCE: "She was pregnant when she got married. Lu Buwei is the true father!"

The whispers grew louder when Lu Buwei manipulated events so that Prince Yiren and later Ying Zheng became king. Prince Yiren's grandfather, Zhaoxiang, was the king of Qin (306–251 BCE). Yiren's father, Xiaowen, was the crown prince. However, Yiren's mother, Lady Xia, was only a concubine, which typically meant that Yiren would not be the next king. However, Xiaowen's queen, Lady Huayang, had no children. Lu Buwei convinced Lady Huayang to adopt Yiren, which put him in the line of succession. About a year later, Yiren's grandfather died. Zhaoxiang's death brought Yiren's father, Xiaowen, to the throne, but he died three days later. Yiren became king after his father's suspiciously sudden death.

Yiren, now King Zhuangxiang (250–247 BCE), made Zhao Ji his queen, placing Ying Zheng next in line as king. He also made his wife's former lover, Lu Buwei, his prime minister. Zhuangxiang only ruled for three years before he died. Ying Zheng was only twelve or thirteen at the time, not old enough to rule independently. Lu Wei, the prime minister (and possibly Ying Zheng's father), was his regent for nine years.

China's states before its first empire [11]

How Did Ying Zheng Unify China?

Although only a young teen, Ying Zheng envisioned a unified China. His grandfather, King Zhaoxiang, had annexed the Chu and Zhao states on Qin's southeastern and northeastern borders. When Yeng Zheng was in his twenties and no longer under a regent, he began his campaign to bring all of China under Qin dominance. He revived Shang Yang's military reforms, such as incentivizing valor and rewarding soldiers who fought well.

In 230 and 228 BCE, he captured the small yet formidable Han and Wei states. The last states to fall in 221 BCE were the Qi and Yan in the northeast. The Qin now ruled all of China's major states. China's former rulers had called themselves "Wang," meaning "king." However, Ying Zheng took the title "Shi Huangdi," meaning "First Emperor."

While conquering all of China, Ying Zheng survived two assassination plots. When he marched on Yan, its crown prince, Dan, sent two assassins posing as diplomats to Ying Zheng's lodgings. They carried the severed head of Fan Yuqi, a former Qin general who had betrayed Ying Zheng. They also had a map of Dukang, a fertile region in Yan that Ying Zheng was determined to capture. The younger assassin, Qin Wuyang, was only twelve or thirteen. He lost his nerve, sweating and shivering, and could not go near the king.

As Ying Zheng unrolled the map, the assassin Jing Ke lunged at him with his poisoned knife. King Zheng pulled away, although the blade sliced through his sleeve. He ran from the assassin, trying to pull his long sword from his belt. As Jing Ke chased him around a pillar, the royal physician, Xia Wuji, happened to walk in. He flung his medicine bag at the assassin, giving King Zheng time to pull out his sword. The king stabbed the assassin nine times, killing him, then slumped on his throne, catatonic, with his sword lying across his legs. From that moment on, he always kept his sword unsheathed on his lap.

Shortly after, Jing Ke's close friend, Gao Jianli, plotted to kill King Zheng in revenge. He was a famous player of the zhu, a Chinese stringed instrument. He appeared at Ying Zheng's camp, offering to play his instrument for the king's amusement. However, one of Zheng's attendants recognized him. Instead of killing him, King Zheng gouged Gao Jianli's eyes out so he could still play the zhu for him. He permitted the musician to sit close to him while playing. Suddenly, Gao Jianli grabbed his instrument and swung it at Zheng's head, but he missed since he was blind. Zheng had to execute him, after all.

Terracotta warrior unearthed near Qin Shi Huang's tomb [19]

What Reforms Did Qin Shi Huang Bring to China?

Qin Shi Huang reorganized his administration based on the teachings of Han Fei, a teacher of Legalism like Shang Yang. Qin Shi Huang divided his vast empire into thirty-six commanderies (provinces), subdivided into districts. Previously, members of the royal family served as provincial rulers. However, Qin Shi Huang chose administrators based on competence. He also introduced the Censorate as his watchdog, investigating corruption, misconduct, subversion, and judicial procedures.

The emperor's ancestor, King Huiwen, had begun minting round bronze coins. Qin Shi Huang made these coins the standard currency for all of China, displacing regional forms of money. Qin Shi Huang also introduced standard weights and measures. He sent bronze models of the new measurements to all the provinces so they could copy them.

The earliest surviving examples of Chinese writing are "oracle-bones"—inscriptions carved into bones and turtle shells around 1250 BCE. They started as pictographs and evolved into symbolic characters. Qin Shi Huang's scholars standardized the characters, and Prime Minister Li Si sent orders mandating this script throughout China.

Qin Shi Huang also built an incredible web of roads and canals connecting China's far-flung cities. He specified the axle width for wagons and chariots to fit his roads' standardized width. Enhanced transportation improved trade and made it easier to move his armies around as needed.

How Did Qin Shi Huang Build the Great Wall?

As previously mentioned, the Chinese built sections of walls along their northern and western borders to keep out hostile nomadic tribes like the Xiongnu, the Ordos, and the Xianyun. The Chinese had built the earliest parts of the wall by at least the seventh century BCE. The *Book of Songs*, an ancient Chinese poetry collection, has a poem about King Xuan (827–782 BCE), who ordered his general to build a wall in the north to keep the Xianyun out.

The Great Wall slithers over the mountains near Beijing. [18]

Qin Shi Huang masterminded the gargantuan task of connecting the existing sections into one wall, like a dragon creeping over the mountains and valleys. He sent General Meng Tian with 300,000 soldiers to begin bridging the gaps between wall sections and shoring up the older walls. The emperor sent 500,000 more non-military men. All Chinese men had to dedicate one year to building the wall; he also sent criminals to work on the wall. Up to a million men simultaneously labored on the wall at any given time.

The laborers endured grueling weather conditions, sandstorms, and food shortages. Countless men died from backbreaking work in near-starvation conditions. Landslides in the mountains swept them away, and they faced the constant threat of attack by wild animals.

Their construction technique was to build two parallel walls using stone, brick, or wood, depending on local resources. They filled the gap between the walls with packed earth and built beacon towers and forts at intervals. Building, rebuilding, mending, and improving the wall continued for two millennia. The Great Wall protected China and showcased a monumental human effort.

How Did Qin Shi Huang's Obsession with Immortality Play Out?

Immortality dominated the first emperor's thoughts and plans. He wanted to live forever in his mortal body if he could find a way. Otherwise, he wanted to ensure he had a happy afterlife. Chinese philosophy was vague about what happened after a person died. Legalism focused on the here and now. Confucius had little to say about life after death other than encouraging ancestor worship. Yet, for Confucius, ancestor worship was mainly about respect for their legacy. Daoism taught that when a person died, their spirit was reabsorbed into the Tao, the unknowable source of all things.

Chinese mythology told of a white spirit mountain called Mount Penglai in the middle of the sea. Eight immortal people lived in a gold and silver palace on the mountain. Fruit growing on the island's trees could cure any disease, keep a person young forever, and bring the dead back to life. The emperor sent his court sorcerer, Xu Fu, over the eastern sea in ten beautiful ships with five hundred boys and girls, commanding them, "Find the mountain and return with the magical fruit!"

An ancient painting of one of the ships in search of Mount Penglai [14]

Sorcerer Xu Fu found Japan and thought Mount Fuji was Penglai. However, unable to find the immortals or the fruit, he returned home. He set off on a second quest and never returned. When the first emperor realized Xu Fu was not coming back, he withdrew into seclusion, constantly searching for a magical herb or potion to give him immortality. As our earlier story indicates, he may have died from consuming mercury or a toxic herb.

Qin Shi Huang's "plan B" was a happy existence in the next life. He pursued both plans simultaneously. Soon after ascending the throne, he ordered over a half million laborers to build his tomb and make an army of terracotta warriors to guard it. The life-size clay figurines even included horses and his favorite pets. His tomb remains untouched to this day, as ancient inscriptions hinted at poison and booby traps that would harm any tomb robbers.

However, in 1974 CE, farmers unearthed one of the clay warriors. Since then, archaeologists have found vaults with over eight thousand terracotta soldiers, horses, bronze chariots, and weapons. The warriors have distinct facial features, suggesting they were modeled after real people.

Terracotta soldiers from a pit near Qin Shi Huang's tomb [15]

What Happened to the Dynasty after Qin Shi Huang Died?

As the story relates, after the first emperor died suddenly in 210 BCE, his prime minister, Li Si, and chief eunuch, Zhao Gao, schemed to bring a younger son, Ying Hu Hai, to the throne. Zhao Gao had tutored him from infancy and held significant sway over the teenager. Hu Hai took the throne name Qin Er Shi ("Number Two" Qin), but Zhao Gao and Li Si were the shadow government.

Lacking a strong leader at the helm, the Qin dynasty plunged into a tailspin. Widespread rebellion arose, spurred by harsh laws, heavy taxation, and forced labor. In the chaos of civil war, the empire lost 300,000 soldiers in the Battle of Ju Lu. It desperately needed more men. Li Si asked the young emperor to divert the enormous sum he was spending on building a new palace toward hiring a new army. In a fit of rage, the emperor ordered Li Si's execution.

Zhao Gao held on to power but knew he would be the erratic emperor's next target. When Qin Er Shi came to the bitter realization that he really did need more soldiers, he tried to blame Zhao Gao. However, the chief eunuch was one step ahead of him. He surrounded the emperor with his loyal men.

"Why didn't you tell me we were out of men? You should die like Li Si!" Qin Er Shi screamed.

"You killed Li Si because he *did* tell you the truth!" Zhao Gao retorted. "You are the only one to blame. You must accept responsibility and commit suicide. It is the only honorable thing to do."

Thus, after only three years on the throne, the twenty-two-year-old emperor ended his life. Zhao Gao appointed another young family member, Ying Ziying, as king, *not* emperor, as the empire had crumbled. However, on his coronation day, Ying Ziying turned on Zhao Gao and killed him. Ziying's reign was short, lasting only forty-six days before surrendering to Liu Bang, a rebel leader. Liu Bang became the emperor of the new Han dynasty, which replaced the Qin dynasty in 202 BCE.

Chapter 3: The End of the Roman Republic

Blood pooled under Lucretia from the knife she had just plunged into her chest. Her husband and father both screamed in horror, but Brutus pulled the knife from her body and held it in the air.

"By this blood, I swear, I will pursue Lucius Tarquinius Superbus and his wicked wife and children. I will not let them, nor any other, be king of Rome!"[6]

The other men raised their swords, swearing to erase Rome of its kings. They carried Lucretia's body to the Forum as an outraged crowd gathered. When they heard the king's son had violated Lucretia, they vowed to avenge her. King Tarquin fled Rome as the Romans decided to go in a new direction politically.

Thus, the Roman Republic began. Over the next five centuries, Rome morphed from an unassuming city-state into a vast realm on three continents. Yet, how did it end? What led to the Roman Republic's collapse and the Roman Empire's rise? How did social unrest and class tensions destabilize the longstanding republic? What unbridled ambition led to the political intrigues that culminated in imperial rule under Augustus? Let's explore the answers in the chapter on the Roman Republic.

---

[6] Livy, *The Rise of Rome: Books One to Five* Volume I (Oxford University Press, 2009).

How Did the Roman Republic Govern?

In 509 BCE, the idea of a republic was new. Most city-states had kings or the occasional queen. Greece's city-states had kings, tyrants (absolute rulers who seize power unconventionally), and oligarchies (rule by an unelected group). Athens was experimenting with a democracy in which all male citizens could vote.

Consul Appius Claudius Caecus enters the Senate in Roman Republic [16]

At the Roman Republic's inception, the elite patrician class ruled the working-class people called plebeians. The Republic changed with the times to deal with crises like the plebeians demanding a say in government. Rome also had to figure out how to govern all the lands it was conquering. The Republic introduced novel political concepts like checks and balances, elections, impeachments, separation of powers, term limits, and vetoes.

In the Roman Republic, two elected men, called consuls, ruled Rome together for a one-year term. Since the Republic kept busy conquering other lands, one consul typically led the army while the other handled administrative affairs. The military Centuriate Assembly elected the consuls. (In the Roman army, a century was one hundred soldiers, and each century got a vote.)

The consuls appointed the senators in the early days of the Republic. The senators advised the consuls and voted on bills. They controlled the Republic's finances, foreign policy, and day-to-day administration. If Rome had a crisis, the Senate could appoint a temporary dictator with emergency powers for a maximum of six months.

Later, the Republic added an Assembly of Tribes, representing geographic areas. This assembly could elect some officials, make laws, and judge some crimes. The working class finally got a voice in government in 494 BCE when the Republic formed the *Concilium Plebis*, or Council of the Plebs, which could propose or veto laws.

How Did Rome Expand during the Republic?

At the beginning of the Republic, Rome was a modest city-state covering about three hundred square miles, with a population of around 83,000 people. At the end of the Republic, the city of Rome had about a half million people. An estimated ten million people lived in its provinces on three continents.

During Rome's first 250 years as a monarchy, it quickly took control of central Italy. Meanwhile, Greece was establishing colonies in southern Italy. After forming its Republic, Rome began conquering the local tribes and the Greek colonies in southern Italy. By 264 BCE, Rome controlled the entire Italian peninsula. It then focused on Sicily, the large island at the toe of Italy's boot.

Up to this point, Rome had no navy. Most cities in Sicily were colonies of Greece or North Africa's Carthage, which had the world's strongest navy. From 264–146 BCE, Rome fought three Punic Wars against Carthage to take control of the Mediterranean. "Punic" comes from the word *Punicus*, Latin for the Phoenicians, a people from Lebanon who settled Carthage.

Always up for a challenge, in 261 BCE, the Romans built 120 warships for their brand-new navy. They knew the Carthaginians and Greeks had superior maneuvering skills, so they built long gangplanks to board enemy ships and fight one-to-one, which was the Roman military's superpower. They also made catapults to fling fiery projectiles at their adversaries. The Mediterranean world gasped when Rome beat Carthage in its first two sea battles. Rome even won the world's largest sea battle of all time, the Battle of Cape Ecnomus, in 256 BCE, involving 680 ships.

An ancient Roman trireme warship [17]

However, Rome suffered humiliating losses in the next few years. Two killer storms sunk 470 Roman ships. And then, in 249 BCE, Consul Appius Claudius Pulcher's sacred chickens, which he used to foretell the future, gave him news he did not like. He tossed them off the ship, cackling and squawking. When Pulcher lost the battle against Carthage, Rome stripped him of his position and charged him with sacrilege for killing the chickens.

In 218 BCE, the brilliant General Hannibal of Carthage scaled the 13,000-foot Isère Alps with his elephants and horses, invading Italy from the north. Rome barely survived Hannibal's surprise invasion but finally obliterated Carthage in 149 BCE.

Rome had been warring against the Greek city-states and colonies while simultaneously fighting Carthage. With Carthage razed to the ground, it was time to crush Greece. In 146 BCE, Rome burned Corinth to ashes, completing its conquest of the entire Greek subcontinent.

What Was the First Triumvirate?

Gnaeus Pompeius (Pompey) Magnus was a ruthless Roman general who served as consul three times. He won fame by scoring military wins in North Africa and Spain. He rounded up eight hundred pirates wreaking havoc in the eastern Mediterranean and rehabilitated them as farmers. Pompey conquered his way through Anatolia (Turkey), Syria, and Judea, consolidating Roman rule in the Middle East.

Despite capturing nine hundred cities, his loyal soldiers had little reward for years of service. Pompey wanted his men to receive farmland in the territory they had conquered so they could settle down and raise families. However, the senators in Rome were ignoring his request for land grants.

"And that's not all, Caesar!" he complained to his friend. "After all that time I spent settling affairs in the Middle East, the Senate has yet to ratify the treaties I made. Those Syrians are already stirring up trouble!"

Julius Caesar was a rising star in Roman politics who had just returned to Rome after a stunning victory in Spain. He nodded. "I feel the same way about my own troops. Our senators are only enriching themselves from our victories. Unless we transform the government, they will never pass that land allotment bill."

"Transform the government?" Pompey frowned.

"A triumvirate," Caesar explained. "You wield your influence to get me elected as consul. Everyone loves and respects you. As consul, I'll get that land bill passed for your soldiers and mine."

Pompey smiled, yet raised his eyebrows. "Who's the third person in this triumvirate?"

"Well, you and I have no money. We need someone rich enough to persuade the senators. We need the richest man in Rome," said Caesar.

"Meaning that deplorable, Crassus!" Pompey scowled. "I suppose I can endure him if it means getting farms for my men. I'm in, on one condition."

"Which is?" inquired Caesar.

"The hand of your daughter in marriage. I think I've fallen in love."

"Pompey! You're thirty years older than Julia!" came Caesar's incredulous response.

"I know, but she will have the most devoted husband in the Republic!"

Caesar laughed. "All right! It's a deal!"

The First Triumvirate: Pompey, Crassus, and Caesar [18]

After the First Triumvirate formed in 60 BCE, Pompey used his strategic friendships, and Crassus used his money to get Caesar elected. However, when Caesar tried to pass the land bill, the other consul, Bibulus, said he would veto it. An angry mob surrounded Bibulus and poured a bucket of feces over him. Bibulus slunk home and stayed there for the rest of the year, leaving Caesar in charge. Pompey threatened to unleash his soldiers on anyone trying to block the bill. It passed, along with Caesar's other bills for the working classes.

What Did Julius Caesar Accomplish in Gaul?

After his one year as consul, the Senate appointed Caesar as the proconsul (governor) of Gaul (northern Italy and southern France). He launched a campaign to subdue the Gallic (Celtic) tribes, expanding Rome's territory to include all of today's Belgium and France. He brutally massacred the Germanic Tencteri and Usipetes tribes that were migrating to Gaul. Caesar also sailed to Britain in 55 and 54 BCE, exploring the coast and marching inland as far as present-day London.

Caesar kept a running account of his exploits in his book *Bellum Gallicum* (*Gallic Wars*). At the end of each year, he sent a section of his book back to Rome with lively tales of his daring conquests. Although probably embellished, the stories enhanced Caesar's popularity.

How Did the First Triumvirate End?

The First Triumvirate crumbled while Caesar was in Gaul. In 52 BCE, Pompey's wife (Caesar's daughter, Julia) died in childbirth. The strain of grief and a growing rivalry between the two men dissolved their friendship. The following year, Crassus was decapitated in the Battle of Carrhae in Anatolia.

Caesar was now a renowned war hero with a seasoned army. Meanwhile, Roman politics had fallen into scandalous disarray. Politicians publicly accepted bribes. Senators fought for their bills with swords, staining the Senate floor with blood. The chaos in Rome made it increasingly apparent that the Republic was no longer functioning.

People whispered, "Perhaps we should return to a single, strong leader, like what Rome had in its earliest days."

The Romans who were entertaining ideas of a monarchy favored Pompey. Yet, Caesar wanted that ultimate power.

Roman Republic, 50 BCE [19]

How Did Caesar Trigger a Civil War?

Caesar finished his tour of duty in Gaul and marched back to Rome in 49 BCE. The Senate demanded that he disband his legions before entering Rome. Yet, Caesar crossed the Rubicon River into central Italy with five thousand men. He knew the Senate was planning to prosecute him for legal irregularities when he had been consul. He had reached the point of no return. It was either endure punishment from the Senate or take control of Rome.

Who Won the War?

As Caesar closed in on Rome, most senators fled to southern Italy. Caesar helped himself to the state treasury but harmed no one. His priority was eliminating Pompey, who had sailed to Greece yet left most of his legions in Spain. Caesar marched to Spain with less than one thousand men, defeated Pompey's army, and returned to Rome.

After having himself declared a temporary dictator, Caesar presided over the elections that made him the new consul. Now, it was time to sail to Greece and confront Pompey. Caesar put his relative, Mark Antony, in charge of Italy in his absence. In 48 BCE, Caesar and Pompey faced off in the Battle of Pharsalus in the Thessaly region of Greece. It was an epic win for Caesar. He reported that he lost only two hundred men while killing sixty thousand of Pompey's soldiers.

Pompey escaped to Egypt, a fatal mistake. Egypt had two pharaohs: thirteen-year-old Ptolemy XIII and his older sister and wife, Cleopatra VII. The siblings were at war, each wanting total control. Ptolemy XIII killed Pompey, knowing he was on the run from Caesar. Ptolemy guessed that Caesar would ultimately rule Rome and wanted to be on the right side of history.

When Caesar arrived shortly after, Ptolemy handed him Pompey's head, hoping Caesar would help him fight Cleopatra. Yet, Caesar was appalled at his one-time friend's shameful death. He mourned Pompey and organized a state funeral. Cleopatra arrived soon after and won over Caesar with her sexual wiles. The two lovers fought against Ptolemy XIII, who drowned while escaping their armies.

What Happened When Caesar Became "Dictator for Life"?

Caesar's only biological son, Caesarion, was born to Cleopatra in 47 BCE. Caesar returned to Rome and installed Cleopatra and her baby in his country villa. He ruled Rome for the next three years as consul or dictator. Caesar introduced reforms to relieve debt for the working class and help with unemployment. He was popular with ordinary people but hated by the aristocratic politicians. Caesar devised the "Julian calendar" with 365 days and a leap year every four years, adding a day in February. We use this calendar today with slight modifications.

Cleopatra VII and her son Caesarion on a mural in Pompeii[20]

Rome's dictators were not supposed to serve more than six months, yet Caesar became "dictator for life" in February 44 BCE. He was essentially a king, although he refused to wear a crown. Around sixty senators plotted to kill Caesar and restore the Republic. They murdered him on March 15 (the Ides of March), 44 BCE, in the Senate, stabbing him twenty-three times. However, his funeral ended in an uproar by the plebeians, who chased the senators out of Italy.

What Was the Aftermath of Caesar's Assassination?

Although Caesar named his nephew and adopted son Octavian as his heir, Mark Antony, Rome's new consul, tried to block Octavian's inheritance. Rome staggered on the brink of civil war with the plebeians supporting Octavian against Mark Antony. After his one year as consul ended, Antony was appointed as Macedonia's governor by the Senate. However, he wanted to be governor of northern Italy (Cisalpine Gaul) instead and marched there with his army. The Senate sent Octavian to bring him back. Before Octavian got to northern Italy, Antony crossed the Alps into France (Transalpine Gaul) and launched a conspiracy with its governor, Lepidus.

How Did the Second Triumvirate Form?

Octavian returned to Rome to discover that the underhanded senators were planning to kill him and had already appointed Brutus, one of Caesar's murderers, as the army's commander. Yet, about half of the military had fought under Caesar and transferred their ardent loyalty to his adoptive son, Octavian. With military support, Octavian announced he was Rome's consul. Yet, he needed an alliance to confront the treacherous senators. He reached out to his former enemy, Antony, and allied with him and Lepidus. Octavian sweetened the pot by offering Antony rule over Rome's eastern provinces. Thus, the Second Triumvirate burst onto the political scene in 43 BCE.

The Second Triumvirate successfully squelched the senators, but it was short-lived. Octavian and Lepidus quarreled. Then, Antony fell under Cleopatra's spell and agreed to appoint Caesarion, her son by Caesar, as Caesar's heir. Their plan was for Antony and Cleopatra to rule Rome as Caesarion's regents. When Octavian uncovered the plot, he declared war on the lovers.

How Did Octavian's Victory End the Roman Republic?

The deciding showdown was the massive Battle of Actium in the Ionian Sea off Greece's coast in 31 BCE. Octavian's maritime commander, Agrippa, led 400 ships against the combined 480 ships of Antony and Cleopatra. King Herod of the Jews, King Malchus of Arabia, and the rulers of Libya, Cilicia, and Thrace allied with Cleopatra and Antony.

Antony commanded his captains, "Do *not* try to fight in the open sea! Agrippa's ships are faster, and they will have the advantage there. Stay in the straits." Nevertheless, some of his captains ignored his orders and sailed into the Ionian Sea, where they were easily surrounded by Octavian's ships. Fearing all was lost, Cleopatra ordered her sixty ships to abandon the battle and sail to Egypt. In dismay, Antony watched his lover and her navy disappear over the horizon. He abandoned the battle to follow her, leaving about half his ships entangled with the Roman vessels. Eventually, Octavian chased the co-conspirators down. When Antony's troops abandoned him, he fell on his sword. Cleopatra also committed suicide, and Octavian seized Egypt as a Roman province.

Octavian's long-term plan was to be emperor for life, but he pretended to support the traditional semi-democratic Republic. He introduced changes incrementally. The Senate made his secret ambition easy to achieve. When he was appointed as consul shortly after returning to Rome, the Senate gave him more authority than a consul usually had and extended his term past the one-year limit. They handed the administration of the provinces to Octavian, along with complete control of the military. Octavian conquered more of Africa, Europe, and the Middle East, doubling the Republic's size.

Octavian, who became Caesar Augustus, Rome's first emperor [21]

Octavian pretended humility, refusing to wear a kingly purple robe. Yet, in 27 BCE, the Senate gave him the title of *Augustus* (magnificent) and *Princeps Senatus/Princeps Civitatis* (first in the Senate, first over the citizens). Julius Caesar had been his adoptive father, so he took the name "Caesar" and was called "Caesar Augustus" from that point. The name "Caesar" became a title for future emperors.

In Caesar Augustus's lifetime, Rome transitioned from a republic to an empire, with one man holding power. Most Romans welcomed the transition, treasuring the peace, economic stability, and wealth Augustus brought to Rome.

Chapter 4: Cleopatra's Egypt

Cleopatra VII's Egypt was the end of an era. She and her teenage son were the last pharaohs of Egypt, the end of the Ptolemaic dynasty. Although remembered as a seductress, Cleopatra was a cunning leader, navigating complex and treacherous politics. She was a multilingual scholar, strategist, and diplomat. Her chief goal was to preserve Egypt's independence and her role as pharaoh. Hers is the story of the interplay between personal relationships and political power during a pivotal era in ancient history.

How Did the Ptolemaic Dynasty Begin?

When Alexander the Great rode into Egypt in 332 BCE, his childhood friend and trusted general Ptolemy rode by his side. The Egyptians cheered, welcoming Alexander as their savior from bitter Persian rule. They had no choice. Alexander of Macedonia had already conquered all of Greece, crossed into Asia, and marched down the Mediterranean coastline with his vast army.

Most cities had politely welcomed Alexander, but Tyre resisted, and Alexander crucified their men. Gaza resisted, and Alexander crushed their seemingly insurmountable walls. The Persian king, Darius III, had ambushed Alexander near Syria's northern border. However, Alexander's impeccably trained army swiftly moved into battle formation and put up a formidable defense. An unnerved Darius swung his chariot around and raced off, leaving his soldiers, mother, wife, and daughters behind. The Egyptians pragmatically decided to welcome the Greeks.

Alexander explored Egypt and found the northern Delta region enchanting. This is where the Nile splits into multiple branches, emptying into the Mediterranean. He excitedly made elaborate plans for a new city named Alexandria, where the westernmost branch of the Nile flowed into the sea. Alexandria would be a premier trade hub and a riveting center of art, poetry, and the sciences.

Alexander never saw Alexandria in all its glory. He left no capable heir when he died of fever at age thirty-two. His generals divided up his newly conquered empire, and General Ptolemy took Egypt. He immediately set to work fulfilling Alexander's dreams—and his own. Ptolemy finished building the gleaming city of Alexandria, the "jewel of the Mediterranean," and made it Egypt's new capital.

Ptolemy and his descendants ruled as Egypt's pharaohs for 275 years, Egypt's longest dynasty. This was Cleopatra's Egypt. Although not Egyptian, they created a fusion of Egyptian and Greek culture. The Ptolemies rebuilt Egypt's temples, desecrated by the Persians, and built temples to Greek gods in Alexandria. They introduced stunning innovations that rocked the world.

How Did the Ptolemaic Dynasty Enrich the World?

Egypt soared to unprecedented heights under its first three Ptolemaic pharaohs. Ptolemy built Alexandria's Great Library for his lofty goal of collecting every book in the world. The Library at Alexandria held 490,000 books by his grandson's reign. Ptolemy imported scholars who revolutionized math, philosophy, science, art, and literature.

Two scholars at the library were the geometry geniuses Euclid and Eratosthenes. Euclid of Alexandria wrote *The Elements*, a textbook covering number theory, mathematic proofs, and geometry, including the Pythagorean Theorem. Eratosthenes was the lead librarian, renowned for calculating the earth's circumference. On June 21 (the longest day of sunlight), he plunged a stick into the ground at noon and measured its shadow's angle. Meanwhile, his assistant did the same in Syene, south of Alexandria. They compared measurements against the distance between Alexandria and Syene. Eratosthenes calculated the Earth's circumference at 28,000 miles, astoundingly close to today's calculations of 24,901 miles.

The Library of Alexandria was the world's intellectual hub.[22]

One of Eratosthenes's students at the Library of Alexandria was the teenage Archimedes of Syracuse. After returning to Sicily, he constantly exchanged letters with Eratosthenes. Archimedes estimated square roots and pi (π)—the ratio of circumference to diameter in a circle. His estimate for pi was between 3.14585 and 3.14084. (Modern-day mathematicians estimate pi as 3.1415926535.) Archimedes also developed the compound pulley, which he used to move a ship. His fascination with moving big objects led him to introduce the "Law of the Lever," utilizing a fulcrum and stick to move a heavy weight.

The philosopher Strato was Aristotle's student who moved to Alexandria and tutored Ptolemy II. Strato thought the stars were fiery like the sun. Yet, he understood that some "stars" (planets) and the moon reflect the sun's light. One of Strato's students at Alexandria was

Aristarchus of Samos. He was the first to theorize (1,800 years before Copernicus) that the Earth and other planets traveled in orbits around the sun. He taught that the stars were faraway suns and that the Earth revolved on an axis each day.

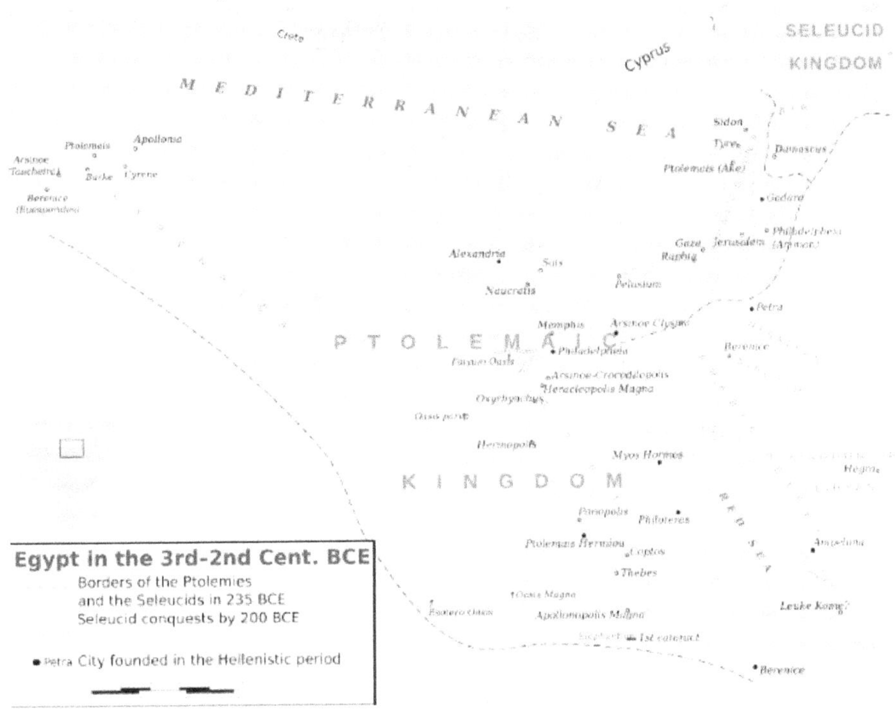

Ptolemaic Empire[28]

Ptolemy I expanded Egypt's realm to include Judea, Phoenicia, and the islands of Rhodes and Cyprus. He built the most powerful navy in the Mediterranean world. His reputation for paying the highest wages and giving land grants to veteran soldiers enabled him to hire elite sailors.

Ptolemy's son, Ptolemy II Philadelphus, became Egypt's next pharaoh in 284 BCE, leading the Ptolemaic dynasty into its golden age.

While some scholars at the library developed metaphysics and math, others dived into literature. One of the librarians, Zenodotus, was an epic poet, an editor of Homer, and a lecturer on Hesiod and Pindar. His assistants edited the Greek comedies and tragedies. Ptolemy II invited the Greek poets Callimachus, Theocritus, and Apollonius of Rhodes to teach at the Great Library's school.

Ptolemy II Philadelphus [24]

Ptolemy II's oldest son, Ptolemy III Euergetes, became pharaoh in 246 BCE. Ptolemy III's sister, Berenice Syra, was married to the Seleucid Empire's king, Antiochus II Theos. When Antiochus suddenly died, probably by poison, Berenice desperately messaged her brother. She was terrified that her husband's other wife, Laodice, would kill her and her baby son. Ptolemy III marched north to Antioch in Syria but arrived too late. Laodice had murdered his sister and her baby. Ptolemy III had Laodice killed and took over Syria, Anatolia, and ancient Iraq. He retrieved treasures the Persians had stolen centuries earlier and returned them to Egypt's ancient temples.

Ptolemy III expanded Ptolemaic Egypt to its greatest extent, controlling the Mediterranean coast from Libya to today's Turkey.

What Plunged the Ptolemaic Kingdom into a Tailspin?

After Ptolemy III, the dynasty went downhill. Ptolemy IV Philopator, son of Ptolemy III, lacked interest in leadership. His friends, Agathocles and Sosibius, ran a shadow government. Southern Egypt rebelled and declared independence in 205 BCE. The following year, Ptolemy IV and his wife both died about the same time, possibly assassinated.

With Agathocles as his regent, the dead couple's little son, Ptolemy V Epiphanes, became Egypt's pharaoh at age five. In 202 BCE, Alexandria's citizens rebelled, ripped Agathocles apart, and installed a new regent.

With Egypt destabilized, Antiochus the Great of the Seleucid Empire conquered Syria. When he marched south to Judea, the Jews opened the gates of Jerusalem to him. They cheered him as their liberator from the Egyptians with no inkling of the horror to come.

At age fourteen, Ptolemy V officially became Egypt's pharaoh. The Egyptian priests inscribed the event on the Rosetta Stone in Greek, Egyptian hieroglyphics, and the Egyptian Demotic script. Two thousand years later, scholars used the Greek inscription to translate the Egyptian hieroglyphics, unlocking Egypt's ancient history.

Ptolemy V and Antiochus declared peace, yet Antiochus kept Judea, Syria, and Anatolia. Ptolemy V married Antiochus's daughter, Cleopatra Syra. Ptolemy V then warred against the southern Egypt rebels and reunited the country in 186 BCE. When he died suddenly in 180 BCE, the rumors erupted:

"He was only thirty! They must have poisoned him."

"Who? And why?"

"Antiochus the Great just died, and Ptolemy planned to recapture Judea and Syria. Yet, his advisors didn't want the war debt."

Coin of Ptolemy V Epiphanes [25]

The Ptolemaic Kingdom plunged deeper and faster into chaos. Ptolemy V's six-year-old son, Ptolemy VI Philometor, became pharaoh with Cleopatra Syra as his regent. At sixteen, Ptolemy VI married his sister, Cleopatra II. Their unhinged uncle, Antiochus IV Epiphanes, ruled the Seleucid Empire in West Asia. He attacked Egypt, taking the southern regions and capturing Ptolemy VI. The Alexandrians crowned Ptolemy VI's younger brother, Ptolemy VIII, their new pharaoh.

Antiochus Epiphanes left for Syria in 169 BCE, leaving Ptolemy VI as pharaoh in the south, while Ptolemy VIII ruled the north. Finally, their sister, Cleopatra II, devised a plan in which the three would rule together over a united Egypt. That brought Antiochus Epiphanes back to Egypt in a rage.

However, Rome inserted itself to get a foothold in Egypt. The Roman proconsul, Popillius, stopped Antiochus Epiphanes outside Alexandria. He drew a line around him in the sand. "The Roman Senate orders you to leave Egypt. Don't leave that circle until I have an answer for the Senate!" he demanded.

Antiochus had no choice but to return to Syria, taking out his wrath on Judea on the way home. He killed forty thousand Jews, placed a statue of

Zeus in Jerusalem's temple, and sacrificed a pig to it. The outraged Jews started the Maccabean Revolt, won independence, and negotiated a friendly relationship with Egypt.

The following nine decades involved constant intrigue, murder, and mayhem. Two or three family members usually ruled Egypt together, but Egypt grew weaker. Meanwhile, Rome grew stronger, conquering most of the Greek world and leaving Egypt with few allies. The siblings in the royal family continued to marry each other but fought so bitterly that, by 80 BCE, they had killed each other off, leaving no legitimate heir to Egypt's throne.

How Was Cleopatra VII's Childhood Upended?

Ptolemy XII Auletes was a pharaoh's son, but his mother was only a concubine. He normally would not have become pharaoh in 80 BCE, but Egypt had no one else. Cleopatra VII, born in 69 BCE, was the second of his five children. When she was a toddler, Crassus and Julius Caesar wanted to conquer Egypt but could not convince the Senate.

When Cleopatra was six, the Roman general Pompey conquered Anatolia and Syria. Only Judea stood between Pompey and Egypt. Cleopatra's father bribed Pompey with eight thousand cavalry and a gold crown to leave Egypt in peace. Judea fell to Rome, but Egypt survived.

When Cleopatra was nine, Rome's First Triumvirate formed. Her father traveled to Rome with a bribe that equaled Egypt's annual revenue. This broke Egypt's treasury, but Julius Caesar declared Ptolemy XII as *socius et amicus* (ally and friend), and Rome formally allied with Egypt.

Yet, the following year, Rome snatched the island of Cyprus, which belonged to Egypt. This infuriated the Egyptians, and they kicked Ptolemy XII out of Egypt in 58 BCE. He fled to Rome with Cleopatra VII, now eleven years old. Her older sister, Berenice IV, became pharaoh. General Pompey took Cleopatra and her father into his home.

Ptolemy XII borrowed a fortune to bribe Aulus Gabinius, the Roman proconsul of Syria, to help him take Egypt back. In 55 BCE, Gabinius's army, led by Mark Antony, restored Cleopatra's father to Egypt's throne. Her father killed her older sister, Berenice IV, who had been trying to convince Rome to keep her on the throne and her father out of Egypt.

This was the milieu in which Cleopatra grew up. Despite the turmoil of her childhood, Cleopatra received a stellar education, with the Greek philosopher Philostratus as her tutor. Unlike most Ptolemaic pharaohs, who only communicated in Greek, Cleopatra learned to speak, read, and write in Egyptian. Having spent her early teen years in Rome, she had also learned Latin. Additionally, she knew the Syrian, Aramaic, and Ethiopian languages.

Why Did Cleopatra Become Julius Caesar's Lover?

In 51 BCE, Cleopatra's father died when she was eighteen. She married her eleven-year-old brother, Ptolemy XIII Theos Philopator, and they ruled as co-pharaohs. At least, that was their father's plan. However, Ptolemy XIII and his regent, Pothinus, plotted against Cleopatra, and a civil war raged for several years. When her brother prevailed, Cleopatra fled to Syria for reinforcements.

While Cleopatra was in Syria, Pompey arrived in Egypt, and her brother's men ambushed and killed him. When Julius Caesar got to Egypt shortly after, he was furious that Ptolemy XIII had killed Pompey. Ptolemy XIII escaped, but Caesar executed Pothinus. At this point, Cleopatra sailed back to Egypt and heard what had just happened. She decided her best scheme was to ally with Caesar against her brother.

Cleopatra charms Caesar [26]

Cleopatra wasn't a classic beauty, but she knew how to make an entrance. The Greek historian Plutarch said Cleopatra had a servant smuggle her in a sack into the palace where Caesar was staying. Caesar looked up to see her gracefully rising from the bundle in a diaphanous gown. One glance, and she captured Caesar's attention and held it until he died.

Caesar and Cleopatra won the war, and she was reinstated as Egypt's pharaoh, co-ruling with another younger brother, Ptolemy XIV. Cleopatra gave birth to Caesar's son, Caesarion, in 47 BCE. Three years later, Cleopatra was staying in Caesar's villa near Rome when the senators murdered him. She fled back to Egypt. Three months later, her brother and co-pharaoh Ptolemy XIV died. He was only fifteen, and people speculated that she poisoned him to elevate three-year-old Caesarion as her co-pharaoh.

How Did Cleopatra Seduce Mark Antony?

Before Caesar's murder, Mark Antony had been his right-hand man. Antony officiated at Caesar's funeral and assumed he would be his political heir. However, Caesar's will crushed his expectations. Caesar named Octavian as his adopted son and heir to his estate. At first, Mark Antony opposed Octavian. Yet, as the last chapter covered, he soon realized it was better to be allies than enemies, so he formed the Second Triumvirate with Octavian and Lepidus.

Octavian gave Mark Antony rule over Rome's eastern provinces, so he sailed to Tarsus on Turkey's southern coast. In 41 BCE, Mark Antony messaged Cleopatra to meet with him to renew Egypt's alliance with Rome. Cleopatra decided to make another unforgettable entrance. Flutes and lyres played as she sailed into the harbor in an exquisite boat propelled by silver oars and purple sails. Dressed as the goddess Aphrodite, she reclined in the ship, fanned by small boys dressed as cupids. Antony immediately fell under her spell. He sailed back to Egypt with Cleopatra, and in the following year, she gave birth to twins, Alexander Helios and Cleopatra Selene. Cleopatra also provided Antony with ships for his Parthian campaign against ancient Iran.

Cleopatra gave birth to another son by Antony, Ptolemy Philadelphus, in 36 BCE. Rome bristled when they heard of a celebration the couple staged in 34 BCE, called the Donations of Alexandria. Antony and Cleopatra dressed as deities and named their children as rulers of Roman provinces.

Bust of Cleopatra VII[27]

Disaster loomed for the lovers when Octavian found Antony's will in 32 BCE. Antony had left it with the Vestal Virgins at Rome's Temple of Vesta. Octavian was shocked when Antony announced that Cleopatra's son, Caesarion, was Caesar's biological son and rightful heir. That directly challenged Octavian's status as Caesar's adopted son. Octavian declared war on the couple, which ended in disaster for Antony and Cleopatra at the Battle of Actium, as we shared in the last chapter.

How Did Cleopatra's Egypt End?

Back in Egypt and full of restless energy, Cleopatra desperately tried to find a way to escape. She needed to find a place of safety with her children, but where? No viable solution emerged. Antony sat like a statue, drunk and drained of emotion. He finally roused when Octavian's ships appeared on the horizon in July 30 BCE. Antony led his troops to battle, and, at first, they were winning. Yet, his troops seemed to realize they were on the wrong side of history and deserted to Octavian.

All hope was gone. After stabbing himself, Antony bled out in Cleopatra's arms. Cleopatra knew she would be dragged to Rome and forced to march in chains at a triumph parade. That was unthinkable. When Octavian arrived, he found Cleopatra dead as well. Although legend says she died from a snake bite, none of the Roman-era historians mentioned it. A mural in Pompeii, painted several decades later, shows her wearing her crown and holding a bowl, presumably of poison. Her teenage son Caesarion, also wearing his diadem, supports her from behind.

A mural from Pompeii, probably of Cleopatra's suicide [28]

Mark Antony had requested burial in Egypt in his will, and Octavian honored that. He buried Antony and Cleopatra in the same tomb in Alexandria. Octavian killed Cleopatra's oldest son, Caesarion. As Caesar's biological son, he would complicate things for Octavian's planned future as Rome's emperor. Octavian took Cleopatra and Antony's three young children back to Rome, and his sister raised them in her home.

Cleopatra's Egypt had reached the end. It was no longer independent or ruled by the Ptolemaic dynasty. It was now *Aegyptus*, a Roman province, although Alexandria's Hellenistic culture continued to thrive.

Chapter 5: Genghis Khan and the Mongol Empire

How did a nomadic herder named Temujin rise from obscurity to unite the Mongol tribes and reshape the geopolitical landscape of Asia and Europe? What genius military and administrative strategies enabled him to impact history so powerfully? This chapter explores the legendary Genghis Khan and the Mongol Empire.

Who Were the Mongols?

The Mongol tribes herded sheep, goats, long-horned cattle, yaks, and Bactrian camels. They raced their short, pony-like horses over the steppes of Central Asia. From their humble origins in the Khentii Mountains of northern Mongolia, they eventually ruled from China to the Danube River in Eastern Europe. The Mongols blended ancestor worship, shamanism, and the worship of spirits in nature. Their primary god was Tengri, ruler of the sky and heaven. Some Mongols eventually adopted Islam or Christianity.

Temujin, later known as Genghis Khan, was born into the Mongolian Borjigin clan in 1162 CE. *The Secret History of the Mongols*, written by an unknown Mongol in Temujin's lifetime, said his ancestor, Qaidu (Kaidu), was the first to unite the Mongol people. Qaidu joined forces with the Jurchen Jin people of Manchuria in northeast China to overthrow the Liao dynasty. Qaidu also feuded fiercely against the Tayichiud, a clan formed by his wayward youngest son, Charaqai Lingqu.

Qaidu's grandson (Temujin's great-grandfather) was Khabul (Qabul) Khan. When he visited the new Jin emperor, Xi Zong, his gluttony scandalized the Chinese. Worse yet, he got roaring drunk and pulled the emperor's beard. After expelling him in disgrace, the Chinese realized they had forgotten to get his oath of loyalty to the emperor. That was the point of inviting him in the first place. "We need to bring him back!" they said.

When Khabul noticed the Chinese were following him, he suspected treachery. He and his companions ambushed and killed the Jin group, leading to brutal warfare between the Mongols and the Jin. Curiously, although Khabul had seven sons, he named a Tayichiud clan leader, Amba Ghai, as his successor. Amba Ghai captured twenty forts along the Great Wall of China, giving the Mongols the upper hand.

Mongol warriors painted by Rashid-ad-Din, a physician and advisor in the Mongol court [29]

The Jin reached out to the Tartars, another steppe tribe. The Tartars tricked Amba Ghai into thinking they wanted a marriage alliance. However, when Amba Ghai arrived with his daughter, they captured him and handed him over to the Jin, who crucified him. As he was dying, Amba Ghai screamed for his fellow Mongols to avenge his death.

The Borjigin clan reclaimed their rulership over the Mongols and elected Khabul's son, Qutula (Hotula), as their leader. However, the feud between the Borjigin and Tayichiud clans raged on. In 1161 CE, a year before Temujin was born, the Jin and Tartars attacked the Mongols, nearly annihilating the Borjigin clan and killing Qutula.

Yesugei, Temujin's father and Khabul's son, became the next Mongol leader. He had been leading a ragtag guerilla band of Mongols. Although he had a wife and concubines, a girl named Hö'elün caught Yesugei's eye. Hö'elün was already engaged to Yehe Chiledu, chief of the Merkits. Undeterred, Yesugei swept in and carried Hö'elün off, igniting a blood feud between the Merkits and the Borjigin.

What Were the Harsh Realities of Temujin's Childhood?

Temujin was born into this messy situation as Hö'elün's oldest son by Yesugei. He had two older half-brothers by his father's official wife. A typical Mongol boy, Temujin learned to ride a horse as a toddler and sped over icy lakes on skates made from bone. He learned herding, hunting, and hand-to-hand combat, but not reading and writing. His best friend was Jamukha (Jamuga). They took an *anda* oath as small boys—a solemn, spiritual vow of perpetual brotherhood and loyalty.

When Temujin was nine, his father arranged his marriage. (Mongolians got engaged as children and married in their teens. Aristocratic Mongol boys typically married high-born girls from the Ongud tribe, a Turkish people who adopted Mongol culture and lived in southeastern Mongolia. Ongud women were the beauties of the steppes.)

The bride-to-be was ten-year-old Börte, daughter of Chief Dai Sechen. However, Yesugei only had one horse for the bride price. Dai Sechen snorted and said, "I'll accept that as a down payment, but you must pay the full bride price before the wedding! Leave Temujin here with me. My son Alchi-Noyan likes him, and the boy can work to earn part of the bride price."

When Yesugei was preparing to leave, Dai Sechen approached him and said, "I had the strangest dream last night. A falcon was clutching the sun in one talon and the moon in the other. Temujin was right there. My vision must mean your boy will rule the world!"

Yesugei smiled. The future looked promising. Temujin spent the next three years as a herder for his future father-in-law. At age twelve, Temujin received devastating news. The Tartars had invited his father to a banquet, then slipped a slow-acting poison into his food. A few hours after leaving the Tartar's camp, Yesugei suffered excruciating stomach cramps. "Monklik," he gasped to his right-hand man, "I'm dying! Go now! Get Temujin."

Monklik raced off as Yesugei died in agony. Dai Sechen scowled at the news and responded, "If I let the boy go now, what will happen to my daughter?"

Monklik reassured Dai Sechen. "They can still marry when they are older. But Temujin needs to assert himself as the new khan."

"Yes, yes. I know," grumbled Dai Sechen. "If he's not there, someone else will grab his position."

By the time Monklik retrieved Temujin and raced with him back to the steppes, it was too late. Temujin's Borjigin clansmen had decided the twelve-year-old was too young to rule. "We're taking back rulership!" the Tayichiud clan announced.

The Mongols abandoned the widow Hö'elün, taking the flocks with them. Hö'elün was left with nothing but several horses and her sons. They had to live off the land—hunting, fishing, foraging for berries, and digging roots. The sons of Yesugei's first wife harassed them, stealing the fish and game they caught.

When Temujin was thirteen, he filled the body of his older half-brother, Begter, with arrows.

Hö'elün tore into Temujin. "What were you thinking, killing your half-brother? You're like a mad dog that eats itself!"

The Tayichiud leader, Tar Gutai, decided to enslave thirteen-year-old Temujin. "He needs to be punished for killing his older brother!" he declared.

Tar Gutai put Temujin in a cangue, or "Chinese death cage," something like stocks (a large board with a hole in the middle for the person's head). One night, the guard fell asleep, and Temujin snuck off and hid in the river reeds. The next day, Sorqan Shira, a man from the Suldus tribe, found Temujin and hid him in his tent. Temujin made his escape that night and returned to his family.

When Temujin was fourteen, the Tayichiud stole eight of his family's nine horses. With the remaining horse, Temujin charged after them, tracking the raiders for four days. He met a young teen named Bo'orchu, who gave him food, water, and a fresh horse. Bo'orchu rode with Temujin for three more days until they caught up with the Tayichiud.

They snuck into the Tayichiud campsite by night, taking back the stolen horses. The Tayichiud awakened and chased after the young teens. Their chieftain rode the fastest stallion and pulled ahead of his men. As the chieftain approached, Bo'orchu twisted around in his saddle and shot an arrow into his chest. His companions stopped to tend to their chief, giving the boys time to escape.

Bo'orchu's father provided the boys with more horses and warriors. Temujin's future father-in-law, Dai Sechen, also sent reinforcements. Suddenly, Temujin segued from foraging for a living to becoming a young warlord. His experiences up to this point armed him with resilience, strategic thinking, and a relentless drive for power.

How Did Temujin Unify the Mongol Clans?

Temujin redeemed his bride when he was fifteen. Börte's mother gifted Temujin's mother with an exquisite sable coat to honor the family union. However, over a year passed, and Börte did conceive.

Meanwhile, the Merkits plotted revenge for Temujin's father stealing Hö'elün from their chief years earlier. About two years after Temujin's marriage, the Merkits kidnapped Börte.

Temujin allied with his father's friend, Toghril (Toghrul), chief of the Keraites, a powerful Turkish Mongolian tribe. He regifted the sable coat given to his mother to seal the deal. Temujin was delighted to discover his beloved childhood friend, Jamuga, had joined Toghril's band. With Toghril's substantial military force, they launched a campaign, scattering the Merkits and almost exterminating them.

Temujin got Börte back, yet he was disturbed to discover she was pregnant by a Merkit chieftain. Temujin spread the story that she was already pregnant when captured. He accepted the baby as his own and named him Jochi.

Temujin's old friend Jamuga had nearly twenty thousand troops, far more than Temujin. "He's a loose cannon!" Börte warned. Hö'elün backed her daughter-in-law's opinion.

The women were right. Jamuga picked a quarrel with Temujin, something about Temujin's sheep and Jamuga's horses. Deeply hurt, Temujin packed up his people and herds and slipped away one night, setting up a new camp.

The Mongols had to decide who they would follow. About thirteen thousand Mongols defected to Jamuga, but the rest supported Temujin, including the Borjigin clan. Temujin immediately began training his men and promoting those who proved themselves. He consistently rewarded merit over social status.

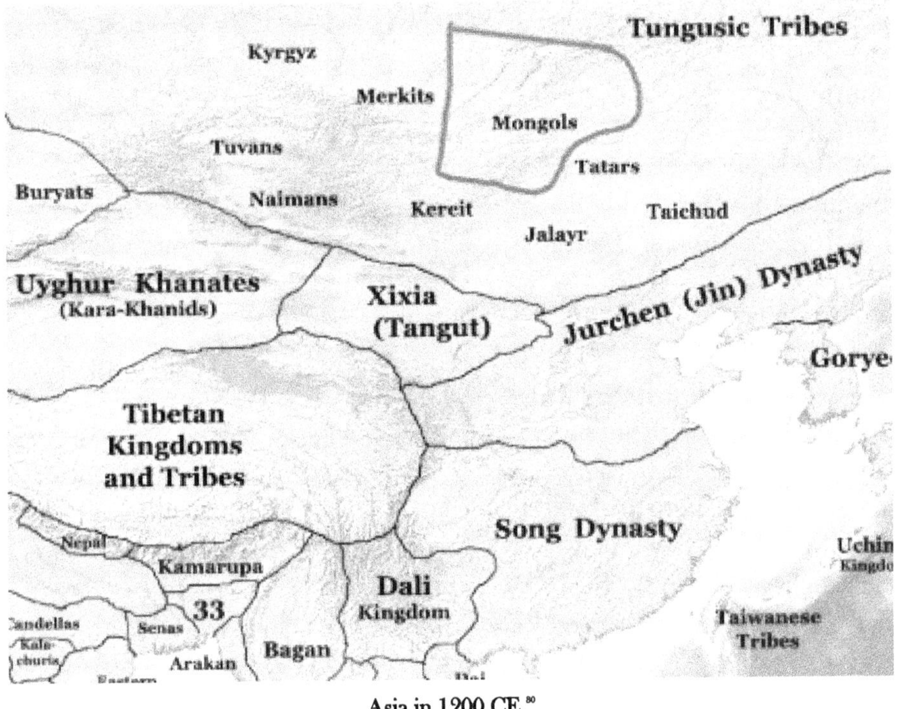

Asia in 1200 CE [80]

In 1186, after nine years of marriage, Börte gave birth to her second son and Temujin's first. He named him Ögedei. A year after that, Temujin's friend killed Jamuga's brother because he stole his horses. "This calls for war!" Jamuga screamed. With his fighting force outnumbering Temujin's three to one, Jamuga won the battle but suffered a debilitating loss of men.

How Did Temujin Become "Genghis Khan" or "Universal Ruler"?

The Chinese Jin recruited the Tartars to help them subdue the Ongud tribe, who lived close to China's northern border. The Chinese-Tartar coalition won the battle, but then the Tartars and Jin fought over the battle spoils. When the Ongud tribe heard, they swept in and utterly defeated the Jin in 1196 CE.

Ever the opportunist, Temujin approached the Jin frontier commander with an offer: "I'll take care of those Tartars and subdue the Ongud tribe for you."

The Chinese commander agreed, and the coalition army of Jin and Mongols crushed the Tartars. For Temujin, this was vengeance for his father's death. He also amassed staggering treasure from the loot.

At this point, Toghril arrived. The two commanders allied against their common enemies, starting with the Merkits, who had regained strength. Temujin had a young man in his army named Subutai (Subedei) who was from the "reindeer country" (northern Russia). Although unschooled in horsemanship and Mongol warfare, Subutai was a genius at strategy. As a non-Mongol, Subutai managed to infiltrate the Merkit camp and spy out their battle plans. The Mongols pulverized the Merkits, and Temujin made Subutai a general and his master strategist.

In 1199 CE, Temujin and Toghril attacked the Naiman people of western Mongolia, who outnumbered the Mongols. At this point, Temujin and Jamuga formed an uneasy truce to fight the Naiman people. The timing would never be better, as the Naiman ruler had just died, and his sons were engaged in civil war.

However, when it was time to ride out to battle, Jamuga was missing in action. Temujin and Toghril fought through the day, defeating one Naiman prince before nightfall. When Temujin awakened the next morning, he was shocked that Toghril and his men had slipped away during the night. Jamuga had snuck in and convinced Toghril to abandon Temujin. The tables swiftly turned for Toghril when the other Naiman prince, Koksu-Sabrak, chased him down, killing or enslaving half of Toghril's army and capturing its cattle, food, and supplies. Toghril had to swallow his pride and go to Temujin.

Despite Toghril's desertion, Temujin needed Toghril's Keraite tribe to keep the Naiman people in check. He sent his top generals after the Naiman army. They arrived in time to save Toghril's son, Ilkha, from destruction and recaptured the stolen cattle.

Temujin and Toghril were a team again, facing off against the Merkits and Tayichiud, who had just allied. Temujin defeated their coalition forces, executed their nobles, and captured thousands of their women and children. However, Toghril's brother conspired against him and forced him into exile in China.

With Toghril gone, Temujin's adversaries made their move. Fifteen tribes, including the Tayichiud, Merkit, and Ongud, formed a coalition to take Temujin down. They were led by Jamuga, their "gurkhan," or universal ruler. All of Mongolia was at war.

However, not everyone in the fifteen tribes was happy about the situation, especially Dai Sechen, Temujin's father-in-law. He and several others leaked valuable information about battle plans to Temujin.

"I need you now!" Temujin desperately messaged Toghril, who was sulking in exile. "Get back here!"

Reproduction of a 1278 Chinese painting of Genghis Khan[81]

Jamuga decided to attack Temujin before Toghril could return. However, he moved too fast, not waiting for all the allied tribes to gather. He rode into battle with only his men and some of the Tayichiud. Jamuga commanded his wizards to produce a storm to blow Temujin's army away. Yet, their magic went awry. The snowstorm enveloped Jamuga's forces, blinding them.

Toghril arrived just in time, and Temujin scored an epic victory in the Battle of Dalan Balzhut, scattering the rebel forces. Yet, a poisoned arrow struck Temujin in the neck, piercing his artery. One of his generals, Jelme, sucked out the poison as Temujin faded into unconsciousness. At midnight, he awakened and weakly asked for milk. Jelme snuck into the Tayichiud camp and stole milk for his commander.

Meanwhile, Jamuga's coalition was dissolving. The Tayichiud were no longer a threat. In 1203 CE, another Naiman confederation attacked, joined by Jamuga and the few remaining Merkit and Tartars. It even included Temujin's uncle and two brothers. Temujin swallowed his feelings of betrayal and focused on strategy. He outwitted the enemy's plans at every turn, displaying incredible versatility. His orders seemed odd, but his men had learned to follow them, aware of his keen instincts.

In this war, Toghril adopted Temujin as his son, making him the crown prince of the Keraite tribe. This deeply offended Seng Gum, Toghril's son, who talked his father into betraying Temujin. The Keraite army caught Temujin by surprise, but Seng Gum was injured in the ensuing fray, and Temujin slipped away. Shortly after, Temujin launched a surprise night attack on Toghril's camp. Toghril escaped, but a random Namaan soldier killed him days later.

Temujin's army swelled to sixty-six thousand warriors. Once again, Jamuga rallied the Merkits, Keraites, and Naiman people against him. In the 1204 Battle of Chakirmaut, Temujin arrayed his soldiers in a long front line called a "lake formation." Guessing he meant to outflank them, the Naiman people also stretched their soldiers out to face him. Temujin suddenly launched a frontal assault in a "chisel battle," breaking through the thinned enemy line. Jamuga snuck away, but Temujin killed every man on the enemy side.

Temujin captured a Merkit princess named Töregene, who married Ögedei, his oldest biological son. Decades later, when her husband died, Töregene became regent of the Mongol Empire. Temujin also attacked the Western Xia in 1205 CE, a Sichuan Chinese-Tibetan people who ruled northwestern China's Tangut Empire from 1038 to 1227 CE. They put up no defense, and he plundered their herds and left.

Temujin is pronounced Genghis Khan; painting by Rashid al-Din, a late thirteenth-century physician who wrote a history of the Mongol and Turkish tribes.[32]

By 1206 CE, Temujin had conquered all his adversaries and killed Jamuga. The Mongol tribes gathered at the Onon River, where the shaman Koko Chu pronounced Temujin "Genghis Khan," or "Universal Ruler." Temujin now ruled the entire Mongol tribe and the other steppe tribes in Mongolia. The great empire had begun.

What Set the Mongol Army Apart?

The Mongol army fought almost entirely on horseback, with composite bows as their primary weapons. The Mongols were incredibly tough soldiers, able to ride for days with little food or water. Their stocky horses were also rugged. Each Mongol warrior rode one horse and had spares, changing out when their mount got tired or injured.

The Mongols were innovative, highly adaptable military strategists. They embraced innovations, such as adopting gunpowder from China. They had a stellar communications network called the *örtöö* or *yam*, which used horseback couriers and relay stations. By frequently changing to a fresh mount, the couriers could cover a jaw-dropping distance in one day. This became especially essential when the Mongolian Empire expanded to two continents.

Mongol warriors often feigned retreats. They pretended to give up and raced off the field, with the enemy in hot pursuit. They would usually ride their horses up a hill, then suddenly swing around and attack their chasers from an uphill advantage. Another favorite tactic was luring their enemies into an ambush.

The Mongols used psychological warfare to instill fear in their enemies. When they won a battle, they would leave several enemy survivors behind to relay the cruel deaths the Mongols inflicted on their captives. Sometimes, they captured a city, killed every living soul, and then warned nearby cities that the same thing would happen to them if they did not surrender.

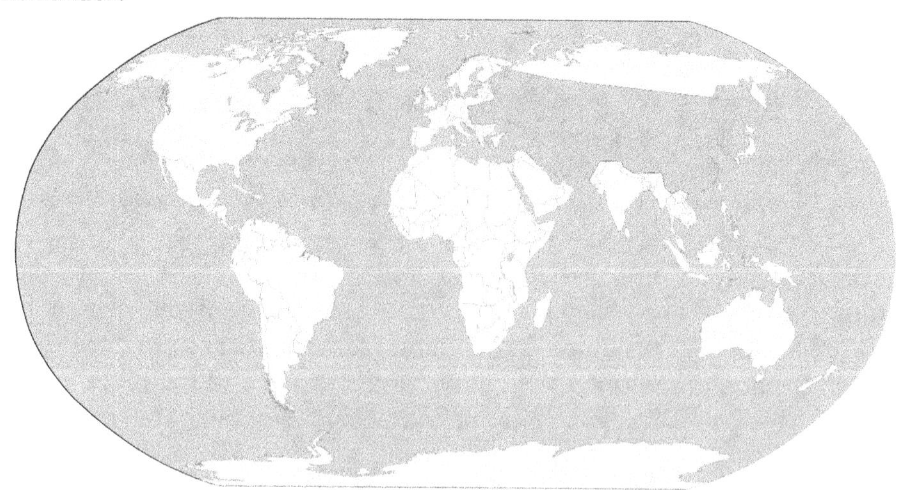

The Mongolian Empire at its height[88]

How Far Did the Mongolian Empire Extend?

After consolidating his leadership over the steppe tribes, Genghis Khan targeted China, attacking the Jurchen Jin dynasty in 1209 and 1211 CE. The Jin signed a peace treaty, agreeing to pay tribute to Genghis Khan. Yet, when they moved their capital south to Beijing (Zhongdu) in 1215 CE, he accused them of breaking the treaty and burned Zhongdu down. Genghis Khan also attacked the Western Xia in 1215 CE. After continued assaults by the Mongols, the Jurchen Jin state collapsed in 1234 CE. Genghis Khan did not live to see the great Mongol victory, having died in China in 1227 CE. His body was carried back to Mongolia and buried in a secret tomb.

Between campaigns in China, Genghis Khan targeted the Khwarazmian Empire, which covered today's Iran, Turkistan, and Uzbekistan. When he sent ambassadors demanding the shah become his vassal, the shah killed the ambassadors. Genghis sent a hundred thousand warriors into Persia, and the shah escaped to an island in the Caspian Sea. Genghis ruthlessly reduced city after city to ashes, killing men, women, and children. In 1221 and 1222 CE, he invaded today's Afghanistan and took control of the regions around the Caspian Sea.

Genghis Khan and his descendants had a reputation for massive destruction and abject violence. However, he allowed leaders to stay in power if they acknowledged him as their overlord and paid tribute. He also showed religious tolerance to Buddhists, Christians, Muslims, and other faiths. Genghis Khan established the Yassa, an unwritten law code that promoted unity, obedience to authority, and harsh punishment of anyone stepping out of line. He rewarded loyalty by elevating people of humble origins to high positions.

Following his instructions, his mighty empire was divided among his three living sons after he died, with his oldest biological son, Ögedei, as the next "great khan." Genghis Khan's grandson, Kublai Khan, conquered the rest of China in 1279 CE—collapsing the Song dynasty, creating the Yuan dynasty, and declaring himself China's emperor. The Mongols also invaded Korea, Japan, Pakistan, and the Middle East. At their peak in the thirteenth century, they pressed into Eastern Europe, conquering parts of today's Russia, Armenia, Georgia, Hungary, and Ukraine, stopping only at the Danube River.

Hulegu, Genghis Khan's grandson, and his wife, Doquz Khatun, Toghril's granddaughter. [84]

The Mongol Empire played an extraordinary role in connecting the East and West before it dissolved in the mid-1400s. One empire ruling such an astonishing swathe of the world enabled knowledge and technology to transfer freely. Protected trade routes encouraged cultural and economic exchange along the Silk Road.

Chapter 6: The Aztec Empire

Aztec folklore, written on picture books called codices, said the Mexica-Aztecs were one of seven Aztec tribes that emerged from seven caves in Colhuacan Hill on the idyllic island of Aztlan. The other six tribes had already crossed over the Lake of the Moon to the mainland. Yet, the Mexica remained in their peaceful paradise, where snowy white herons graced the shoreline, and ducks and large fish were easily caught in the sparkling lake water. No one ever grew old in Aztlan.

The seven caves on Aztlan; illustration from the Historia Tolteca-Chichimeca[85]

However, something mysterious and unexplained impelled them to leave their life of ease. When they crossed the lake, a hummingbird sang to them each night. It was Huitzilopochtli, the god of the sun and war:

"You are my people now. I will lead you to your new home and give you the tools you need for your journey," Huitzilopochtli said. "I will sing to you at night with instructions. You will become preeminent and prosperous, ruling over the other tribes. Yet, I require one thing in exchange: human sacrifice."

Xiuhcoatl, the Turquoise Serpent, was wielded by Huitzilopochtli against evil forces[86]

The Mexica-Aztecs eventually ruled eighty thousand square miles of central Mexico from their spectacular city built on an island in a swamp. Tenochtitlan, their capital, was among the world's largest cities from the fourteenth to the sixteenth century CE. It presided over five hundred city-states with six million people from multiple tribes. The Mexica created a sophisticated society with advanced agriculture, complex social hierarchy, and vibrant—albeit depraved—social practices.

What Happened as the Mexica Migrated from Atzlan to the Valley of Mexico?

After leaving Atzlan, the Mexica captured two men and a woman from the Chicomóztoc-Mimixcoa tribe and sacrificed them, laying their bodies across two cacti and a bush. Then, they traipsed through the harsh Mexican desert in a land turned against them. Thistles and thorns tore their skin, and poisonous lizards and snakes slithered across their path.

The first sacrifice, from the Codex Boturini[87]

When the Mexica finally reached the Valley of Mexico, their Aztec relatives and other tribes had already settled around Lake Texcoco, which covered over two thousand square miles. The Mexica had to carve out a place for their tribe. They hired themselves out to the other tribes as construction workers and mercenary soldiers. They made strategic marriages to build up allies.

The Colhuacan tribe gave the Mexica land to settle in exchange for military service. But the Mexica quickly wore out their welcome. After winning a stunning battle against the Xochimilca tribe, they asked the Colhuacan king for his daughter so they could worship her as a goddess. The chief was horrified to discover that the Mexica concept of worshiping her involved killing and skinning the young woman. He arrived at their village to find a priest wearing his daughter's skin!

The enraged Colhuacans drove the Mexica out. No one else wanted the macabre Mexica around either. The Mexica had to creep around, hiding in the mosquito-ridden swamps, trying to scavenge for food. When all hope seemed lost, Huitzilopochtli spoke to a Mexica priest in a dream: "In the morning, look for a prickly-pear cactus growing among the reeds. You will see an eagle perched on it, with a snake in its claws. That is where you will settle down and build your city, Tenochtitlan. From there, you will conquer all your enemies."

The following day, the Mexica set off in search—and there it was! On an island on Lake Texcoco's western shore was a prickly pear cactus with an eagle sitting on it, holding a snake in its talons. They laughed and cried. It was 1325 CE, and their forefathers had left Aztlan almost 150 years earlier. Now, they had an island for a new city and a bright future.

Mexico's coat of arms features an eagle on a cactus holding a snake. [88]

How Did Tenochtitlan Grow into a Sprawling Metropolis?

A bog sounds like an odd place for a new city, but the Mexica-Aztecs made it work. They had abundant fish and waterfowl. The Mexica used chinampas, or floating gardens, to grow corn, beans, and squash. The chinampas had underwater wooden stakes supporting woven reed platforms on the lake's surface. The Mexica dredged fertile mud from the lake bottom and piled it on the platforms, where they grew their produce.

The farmers paddled canoes around their floating gardens, and they could stand on the platforms to plant or harvest. In the warm lake region, they could grow multiple crops each year. Just south of Tenochtitlan was a waterway connecting Lake Texcoco to Lake Xochimilco, with more extensive floating gardens.

The Mexica-Aztecs built a gleaming city of adobe brick houses, palaces, and temples on their island. Instead of roads, they had canals, which they navigated by canoe. In the city center was the lavish Templo Mayor, the city's main religious center. It was a pyramid topped by two temples, one for Huitzilopochtli and the other for Tlaloc, the rain god. Glistening palaces for the city's nobility encircled the temple complex. Around the temples and palaces were four residential districts housing 200,000 people. Few European cities in the 1300s to 1500s were larger than Tenochtitlan, and they certainly were not as clean!

When the Spaniards arrived, they noticed how pristine Tenochtitlan was. It had an advanced waste management system, and its citizens kept the streets and their homes spotless. Dams and dikes provided flood control, and since the water around the city was slightly saline, an aqueduct brought in fresh drinking water. Causeways connected the city to the mainland.

Mural of Tenochtitlan by Diego Rivera [89]

What Was Remarkable about the Aztec Social and Economic Structure?

Aztec society had clearly defined social levels, with nobility, priests, and military commanders at the top. The second level included merchants, architects, and artisans. The third level was farmers and laborers, and at the bottom were enslaved people.

All young teens in Tenochtitlan, both boys and girls, attended school. The boys lived in dormitories and learned military arts. The upper-class boys also studied reading, writing, astronomy, and religion. The working-class boys studied religion and honed their skills in a trade. Teen girls learned dancing, singing, and theology at day school. Some learned medical arts, like midwifery.

Most enslaved people were war captives or people sent as tribute from conquered city-states. Occasionally, Aztec citizens sold themselves into slavery if they got into deep debt. The destiny of some enslaved people was human sacrifice, as the Aztecs sacrificed thousands of adults and children each year. Enslaved children were usually household servants, while enslaved males did farm and construction work. The educated often managed their owners' businesses. Enslaved people were rarely resold and could buy their freedom.

Most Aztecs were farmers who also fought in the military between the planting and harvest seasons. Additionally, farmers helped build temples, roads, and water systems in the off season. The Aztecs had complex irrigation canals, diverting water from rivers and lakes. In addition to farming the floating chinampas, they built terraces up the sides of mountains for planting.

The Aztec artisans had large workshops for carpentry, metalworking, ceramics, stone carving, and other skilled crafts. Since the Aztecs were almost constantly at war, they made many weapons, such as six-foot-long blowguns. They dipped blowgun darts in poisonous secretions from the skin of the Colorado River toad and the Mexican tree frog. Artisans also made war clubs embedded with razor-sharp obsidian, a black volcanic rock.

Some artisans were boat builders, as the Aztecs needed canoes to navigate around their canal city of Tenochtitlan and travel to other cities via the lake and river systems. The Aztecs had engineers and skilled craftsmen designing and building their aqueducts, dikes, canals, and causeways.

The traders and merchants were the fastest-growing class in Aztec society. They were becoming so rich and powerful that they might have upended the Aztec social system if the Spaniards had not arrived and disrupted everything.

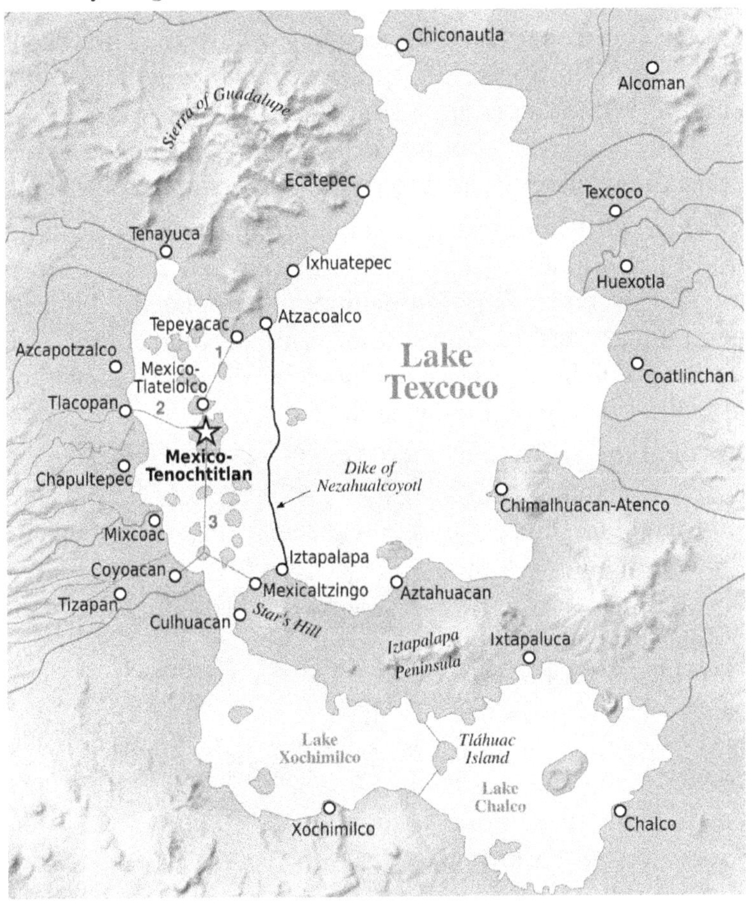

Cities around Lake Texcoco in the Aztec Empire [40]

After building Tenochtitlan in the southern marshes of Lake Texcoco, the Aztecs soon controlled most of the cities around Lake Texcoco. (Today, the lake is drained, and Mexico City sprawls over the region.) Through military conquest and strategic alliances, the Aztec Empire ultimately stretched from the Gulf of Mexico to the Pacific Ocean and reached south to Guatemala's rainforests. The conquered people enriched the empire through tribute, usually products made or grown in their region. Aztec merchants traded in goods from around the empire, like cotton cloth, precious gems and metals, featherwork, rubber, exquisite carvings, and brightly colored bird feathers.

How Did the Aztecs' Religion and Mythology Shape Their Culture?

The Aztecs worshiped many of the same gods as other Mesoamericans (people in the area from central Mexico to Costa Rica). The exception was their chief deity, Huitzilopochtli, the hummingbird god of the sun and war. Only the Aztecs worshipped him until they started building their empire. They forced conquered people to build temples to Huitzilopochtli but allowed them to continue worshiping other gods.

The Aztecs also adopted the deities of nearby civilizations. Their second-most important god was Tlaloc, the fanged, goggle-eyed rain god that virtually everyone in Mesoamerica worshiped. Huitzilopochtli demanded human sacrifice in increasing numbers, and so did Tlaloc. Yet, Tlaloc wanted children. About 20 percent of Aztec baby boys were drowned in the worship of the rain god.

The myth of the "Fifth Sun" was the Aztec creation story. The gods had to create a world, a sun, and people. Huitzilopochtli and his brother, Quetzalcoatl, created the first world. Its people were acorn-eating giants. Another brother, Tezcatlipoca, volunteered to be the sun. However, he was the smoke and mirrors god of darkness, so he did not shine brightly. The new world was always dim.

"This is no good!" the other gods muttered.

Exasperated, Quetzalcoatl threw his club at Tezcatlipoca, knocking him out of the sky. He fell into the ocean and

A turquoise mask of Tezcatlipoca[4]

shapeshifted into a jaguar who ate the giants, ending the age of the first sun.

Now, it was Quetzalcoatl's turn to be the sun. He created people who ate pine nuts, and his sun shone brightly. Sadly, his people stopped praying. They became corrupt, greedy, and violent. Tezcatlipoca got his revenge on Quetzalcoatl by blowing all the people away in a hurricane. The survivors turned into monkeys and lived in the jungle.

In the third world, Tlaloc was the sun. This time, the humans prayed and lived morally. Unfortunately, while Tlaloc was giving light and warmth to the earth, Tezcatlipoca stole his wife. Heartbroken, Tlaloc forgot to send rain to his world. In desperation, the people prayed for rain, but Tlaloc ignored them. The harvest failed, and the starving people screamed out to Tlaloc. Tlaloc's grief turned to rage. "Here's your rain!" he snarled. Instead of water, he rained fire down on the earth, burning up the people. The survivors turned into turkeys.

Tlaloc's new wife, Chalchiuhtlicue, was the sun in the fourth world. She shone benevolently over the people. Yet, Tezcatlipoca, the troublemaker, played on her emotions: "Ha! You're pretending to love the humans, but you don't know what love is!" Deeply hurt, Chalchiuhtlicue began to cry. She was the water goddess, so her tears became rain. She kept weeping, and the rain caused a flood that swept over the earth, covering the mountains and drowning the turkeys. The surviving people morphed into fish to survive. Chalchiuhtlicue fell to the earth.

The gods were remorseful. "Our infighting has destroyed four worlds!" they cried. Quetzalcoatl and Tezcatlipoca apologized and transformed into giant oaks that pushed the sky back into place. The gods gathered around a great fire, discussing how they would create the fifth world. "Someone must sacrifice themselves to become the new sun!" they decided.

Tecuciztecatl, handsome yet vain, volunteered to jump into the bonfire. But he kept losing his nerve. Then, the ugliest and smallest god, Tonatiuh, leaped into the fire. Suddenly, the gods looked up to see a radiant new sun lighting the sky. Their cheers made Tecuciztecatl jealous. He finally got the nerve to leap into the fire. A minute later, two suns shone side by side.

"We can't have two suns!" grumbled one god. He snatched a rabbit and threw it at Tecuciztecatl. When the rabbit hit the second sun, Tecuciztecatl turned into the moon, with the imprint of the rabbit on his face. Now, only Tonatiuh shone as a brilliant sun; however, he was so frail he could not move across the sky. The other gods sacrificed their blood to give him the strength to orbit through the galaxy. Thus, for the Aztecs, sacrifice was imperative to maintain cosmic order.

This replica of the Sun Stone is painted in its original colors. [49]

In 1790, while repairing the Mexico City Cathedral (built over the Aztec Templo Mayor), workers discovered a twelve-foot-wide stone disk buried in the rubble. The Aztec Sun Stone had intricate carvings illustrating Aztec cosmology. Rays spread out from the sun god Tonatiuh, grimacing in the center. Four images representing the first four suns surround him. Further out on the disk is a circle of twenty glyphs (pictographs) representing the twenty days in an Aztec month. The glyphs on the outer ring relate to the solar calendar.

How Did Cortés and the Spanish Conquistadors Defeat the Aztec Empire?

In 1517 CE, the Spaniards discovered Mexico's Yucatan Peninsula when a storm blew one of their ships off course. Two years later, Hernán Cortés sailed eleven ships to the area to explore. After fighting the Maya in the Yucatán, he sailed north along Mexico's Gulf Coast, picking up several translators, including a shipwrecked friar. When the Spaniards arrived in Aztec territory, the Aztec Emperor Moctezuma sent them gold, politely asking them to go away. That did not work. Cortés only wanted more gold. He marched inland with his army, horses, and cannons.

Despite never having seen horses or cannons, the Aztecs were fearless warriors determined to fight for their empire. The Spaniards met other tribes—the Totonacs and Tlaxcalans—as they traveled inland to the Aztec capital of Tenochtitlan. Cortés convinced these tribes to ally with him against the Aztecs. These tribes hated the Aztecs for sacrificing their children and demanding heavy tribute payments.

In 1519 CE, Cortés met Moctezuma on the causeway leading to the island city of Tenochtitlan. The Aztec emperor cordially hung flowers and a gold chain around the conquistador's neck. Yet, Cortés had his guard up. Several days later, after learning that the Aztecs had attacked his men whom he had left at the coast, Cortés placed Moctezuma under house arrest.

Open war broke out a few months later when nineteen more Spanish warships arrived carrying fourteen hundred soldiers. Two thousand Tlaxcalans fought on the Spanish side. Moctezuma was killed in mysterious circumstances, and the Aztecs made his brother Cuitlahuac their new emperor. On La Noche Triste, or Night of Tears, the Spaniards and their Tlaxcalan allies fought a desperate and losing battle on the causeway leading out of the city. They lost about a thousand Spaniards and twice as many Tlaxcalan warriors.

Cortés spent the next few months convincing the other city-states around Lake Texcoco to ally with him against the Aztecs. Smallpox, brought to the New World by the Spaniards, hit Tenochtitlan in September 1520 CE, killing many warriors and the new emperor. The Aztecs made the emperor's cousin, Cuauhtémoc, their next (and last) emperor.

While the Aztecs fought smallpox, Cortés built thirteen small ships armed with cannons to launch a naval battle against Tenochtitlan. In April 1521 CE, his new ships sailed down a secret canal into Lake Texcoco. Meanwhile, a Spanish battalion cut the aqueduct bringing fresh water to the city. Five hundred Aztec canoes surged out of the city toward the new ships, but the Spaniards hoisted their sails and crushed any canoes that could not move out of the way fast enough. Ten thousand Tlaxcalans blocked the causeways leading to the island city, keeping other Aztec cities from joining the battle.

The Spaniards launched cannonballs at Tenochtitlan while the Aztecs shot a hail of arrows at their ships. Tenochtitlan's conquest took months. The Spaniards worked their way through the city, taking a section, burning it down, and then retreating to the causeways or their ships at night. The people in the city had no fresh water or food other than what their allies smuggled in by canoe in the dead of night. Finally, the starving remnant of Aztecs in Tenochtitlan surrendered, only to be viciously attacked by the Tlaxcalans. The Spaniards captured Emperor Cuauhtémoc and his family on August 13, 1521 CE, ending the Aztec Empire.

Chapter 7: The British Empire

How did a modest island nation become history's most extensive empire? What profound influence did Britain have on the world in those four centuries, beginning in the late 1500s? This chapter explores the economic ambitions, naval prowess, and political strategies that propelled Britain to establish colonies around the globe. The British Empire's complex legacy included cultural changes, the global spread of the English language, and new government systems.

All the territory that was once part of the British Empire "

What Were the First British Colonies in the New World?

In 1603, when Queen Elizabeth I died, Great Britain was not great geographically. It was only England and Wales. A century would pass before Scotland officially united with Britain and two centuries before Ireland did the same. Yet, Britain had already begun building an empire in the New World, jumping into competition with Spain, Portugal, and France. Its first attempt failed in 1590 when 117 people mysteriously disappeared from Roanoke Island (North Carolina). A 1604 attempt to settle Guyana in South America also fizzled.

Britain founded its first permanent colony at Jamestown (Virginia) in 1607. One of its leaders was John Smith, who had been captured and enslaved by the Turks. After escaping, he joined the expedition to Virginia, only to be captured again, this time by the Powhatan tribe. Their chief planned to kill Smith, but the chief's daughter, Pocahontas, intervened. The Powhatan tribe helped the colonists survive the first brutal winter.

In 1609, the British ship *Sea Venture* was sailing to Jamestown with supplies and new colonists. A hurricane drove it off course and onto Bermuda's reef. Several British men stayed in Bermuda, establishing a permanent colony on Smith's Island. Using local cedar and the *Sea Venture*'s wreckage, the British built two ships and sailed to Jamestown with 137 people in 1610. They found only 61 colonists still alive.

The Puritans arrived in the New World in 1620, seeking freedom from religious persecution in England. They had a land patent to settle at the mouth of the Hudson River; however, winter gales blew the ship north to Cape Cod (Massachusetts). While pledging loyalty to King James I, they formed the Mayflower Compact, granting themselves self-government. At the Plymouth Colony, they elected their leaders and made their own laws.

In 1634, England's persecuted Roman Catholics settled the Province of Maryland. The Puritans founded Rhode Island in 1636 as a place where everyone could enjoy religious tolerance. In 1639, the Congregationalists, who followed a Reformed, Calvinist faith, settled Connecticut. And, in 1664, the British captured the Dutch colony of New Amsterdam and renamed it New York.

In the West Indies, Britain established colonies in St. Kitts (1624), Barbados (1627), Nevis (1628), and Jamaica (1655). Sugarcane plantations on the islands brought phenomenal wealth to Great Britain. At first, these colonies used indentured servants to farm plantations. Toward the end of the seventeenth century, they began importing African enslaved people.

How Did the British East India Company Impact India and China?

The British East India Company (EIC) controlled half of the world's trade in the 1700s. Incorporated under Queen Elizabeth I, it operated in India, Pakistan, Bangladesh, China, Persia, and Indonesia from 1600 to 1874. The EIC wielded both economic and political power over these nations. It had its own navy and an army twice as big as Britain's full-time army. The British East India Company built staggering wealth by importing cotton, tea, and spices to London. However, one-third of its employees died from tropical diseases, battles with pirates, and violent uprisings in India.

William Fullerton, an East India Company official, receiving a visitor "

Babar, a descendant of Genghis Khan, conquered northern India in 1526. Two hundred years later, his Mughal Empire ruled most of India. The Mughal emperor permitted the East India Company to set up trading posts. In the beginning, the relationship enriched both India and Britain. However, in the early 1700s, the Mughal Empire began to weaken. The East India Company capitalized on that by allying with local rulers to take control.

Soon, the East India Company ruled some of India's cities, like Bombay, Calcutta, and Madras. It was collecting taxes, minting coins, building forts, and running the police forces and justice systems. In 1784, the British Parliament passed the "India Act," giving the EIC control of trade and day-to-day affairs in these regions. Essentially, the EIC was a branch of the British government, especially since about one hundred members of the British Parliament were employees of the EIC.

China was the only country exporting tea then, and Britain wanted trade control. China had banned the import of opium because its recreational use had evolved into a horrific addiction issue. Britain flouted Chinese law by smuggling opium from India to China in exchange for tea and fine porcelain. China cracked down harder, and Britain responded by sending in warships and taking over Hong Kong in 1841.

By 1858, the British East India Company ruled most of India, Pakistan, and Bangladesh. This quickly changed when the Mughal Empire collapsed that year. The British East India Company had about 45,000 British troops and 230,000 Indian soldiers called "sepoys." These disgruntled Indian soldiers led the Sepoy Mutiny against the EIC. The British won, but it spelled the end of the EIC. The British government dissolved the East India Company in 1878 and ruled India directly until 1947.

Sepoy Mutiny [45]

What Was the Role of the Royal Navy in the British Empire?

James Thomson's poem, set to music, rallied the British around their navy as a key element to Great Britain's success as a world empire: "Rule, Britannia! Rule the waves: Britons never will be slaves."

The British Royal Navy did indeed rule the waves. It enabled Britain to become a global power, defend its interests, and move people, goods, and ideas across oceans. The navy's power at sea protected its merchant ships from pirates or attacks by ships of rival nations. It enabled supplies to reach British colonies and goods from the colonies to be shipped to England.

The British Navy's superiority gave Britain a decisive advantage over rival nations as it built its global empire. It spent more time on gunnery practice than other navies. Even when confronted by larger ships, the British Navy was impeccably trained in weaponry and seamanship. In 1675, a British clockmaker, John Harrison, invented the marine chronometer, immensely enhancing navigation through accurate longitude measurements.

How Did the Industrial Revolution Change the British Empire?

The British Industrial Revolution (1760–1840) was an era that experienced breathtaking technological breakthroughs. Exciting manufacturing, transportation, and communication inventions enabled the empire to thrive economically. New technology, like railways, steamships, and the telegraph, changed how people traveled and communicated. Large factories revolutionized world trade.

The invention of the power loom, spinning jenny, and water frame in the late 1700s radically changed cotton weaving. Previously, this was a time-consuming task done in homes or small workshops, all by hand. The fibers and seeds had to be separated, carded, turned into thread on a spinning wheel, and woven into cloth on a loom. These machines could do all this much faster. British factories imported the raw cotton from its colonies, wove it into cloth in factories in Britain, and then exported it worldwide.

Radical changes to the textile industry were not the only advances. Steam engines became much more efficient, requiring less fuel. Factories used stationary steam engines to run machines. Factory furnaces began using coke, a processed form of coal, especially for iron production. Technological advances fueled the British Empire's economic dominance, industrial growth, and global influence.

A London neighborhood near a factory, by Gustave Doré, 1870 [46]

The Industrial Revolution changed the demographics of Great Britain (and many other nations). With the boom in factory jobs in cities, people left their rural farm communities. Cities like Manchester, Birmingham, Glasgow, London, and Newcastle swelled in population. As people's income and standard of living increased dynamically, Britain's population tripled. Yet, there was a downside. City living was cramped, and the air near the factories was polluted. Diseases like typhus and cholera spread easily due to poor sanitation.

Women, who traditionally worked from home, went to work in the factories in droves. So did children—as young as eight. The factories paid women and children less yet preferred them because their small, nimble hands could work some machines better. Half of the textile factory workers were women, and half of Britain's school-aged children worked in the factories. Men, women, and children worked twelve-hour shifts until 1847, when it changed to ten-hour shifts.

In the colonies, the focus became mining or growing products like sugar, cotton, or tobacco. These raw products filled ships sailing to Great Britain's factories. Most colonies lacked the resources or technical knowledge to build their own factories with complicated machines.

What Were the Social and Cultural Dimensions of the Empire?

The British Empire facilitated the global spread of the English language, legal systems, education, and Christianity. By the late 1700s, English was spoken throughout the British colonies. In North America, it became the dominant language. In the Asian and African colonies, many people were bilingual, speaking English and their native language. Schools in the colonies taught the English language, and most taught other subjects like math and science in English. English was the language of trade, technology, and science.

The advantage of the global spread of English was that the world had a common language. Even after the British colonies gained independence, they continued using English as an official language. Today, English is written and spoken by more people than any other language in world history.

The British legal system also spread throughout Great Britain's colonies. The Royal Proclamation of 1763 said all British colonies had to follow English common law. However, places like Quebec and India already had legal systems. Local officials often tailored the British law to align with their existing legal systems.

Most of the earliest schools in Britain's Asian and African colonies were missionary schools. One objective was teaching children to read the Bible, and a second was educating Christian students to lead new churches in their region. A third objective was to educate the general population and lift them out of poverty.

As time passed, the British government began establishing standard schools in its colonies. Many taught basic reading, writing, and math but focused on developing practical skills. Usually, only students from elite families or exceptionally bright students received higher education. However, this was also true of students in Britain.

The British encountered diverse religions in its colonies, like Hinduism in India, Islam in the Middle East, and indigenous religions in Africa. One goal of the British rulers was to spread the Protestant Christian faith. They sent missionaries and gave special privileges to folks who converted. This was especially the case in Africa. The British thought that converting the Africans to Christianity was essential to civilizing them. They also wanted to end practices like witchcraft.

David Livingstone was a famous missionary in Africa. He was born in 1813 to a low-income family in Scotland and went to work in the cotton mills at age ten. Despite leaving school early, he read every book he could find on science, philosophy, medicine, and religion. Eventually, he received some formal training in theology and medicine. He became a missionary doctor and explorer in Central Africa, where he vigorously campaigned against the slave trade.

Most of the Middle Eastern Muslims and people of India refused to change their religion. The British mostly stopped trying to convert them. However, they did outlaw religious practices like *sati*, an Indian custom that expected widows to throw themselves on their husbands' funeral fire. Missionaries like Amy Carmichael built group homes for girls who escaped from the Indian *devadasi*. This was a custom of "marrying" little girls to a god and placing them in service to temples, where they were sexually exploited.

Amy Carmichael with children in her care[17]

How Did Independence Movements Resisting British Rule Play Out?

Britain's colonists in America and other points of the globe became increasingly irritated by what they considered unfair trade policies. The colonies were not allowed to set the prices on items they exported, like tobacco, gold, and cotton. They could usually only export goods to Britain, which set rock-bottom prices. Britain processed the raw goods, then sold them back to the colonies.

Adding insult to injury, Britain began taxing the American colonies on wine, coffee, and sugar to pay its debt from the Seven Years' War. The 1765 Stamp Act taxed documents in the colonies, including newspapers. The Americans seethed: "We have no seats in Parliament. This is taxation without representation!"

Britain continued passing new tax laws, which the Americans felt were unfair. An angry crowd in Boston threw snowballs at the British soldiers in 1770. The soldiers opened fire, killing five colonists. The colonists responded to the tax on tea by boycotting British tea. They grew herbal tea or switched to coffee, which became America's patriotic beverage at that time. Finally, a group of colonists dressed like Native Americans attacked the British merchant ships in Boston Harbor, dumping 342 crates of tea into the water. The British responded to the "Boston Tea Party" by closing Boston Harbor and taking over Massachusetts' elected government.

In 1774, delegates from the American colonies met in Philadelphia for the First Continental Congress. They decided to form their own military and adopt a Declaration of Rights. "We are entitled to life, liberty, and property!" they declared. The British responded in April 1775 by attacking Concord and Lexington, Massachusetts. This did not end well for them. The colonists trounced the British and chased them back to Boston. The American Revolutionary War had begun.

A year later, the American colonists ran the British out of Boston. The Continental Congress signed the Declaration of Independence on July 4, 1776. It said that the government must have the consent of the people being governed. If the government became destructive, the people had the right to change or abolish it.

However, the war was far from over. It dragged on for another fifteen grueling months. Finally, George Washington confronted the British general Charles Cornwallis in Virginia. With assistance from the French, the American colonists won the war and gained independence.

India's quest for independence continued despite losing the Sepoy Mutiny of 1857. Queen Victoria, proclaimed Empress of India in 1876, tried to fix some of the issues. She promised the Indians equal opportunity in public service and that they could join the civil service. She also said she would stop taking land from the native princes and that India would have religious freedom. Nevertheless, she increased the number of British soldiers to outnumber the Indian soldiers in India's army. Furthermore, only the British could shoot high-caliber guns.

Mahatma Gandhi, 1931 [46]

By 1900, India had an all-Indian congress, yet the Muslims felt they did not have enough of a voice. Still, they agreed with the Hindus on one thing—they did not like British rule. Mahatma Gandhi became the leader of the Indian National Congress in 1921. He encouraged peaceful resistance and civil disobedience against the British rather than violence. "Non-violence is a weapon of the strong," he taught. In 1942, the Indian National Congress launched the "Quit India" campaign. "Leave immediately!" they told the British. "Give India independence!" The British threw Gandhi and over 100,000 other nationalist leaders in jail, publicly flogging the protesters.

Eventually, the British agreed to independence in 1947. Yet, they did not think the Hindus and Muslims could peacefully live and rule together. The British split off the northeastern section of India, making it the Muslim country of Bangladesh. Millions of Hindus whose ancestral homes were in Bangladesh relocated to India. They trudged south with the possessions they could carry, passing Muslims who had also been uprooted and were moving to Bangladesh.

World War II (1939–1945) almost broke the British Empire. It devastated its military and left it drowning in debt. Britain had neither the money nor the manpower to resist the independence movements in its colonies. Ceylon (Sri Lanka) won independence in 1948, Burma (Myanmar) in 1948, and Libya in 1951.

In 1952, Princess Elizabeth and her husband, Philip, were in Kenya, touring the Commonwealth. Word came that her father had died, making Elizabeth the queen of Great Britain. The British Empire was already evolving into the "Commonwealth of Nations," an association of independent countries that had once been part of the empire. Twenty-five-year-old Elizabeth II became their symbolic monarch.

Some countries were still in the process of gaining independence. For several, it meant violent uprisings. Malaya and

Queen Elizabeth II, Coronation Day [40]

Ghana became free in 1957. In the 1960s and 1970s, Kenya, Nigeria, Jamaica, and the Caribbean territories won independence. Britain returned Hong Kong to China in 1997, officially ending the British Empire.

Chapter 8: The French Revolution and the Dawn of a New Era

The French Revolution brought profound upheaval, ending the French monarchy. This pivotal event transformed France and changed the course of global history. What ignited the revolution? How did social inequality, economic distress, and Enlightenment ideas all play a part? Who were the major players? This chapter unwraps how the revolution dismantled the old feudal order and paved the way for modern democratic principles.

What Was the State of French Society in the Late Eighteenth Century?

King Louis XVI of France came to the throne in 1774. His government had ingrained issues that seemed unfixable. The most significant problems were finances and social inequality. France had a rigid class structure called the "Three Estates": the Roman Catholic clergy, the nobility, and commoners. The commoners—ordinary working-class people—comprised 90 percent of France's population. They had no voice in government and suffered under crushing taxes. The other 10 percent, the Roman Catholic clergy and aristocrats, got tax exemptions and other social advantages.

France's population grew at an unusual pace in the 1700s. Medical knowledge had improved, so fewer babies died in infancy. Farming technology had also improved, and there were no prolonged dry spells in the first two-thirds of the century. This meant children and adults had enough food. The population increased by about 50 percent to roughly

28,000. France had more people than any other European country, yet about one-third of its population lived in poverty.

The middle-class commoners, the bourgeoisie, did not suffer as badly. They were the merchants, business owners, or more successful farmers. Some grew wealthy and powerful enough to challenge the aristocratic class. New political ideas were filtering in, making them question how things were done. They realized that the elite folks running the country were inept at management. Worse yet, the ruling class were unethical, arbitrary, and cruel.

In 1770, France's fifteen-year-old dauphin (crown prince), Louis XVI, married the fourteen-year-old Marie Antoinette. She was from Austria, the daughter of the Holy Roman Emperor. It was a political marriage, meant to unite two countries that had been enemies in the Seven Years' War. Marie's mother, the Empress of Austria, expected her daughter to manipulate affairs in France to Austria's advantage.

In 1774, France's King Louis XV died of smallpox, making his grandson, Louis XVI, king and Marie Antoinette the queen consort. Shortly after, drought struck, followed by an intense

Marie Antoinette, 1775, by After Jean-Baptiste André Gautier-Dagoty[50]

hailstorm ruining the harvests. Several outbreaks of the viral Rinderpest disease killed over 200 million cattle in Western Europe. The price of bread skyrocketed, leaving the people angry and desperate. Workers went on strike, and rioters filled the streets. The French disliked their Austrian queen and accused her of gambling and reckless spending on lavish clothes and furniture. "We're starving, and she's draping herself in silk and diamonds!" they protested.

Why Was France in a Financial Crisis?

One reason France was in financial trouble was its mountain of debt, which grew to twelve billion livres by 1789. Louis XVI's grandfather had plunged the nation into debt through several European wars. After becoming king, Louis XVI got France involved in the American Revolution, initially as a secret supporter of the colonists. France sent clandestine supply shipments, beginning in 1776. Later, France formed a formal military alliance with the colonists, sending financial, military, and naval support to America.

Meanwhile, Louis XIV and his queen were overspending on fine clothing, an ostentatious lifestyle, and enlarging the opulent Versailles palace. Because France was so deeply in debt, it had to pay astoundingly high interest rates on loans. The interest rates and continuous spending made it almost impossible to repay the loans. Creditors began demanding repayment in the 1780s. Since the upper classes were exempt from taxes, the middle and lower classes carried the tax burden, leading to increasing unrest.

Hall of Mirrors in Versailles Palace [51]

Finally, the king's controller general, Charles-Alexandre de Calonne, recommended revising the tax code to include the wealthy aristocrats. In 1787, Calonne convened the Assembly of Notables to approve his reforms. However, the aristocratic Assembly refused to pass the reforms because they would have to start paying taxes. "We do not have the power to do this," they said. "Only an assembly of the Estates-General can pass legislation like this."

The Estates-General was a governing body of elected officials from three classes of society: clergy, nobility, and commoners. An Estates-General had not been called in 175 years, and it was not something Louis XVI wanted to do. For one thing, the Estates-General was more of an advisory council, not one that passed laws. It made recommendations to the king, who made the decisions and passed any laws. Louis XVI did not want to be in the position of passing an unpopular law that would bring down the wrath of the aristocrats. He fired Calonne and asked the parliaments to consider the tax reforms. In France at that time, aristocrats led thirteen parliaments, or courts. This group also refused to approve the tax reforms. "You must call an Estates-General!" they insisted.

Finally, King Louis called for the Estates-General of 1789. It had 282 representatives for the nobility, 303 for the clergy, and 578 for the "Third Estate," or the commoners. As the Estates-General met, its representatives were challenged by revolutionaries who wanted to turn society on its head. The revolutionaries wanted a new society built on the Enlightenment motto: "*Liberté, égalité, fraternité*" or "Liberty, equality, fraternity."

How Did the Enlightenment Thinkers Change Political Ideals?

The Enlightenment or Age of Reason (1685–1815) was a European movement that questioned old political traditions. It pushed logic, intellectualism, individualism, and science as the path to humanity's improvement. The Enlightenment thinkers' ideas about individual rights, separation of powers, and social contracts inspired people to challenge traditional authority and demand greater freedoms.

Voltaire was a French Enlightenment philosopher who advocated for social equality, freedom of speech, and religious tolerance. He was critical of the Catholic Church and France's absolute monarchy, both of which he believed held the people down. He promoted the separation of the church and the government.

Jean-Jacques Rousseau believed that people are good at their core, but the inequality and injustices of society corrupt their morality. In *The Social Contract*, Rousseau wrote that society should not have slavery and that people in a community should decide together on the common good.

However, he believed in a strong government; otherwise, there would be chaos and no freedom.

Montesquieu taught the separation of powers into the executive, judicial, and legislative branches, which the American Constitution adopted. He warned that if a government becomes too authoritarian, it will essentially enslave the people. He promoted religious tolerance but believed "natural law" should prevail. He taught that the government must guarantee justice and freedom to everyone.

What Key Events Marked the Revolution's Beginning?

The Estates-General of 1789 was floundering. The Third Estate refused to verify the elections of the representatives, which had to happen before they could do anything. The Third Estate wanted individual voting, but the nobility refused to cooperate. They wanted a unified vote from each block of the "Three Estates." The nobility would get one vote, the clergy one, and the commoners one. Thus, the two votes from the nobility and clergy would outnumber the commoners' vote.

On June 4, King Louis's seven-year-old son died of tuberculosis, pulling the king away from involvement. The Third Estate began a roll call on June 13. Technically, they were not allowed to start proceedings without the king's permission and the agreement of the nobility and clergy. Nevertheless, the Third Estate plowed ahead. Four days later, they announced they were now the National Assembly. The clergy and nobility had no choice but to join them.

On June 30, everyone arrived at the assembly hall to find the door locked and guarded by soldiers. "Does King Louis plan to attack us?" they wondered.

Joseph-Ignace Guillotin cleared his throat. He was a physician and the secretary of the National Assembly. Several months later, he would develop the guillotine as a "painless" way of beheading people. "Does it matter where we meet? What about the royal tennis court? We can meet there."

The group nodded and gathered at the indoor tennis court. There, they swore the "Tennis Court Oath," which said the National Assembly could meet anywhere. "We will not disband until we give France a new constitution!" they declared.

King Louis XVI had been mourning his son but finally realized that matters were spiraling out of control. He had to take charge of the "revolutionary" National Assembly. Louis called up thirty thousand soldiers. The people of Paris were in a state of panic. Most supported the reform efforts of the National Assembly, yet rumors circulated that a military coup was imminent. "We need to arm ourselves!" the people warned each other.

Storming the Bastille [52]

On July 12, 1789, the Parisians rioted. In the "Storming of the Bastille," hundreds of people broke into Paris's fortress to get weapons and gunpowder. The French Revolution had begun. To quiet the crowds, King Louis disbanded his soldiers. Yet, the king's brother and other royalty escaped France on July 16. They feared what was to come.

Soon, all of France was in an uproar. The poor farmers revolted against their landlords and tax collectors, looting and burning their homes. France followed the feudal system of aristocratic "lords" owning the land and poor peasants (serfs) farming the land in exchange for "protection" from the lords and the right to keep a small portion of the harvest. The lords essentially "owned" the peasants, who had no right to leave the estate and find work elsewhere. On August 4, the National Assembly banned feudalism. They gave the serfs their freedom and stripped the wealthy landowners of their privileges.

Later in August, the National Assembly passed the Declaration of the Rights of Man and of the Citizen, which was based on Enlightenment thought. It presented a new government based on the people's will, with a representative government. It mandated the separation of powers and universal human rights like freedom of speech.

Writing a new constitution was far more difficult. It took two years to complete. The National Assembly had to hash out questions like how much authority the king would have. Several wondered if a king was even necessary. Meanwhile, Louis XVI was sullenly brooding in his palace. "I should have the right to a full veto of this new constitution!" he raged.

His lack of cooperation angered the ordinary people, especially the women. "We haven't enough bread, and this king refuses to cooperate!" they complained.

On October 4, 1789, a throng of wrathful women from the marketplace marched on Versailles, pounding drums and brandishing knives and sturdy sticks. Someone started ringing a church bell, and more people joined in, swinging by city hall to grab weapons and two cannons. They pressed on through a downpour and arrived at the palace, exhausted and dripping wet. The king had been hunting and got back to the palace just as the horde of citizens arrived. The women's spokesperson was a seventeen-year-old girl who fainted at the king's feet. He immediately knelt to help her, softening the agitated crowd.

"I'll have food sent to Paris from my royal stores!" he promised. He agreed to ratify the decree on feudalism and the Declaration of the Rights of Man.

In the dead of night, the national guard arrived, led by the French military officer Lafayette. He calmed down the people, then met privately with King Louis. "You'll be safer if you and your family return with me to Paris."

"I'll give you my answer in the morning," the king answered.

Yet, before dawn, attackers broke into the palace. "We'll tear the queen's heart out!" they yelled. They killed two guards and mounted their heads on pikes.

Marie Antoinette raced out of her room, barefoot. "Save my children!" she screamed.

Finally, the national guard managed to subdue the rioters, and the king agreed to accompany Lafayette back to Paris with his family. The unrest in Paris quieted, and relative peace reigned for the next year and a half. Yet, in June 1791, the king tried to sneak out of France with his family. They were caught and returned to Paris, but people began seriously discussing whether they needed a king. "Look!" they said. "The American colonists have established a republic with an elected president!"

The French people were divided. The Jacobins did not want a king at all. A second group, the Feuillants, wanted a constitutional monarchy with a king. However, they did not want him to hold absolute power.

In 1792, Austria and Prussia came to King Louis XVI's aid, no doubt worried that France's revolutionary ideas might spread. Furthermore, many of France's nobility had fled to those two countries for refuge and were demanding aid to get France back to the way it was. The French revolutionaries declared war on Austria and Prussia to squelch these counterrevolutionary efforts.

The guillotine, a symbol of the French Revolution [53]

France also had counterrevolutionaries at home. Thousands were massacred in the ensuing violence. In August, the Jacobins raided the palace and captured the king and queen. They put Louis XVI on trial for treason and high crimes against France. He was sent to the guillotine to be decapitated in January 1793. His queen met the same fate nine months later. Horrified, the Dutch Republic, Great Britain, and Spain joined Austria and Prussia in the war against France.

How Did the Reign of Terror Traumatize France?

With multiple factions trying to gain control, France descended into chaos. A radical faction of the Jacobins snatched control of the National Assembly. They issued a new calendar and outlawed Christianity, exiling 30,000 priests and sending hundreds more to the guillotine. Their Committee of Public Safety took almost total power over the government. It first halted the foreign armies on France's borders, then savagely pulverized the other factions in France vying for power.

Beginning in early 1793, a radical Jacobin named Maximilien Robespierre dominated the Committee of Public Safety for ten months. He led the grisly Reign of Terror, in which 16,594 men and women lost their heads at the guillotine. The committee even sliced the heads off sixty-six children.

Finally, the people revolted against Robespierre, sickened by the climate of fear and the daily executions. In July 1794, they sent Robespierre and his closest associates to the guillotine, ending the Reign of Terror. This led to the Thermidorian Reaction, in which the more moderate French people successfully focused on ending the war with other nations.

How Did Napoleon Bonaparte Rise to Power?

General Napoleon Bonaparte became France's hero when he trounced Italy and their Austrian allies in 1797. He staged a coup in 1799, making himself the consul of France, the top political leader. He ended the civil wars and many of the revolution's ideals. Napoleon focused on restoring stability to France, which had been traumatized by years of violence. He reformed France's education, banking, and legal systems.

His government passed a constitutional amendment in 1802, which made him consul for life. In 1804, he declared himself France's emperor and his realm the French Empire. Under his leadership, France dominated much of Western Europe. He met his downfall in 1813 when he attempted to invade Russia. The Russians lured him deep into the country, where he was unprepared for the harsh winter. He lost all but 100,000 of his 600,000-man army. Months later, a coalition force of Austrians, Prussians, Russians, and Swedes defeated him in eastern Germany. Napoleon abandoned his plans to conquer all of Europe and was forced into exile.

Amazingly, France wanted a king again, but this time in a constitutional monarchy. They made Louis XVI's younger brother, Louis XVIII, their new king. After several decades and two more revolutions, France abandoned the monarchy forever and established the French Second Republic.

What Were the Long-Term Impacts of the French Revolution?

The revolution abolished the feudal system, which had kept farmers in a semi-enslaved status for centuries, and set France on the path to democracy. The country underwent a series of transformations until it reached its Fifth Republic in 1958. The revolution also built a long-lasting pride among the French people in their national identity. It reshaped political boundaries and ideologies across Europe. The Roman Catholic Church had held considerable power over France's government, and this mostly ended. Although the French Revolution was a savage time, its ideals influenced other nations worldwide to move from absolute monarchies to more democratic governments.

Chapter 9: The Rise and Fall of the Soviet Union

The Soviet Union's history spanned over seven decades from the Bolshevik Revolution in 1917 to its dissolution in 1991. How did the desire for a classless society lead to the world's first socialist state under Lenin? What did subsequent leaders like Stalin do to consolidate power and expand the Soviet Union? How did the Cold War and the Space Race change the world? This chapter answers these questions and explores the events leading to the Soviet Union's collapse.

Why Were the Russians Unhappy with the Tsar?

Russia's people lived in deplorable conditions, and the strain of war made matters unbearable. Russia entered World War I in July 1914, allied with France and Britain against Austria-Hungary and Germany. Russia had a million-man army and four million reserves, yet they were not well trained. Russia's military technology and skill were lacking. Thus, jaws dropped when Russia invaded East Prussia and won the Battle of Stallupönen and the Battle of Gumbinnen on August 17 and 20.

However, Russia could not hold its edge. The two Russian generals leading the invasion hated each other and refused to communicate. They gave commands to their troops via radio, and the Germans had the technology to listen in. After pinpointing their location, the Germans shelled the Russian troops for a week, killing 120,000 soldiers and capturing 100,000. The Russians retreated in humiliation and dared not strike Germany again.

By April 1916, the mood in Russia was gloomy. Tsar Nicholas II was technically the supreme military commander but had never fought in a battle. General Brusilov wanted to attack Austria. He surprised everyone when his assault succeeded on its first day, netting him 26,000 prisoners. Ultimately, the Germans and Austrians lost over a million soldiers to Brusilov, with another 400,000 captured. However, the assault cost Russia more than a million men.

A Russian WWI poster [54]

In the east, German vessels attacked Russian ships and Black Sea ports. The Ottoman Empire was trying to snatch territory on the eastern side of the Black Sea. Russia lost another million men, leaving the people restless and irritated with their tone-deaf leadership. The Russians had long considered their tsars out-of-touch, unjust, and tyrannical.

Although Russia had eliminated serfdom in 1861, the farmers had to make payments to their former landlords. The payments and occasional bad harvests kept them close to starvation. When the Industrial Revolution struck Russia in the late 1800s, thousands of Russians moved into the cities to work in the factories. Moscow and St. Petersburg nearly doubled in population. Yet, the Russian factory workers lived in ghastly slums with low pay. The incessant poverty of Russia's population made them question their monarchy: "America and France both did away with their kings. Look how they are thriving now! What good is our tsar?"

In 1905, nine years before WWI started, a throng of Russians marched on the palace, insisting that the ordinary people have a voice in government. They demanded better living and working conditions. The tsar's guards opened fire, wounding or killing over a thousand. The Bloody Sunday Massacre led to more revolts and strikes as the factory workers, farmers, and soldiers demanded a say in the government.

Nicholas II agreed to form a Duma, a type of congress with elected leaders—a new thing in Russia. The tsar even agreed to include factory workers and farmers in the Duma. However, Nicholas's seeming support for the Duma melted away when it called for reforms. He disbanded the Duma and dissolved the next one that formed in 1907. The third Duma had only nobility and upper-class people; the fourth had better representation but hardly any power.

How Did the Bolshevik Revolution of 1917 Upend Russia?

The Russians were weary of war. Fighting on multiple fronts had cost them more men than any war in any country up to that point in history. The hard life of Russia's farmers and factory workers grew harder as WWI drove up the price of bread and fuel. The Marxist Bolshevik movement, led by Vladimir Lenin, capitalized on the people's felt needs. It promised "peace, land, and bread" for everyone.

In 1915, Tsar Nicholas made the irrational decision to travel to Mogilev (in modern-day Belarus) and take command of the Russian forces. He had no war experience, yet he hoped his effort would quiet the restless

Vladimir Lenin, 1917[55]

Russians. However, when Germany continued to crush the Russian troops, the blame fell on Nicholas. Both Nicholas and his wife were cousins of Wilhelm II, Germany's emperor. Whispers swirled that the tsar and his wife were secretly colluding with the Germans.

In early 1917, Russia's underdeveloped infrastructure collapsed. Trains that would normally bring grain to Russia's cities now transported troops and supplies to the front. The Germans and Turks blockaded Russia's Black Sea ports, cutting off fuel and other essential raw materials needed to operate the trains. Russia's people were starving and had no fuel for heat, while January temperatures hovered around 11°F (-12°C).

In February 1917, the fuming people of Petrograd poured into the streets, throwing bricks through bakery windows to steal bread. Tsar Nicholas was still in Mogilev as workers went on strike. "End the war! Dethrone the tsar!" they demanded.

In early March, police shot into the crowds, killing more than two hundred. This did not sit well with the Russian soldiers, who were primarily farmers and factory workers before the war. Ten thousand soldiers in Petrograd mutinied, marching with the protestors and burning down police stations.

Petrograd's soldiers fire on police in March 1917. [56]

Nicholas II knew his reign had ended. He started traveling home, but the journey took a week. Although warned to take her children and leave the country immediately, the tsarina waited for her husband to return. When he did, they discussed their options. They hoped to flee to England, where their cousin, George V, was king. The British Parliament was willing to give them refuge, but King George feared political fallout. Britain desperately needed Russia's support in the war. Russia's new government was unlikely to continue allying with Britain if it took in their exiled tsar. Other European countries were equally hesitant.

The Bolshevik Revolution of October 1917 replaced Russia's monarchy with a Communist regime. Factory workers, farmers, and soldiers were in charge, and Lenin was its dictator. War raged between the Bolshevik "Red Army" and the "White Army." The White Army represented a hodgepodge of ideologies ranging from those who still wanted a tsar to those who wanted a different version of socialism than Lenin's. With civil war raging, Russia withdrew from World War I in March 1918. In July, the Bolsheviks shot and bayoneted Nicholas II, his wife, and all their children.

Russia's new Bolshevik government revolved around key principles of Karl Marx and Lenin. They believed a radical revolution that broke the capitalist system was necessary for their Communist utopia. Lenin believed a dictator should lead the country, acting on behalf of the proletariat (working-class people). Marxist-Leninists advocated for the working class to hold economic and political power, equal wealth distribution, and communal land ownership.

A woman named Fanny Kaplan viewed Lenin as a traitor to genuine socialism. She fired three shots from her pistol at Lenin in August 1918. One bullet punctured his lung, and another lodged in his shoulder. She was immediately executed, and the "Red Terror" was unleashed.

The Red Terror was a Bolshevik movement of extreme violence lasting from September 1918 to 1922 that aimed to crush any opposition. The Cheka (the Bolshevik secret police) had unprecedented powers to arrest and torture anyone they considered "anti-revolutionary." They executed people without a trial or sent them to the "Gulag," forced labor camps. The secret police not only targeted outspoken opponents but also religious leaders, intellectuals, and the former nobility.

What Draconian Polices Did Joseph Stalin Pass?

Joseph Stalin joined Russia's revolutionary movement in the 1890s, organizing protests and strikes. He impressed Lenin with his ruthlessness in the underground Bolshevik movement. Stalin was sent to a Siberian labor camp in 1910, but he escaped and helped with Lenin's revolution by publishing *Pravda*, the Bolshevik newspaper. After taking power, Lenin appointed Stalin as General Secretary of the Communist Party.

When Lenin died in 1924, Russia had collective leadership for several years. However, Stalin announced he was Lenin's political heir. Many expected Leon Trotsky, general of the Red Army, to be the next leader. Stalin used his power to exile Trotsky, and by 1929, he was the Soviet Union's dictator.

Russia lagged behind Western Europe in industrialization. Stalin instigated a series of five-year plans to modernize the Soviet Union, making its factories and farms more productive. He succeeded in increasing coal, steel, and oil productivity and stimulating economic growth in Russia. Yet, success came at a great price. If factories failed to meet their quotas, the workers were imprisoned or even executed.

When Russia did away with feudalism in the 1860s, it divided the large estates into small owner-operated farms. This system was in place when Stalin took power. Stalin instituted "collectivism," where the state took over the farms. The farmers rebelled against losing their farms. They hoarded grain and killed their farm animals, resulting in famines in which five million died. Stalin killed or imprisoned millions of farmers.

By the late 1930s, the government had consolidated all the small farms into large, state-owned collective farms. The government expected that introducing mechanized equipment and more organization would increase production. It set unrealistic harvest goals. When the goals were unmet, the government sent the grain and produce to the cities and the military. It did not allot any to the farm workers, and five million starved to death. Thousands of farmers left the rural areas to work in the cities.

A 1935 propaganda poster of Stalin [57]

Stalin promoted himself in the press and on posters plastered everywhere as the Soviet Union's all-powerful hero and its great, all-knowing leader. Poetry, statues, and hymns exalted him as if he had divine status. Yet, Stalin grew paranoid, fearful of potential opposition. From 1936 to 1938, Stalin's Great Purge wrecked the Soviet Union even further. He executed over half the Central Committee members and most of his highest military officers. His secret police enforced his Stalinist cult, killing 750,000 people and sending three million to Siberia's Gulag.

How Did the USSR Catapult to Superpower Status?

In August 1939, Stalin signed a secret pact with Adolf Hitler. They agreed not to fight each other and to divide Eastern Europe between them. At first, all went as planned. One week after signing the pact, Germany attacked Poland from the west. The next day, the Soviet Union attacked Poland from the east. The plan was for Germany and the USSR to divide Poland between them.

In 1940, still following the secret pact, Stalin annexed part of Finland, then moved on to take Estonia, Latvia, Lithuania, and part of Romania. Invading Romania broke the agreement with Hitler, and he reacted. The Nazi blitzkrieg attack tore through Poland and into the USSR in Operation Barbarossa. It decimated the Russian army, leaving Stalin paralyzed with shock as Hitler's forces closed in.

Stalin gathered his wits and joined the Allies. In 1942, the epic Battle of Stalingrad began. "Not a step backwards!" Stalin warned his men. He lost over a million men but trounced the Nazis in 1943, pushing them out of Russia, out of Poland, and back into Germany. It was a turning point in WWII, shifting the balance of power from Hitler to the Allies. The Soviet Union now ruled a vast swathe of Eastern Europe, even the eastern half of Berlin, Germany's capital. The United States, France, and Great Britain occupied West Berlin.

After World War II ended in 1945, the Iron Curtain fell. The Soviet Union had allied with Britain, America, and the other Allies to beat Hitler. After the war, they were rivals in the "Cold War." Political and ideological barriers separated the democratic, capitalist nations and the USSR's totalitarian Communist state.

The Cold War heated up from June 1948 to May 1949 when the Soviets blocked land and water access to West Berlin. The "Berlin

Blockade" was supposed to drive the Allies out. However, the Allies formed the "Berlin Airlift," which flew fuel, food, and medicine to the 2.5 million people in West Berlin. Finally, Berlin formally split into East Berlin and West Berlin and stayed that way, separated by a wall, until 1989.

The Soviet Union had become a superpower, ruling fifteen states and covering one-sixth of the globe's land mass. It was the world's largest nation, geographically.

What Were the Arms Race and Space Race All About?

The nuclear arms race and the Space Race exemplified the competition between the two superpowers. America wanted to keep the Soviet Union from annexing more nations. It built up its weaponry to unprecedented heights. After the United States dropped two atomic bombs on Japan in WWII, it continued developing nuclear weapons. The Soviet Union refused to be outdone. It had captured Nazi nuclear scientists when it invaded Germany. Now, the German scientists were helping the Soviet Union make its own bomb. The USSR tested "First Lightning" in Kazakhstan in 1949.

President Truman's response was to direct the United States's Atomic Energy Commission to develop the "superbomb," a hydrogen bomb. It uses both fused atoms and split atoms, making it a thousand times more lethal than an atomic bomb. The USSR dived into the race for the hydrogen bomb.

Meanwhile, the Soviet Union was enticing nations worldwide to become allies. The Korean War raged from 1950 to 1953, with China and the Soviet Union backing Communist North Korea, and the United States supporting South Korea. North Korea failed to unify the peninsula as a Communist nation.

Cuba had been friendly with its near neighbor, the US. However, Fidel Castro staged a Communist revolution in 1959 and allied with the Soviet Union. President Kennedy made an ill-fated effort to upend Castro's government by using exiled Cubans to invade the island. The Bay of Pigs invasion of 1961 was a fiasco.

This led to the Cuban Missile Crisis of 1962. The Soviets gave nuclear-armed missiles to Cuba, putting the eastern United States in imminent danger. A US reconnaissance pilot spotted the missiles, and President

Kennedy huddled with his executive committee. Kennedy decided to blockade Cuba's waters and warned the Soviet Union to remove the missiles. Soviet vessels sailed close to the US Navy ships surrounding Cuba, yet they did not try to break the blockade.

Finally, Khrushchev, the Soviet Union premier, sent a message to Kennedy: "If you promise not to invade Cuba, I will remove my missiles." With the crisis averted, Kennedy and Khrushchev set up a hotline between their capitals and agreed to treaties on nuclear weapons.

In 1979, the Soviet Union sent troops into Afghanistan to support its fledgling Communist government against Islamic militants, the Afghan Mujahideen. The United States, Pakistan, and other nations supported the Mujahideen in the ten-year struggle. The war drained the Soviet economy and hurt it politically. It also devastated Afghanistan's infrastructure and culture. Atrocious human rights violations occurred on both sides. When the Soviet Union withdrew in 1989, it left a power vacuum, and civil war ensued. The Taliban, a radical Muslim group, took power.

The arms race played out alongside the Space Race as the Soviet Union and the United States competed in the final frontier. The Soviets won the first round in October 1957 when they launched Sputnik I. It was the first satellite to pass out of Earth's atmosphere. Sputnik traveled 139 miles from Earth's surface and circled Earth 1,440 times over three months. Aerodynamic drag finally pulled it out of orbit, and it fell back into Earth's atmosphere, where it burned up in the intense heat caused by denser air levels.

Laika the space dog [58]

The Soviets sent up Sputnik 2 a month later, this time with a passenger—a dog named Laika. The satellite's thermal system malfunctioned, and Laika overheated and died five hours into flight. However, Sputnik 2 orbited Earth for five months before it burned up on re-entry. Three months after Sputnik 2's launch, the US launched its first satellite into space, Explorer 1. The Soviet Union was also the first to send an unmanned rocket to the moon. *Luna 2* hit the moon at 7,400 miles per hour.

In April 1961, the Soviets sent the first man into space three weeks before the Americans sent Alan Shepard into space. Yuri Alekseyevich Gagarin orbited Earth once, then reentered the atmosphere. He ejected four miles from Earth's surface and fell to 8,200 feet; then his parachute opened, and he landed safely.

Why Did the Soviet Union Dissolve?

Economics, political pressures, the Cold War, and even well-intentioned reforms all led to the Soviet Union's fall. The Space Race, the nuclear arms race, and the war in Afghanistan drained the USSR's finances. Mikhail Gorbachev, the Soviet Union's last leader, introduced *perestroika* (restructuring) and *glasnost* (openness). He intended these reforms to revitalize the Soviet system. Instead, the USSR's satellite states demanded more independence. The Soviet Union officially dissolved on December 26, 1991.

Conclusion

From Sargon to the Soviet Union, the rise and fall of empires illustrate the cycle of history. What can we learn from the achievements and failures of these remarkable empires? They all had one thing in common: the burning desire to achieve greatness. Ambition propelled empire-builders forward, enabling them to breach barriers and struggle for superiority. Ambition, innovation, and leadership built these empires. Exploitation and the inability to confront internal or external threats destroyed them.

Empire builders had lofty goals. Although they were power-hungry, many brought reforms. Qin Shi Huang of China chose officials based on competence. He investigated and punished corruption and misconduct. The French Revolution, although horrifically bloody, overthrew feudalism. It introduced democratic principles like representative government and freedom of speech.

However, ambition is self-destructive if it leads to exploitation. Achievements gained in this way eventually crumble, as in the Aztec Empire. Suffering under crushing tribute payments and distraught that the Aztecs took their children as sacrifices to their bloodthirsty gods, the tribes the Aztecs conquered allied with the Spaniards to destroy the empire. Likewise, exploitation led to uprisings in the British Empire's American, Asian, and African colonies. It was too difficult to maintain control of vast territories with rebellious people.

Empires also failed when they strayed from their foundations. The Roman Republic, built on a semi-democratic system of checks and balances, persisted for almost five centuries. It imploded due to the increasing corruption of its senators, who overlooked the needs of the ordinary people, like the soldiers who had been fighting for decades, expanding the empire.

Empire builders like Sargon the Great, Ptolemy I, and Genghis Khan were powerful enough to build empires that lasted 150 years or longer. Their descendants grew their empires through several generations. Sargon and Genghis ruthlessly squelched rebellions, as their successors did. On the other hand, Ptolemy forged a friendship with the Egyptians by respecting their culture, restoring their temples, and honoring their gods. He set the stage for a three-century empire. It ultimately crumbled through the intrigue and weak leadership of the inbred Ptolemy family, leaving them wide open to Rome's ambitions.

Though at times corrupt and destructive, empires came with benefits. Cultural exchange led to tremendous advancements. As people shared ideas, they surged ahead in knowledge, technology, and innovation. Empires enabled large military forces. They could enlarge the empire through invasions and deflect attacks from other countries. The Akkadian Empire and Roman Republic achieved remarkable infrastructure such as postal systems and excellent roads. The relative peace of empires led to lucrative trade. The systems put in place by our world's empires still impact us today.

Part 2: Ancient Civilizations

An Enthralling Journey Through the Great Societies of the Ancient World, Including Mesopotamia, Egypt, the Indus Valley, and Beyond

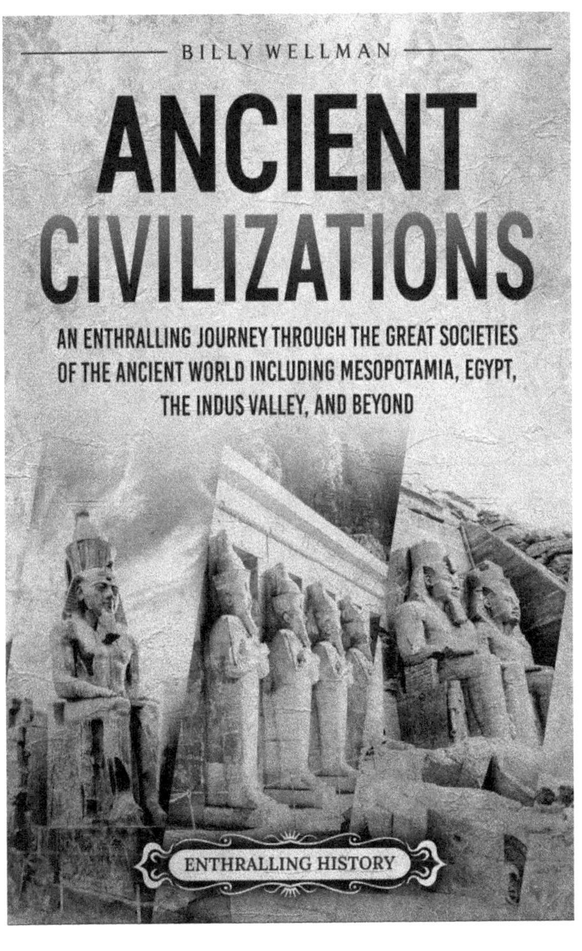

Introduction

What comes to mind when you think of the world's most influential ancient civilizations? This book explores nine ancient cultures that left a lasting legacy. How did they begin? What stunning cultural, technological, and societal innovations did they contribute? How did writing, government, religion, architecture, and other aspects make each civilization stand out? These civilizations gave us the first writing, the first alphabet, the first transportation wheel, the first beer, the first law codes, the first cities, the first mathematics, the first Olympic games, the first republic, and much more.

Did you know people were grinding grain into flour and baking bread at least seven thousand years ago? By approximately 5000 BCE, bread had become a staple food in Mesopotamia. Why did Egypt's first "real" pyramid collapse before its completion? How did Greece lose its written language and most of its major cities? This book will keep you turning pages as it reveals the stories of these exceptional civilizations.

These ancient societies had to adapt to their environment and deal with harsh climate change. They were not islands to themselves. These civilizations all interacted with neighboring cultures through trade, marriage, and yes, warfare.

The spellbinding histories of how these ancient civilizations changed the world are compelling. Their stories help us understand why things are the way they are today in every aspect of our lives. Let's travel back in time and around the globe to learn their breathtaking tales.

Chapter 1:
The Dawn of Civilization

The Ubaid and Sumerian civilizations introduced an awe-inspiring number of "firsts" to our world. These cultures blossomed in southern Mesopotamia—the "land between the rivers." Most of Mesopotamia (today's Iraq, eastern Syria, and sections of Turkey, Saudi Arabia, Kuwait, and Iran) lay between the Tigris and Euphrates rivers. Mesopotamia, "the Cradle of Civilization," stretched

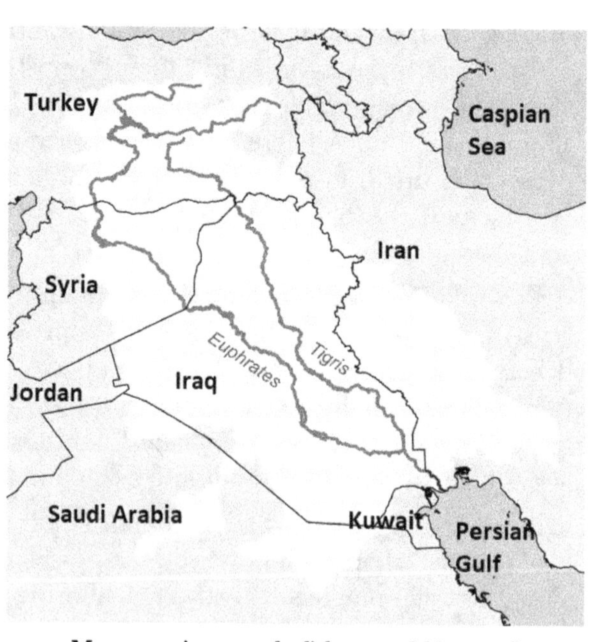

Mesopotamia covers the light area of this map. [59]

from the headwaters of the Euphrates and Tigris to where the rivers joined and emptied into the Persian Gulf.

Around 6500 BCE, the Ubaid culture, a precursor to the Sumerians, emerged in southern Mesopotamia. This civilization may have been related to the Hassuna and Samarra cultures of central and northern

Mesopotamia. The people of the Ubaid civilization migrated south with their cattle, goats, and sheep, eventually reaching the Persian Gulf coast.

They exchanged their tents for reed-thatched huts and settled in villages. By 5500 BCE, they learned to make sun-dried mud bricks to build sturdy houses with flat roofs and arched doorways. The people of the Ubaid culture made clay ovens for baking bread and firing distinctive pottery with linear artwork. The rivers, lakes, and gulf were rich sources of seafood. By 5200 BCE, they built small boats (some with sails) to ply the waterways, even sailing down the Persian Gulf.

An Ubaid pottery jar, circa 5000 BCE [60]

They made their tools and weapons from stone, flint, or obsidian (a type of volcanic glass). Initially, they consumed wild grains, but later they began cultivating barley, emmer wheat, flax, and lentils. From these grains, they made beer, porridge, and bread. By 4500 BCE, they were weaving linen cloth from the flax fibers.

The people of the Ubaid civilization built Eridu, perhaps the world's oldest city, around 5400 BCE. The *Sumerian King List* states that it was the first city to hold "kingship" over the region before the Great Flood swept over.[7] At least two other contenders vie for "first city" status: Jericho (in today's West Bank), built about 8000 BCE, and Çatalhöyük (in today's Turkey), built around 7100 BCE. Yet, both settlements lacked the

---

[7] Sumerian King List, trans. Jean-Vincent Scheil, Stephen Langdon, and Thorkild Jacobsen (Livius, updated 2020). https://www.livius.org/sources/content/anet/266-the-sumerian-king-list/#Translation.

infrastructure that typically defines a city, such as roads and public buildings.

During the Ubaid period, Eridu's central settlement covered an area of approximately twenty-five acres, with a total population of around four thousand people. It had roads, a one-room temple, and other infrastructure. Eridu's irrigation system for crops, using ditches and canals, was probably the world's oldest. Irrigation was a game-changer, enabling agricultural productivity that could feed thousands in a dry climate.

Around 5000 BCE, the people of the Ubaid culture built the city of Ur at the mouth of the Euphrates, twelve miles east of Eridu. They also built Uruk on the Euphrates, about fifty-eight miles north of Ur. Uruk and Ur were chief cities of incredible wealth for the Ubaid culture and later the Sumerians.

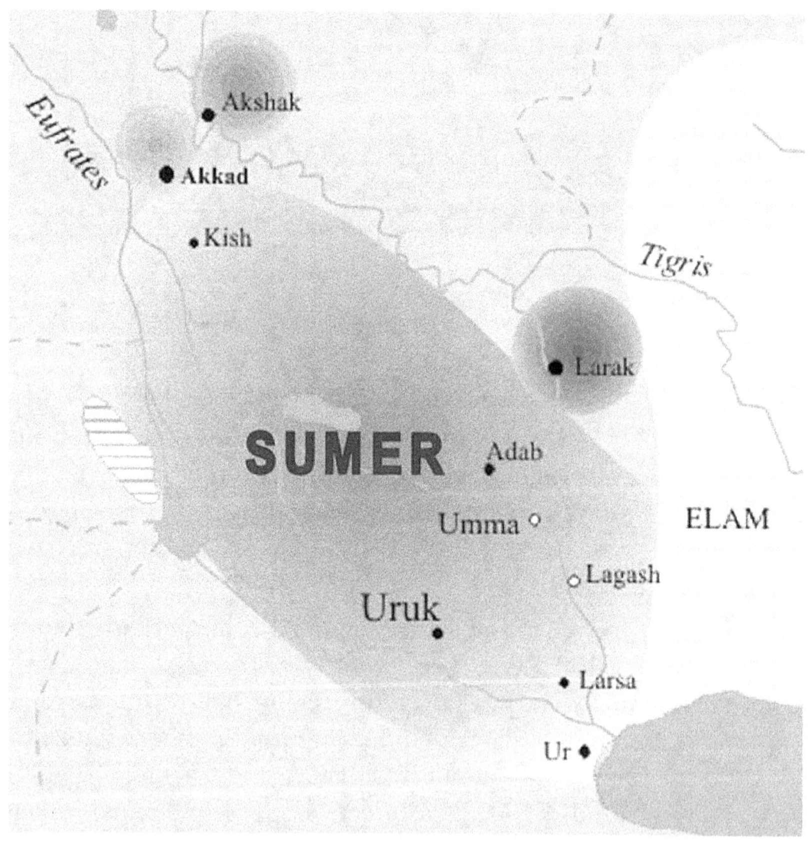

Dominant cities of the Ubaid and Sumerian civilizations [61]

The Ubaid civilization abandoned Ur and Eridu between 3800 and 3500 BCE. Ur suffered a catastrophic flood caused by the rising water levels of the Persian Gulf, which disrupted the Euphrates River delta. Changing weather patterns led to devastating droughts and sandstorms. Eridu depended on Lake Hammar, adjacent to the city, for irrigation. However, drought made the lake's water saline. Without a water source, Eridu became a ghost town, covered by the blowing sand.

By contrast, Uruk thrived thanks to its irrigation canals connected to the Euphrates. Uruk was Mesopotamia's powerhouse in this era, characterized by a hierarchical social system, a well-developed military, pottery factories, and full-time administrative officials. The city may have taken in refugees from Ur and Eridu, as its population grew exponentially in this era.

However, the Sumerians were migrating into southern Mesopotamia and may have driven Uruk's sudden population growth. They called themselves the "black-haired people" and spoke a language isolate unrelated to any other known language. They adopted many aspects of the Ubaid civilization, to the point that some scholars think the Sumerians were an extension of the Ubaid culture. Yet, the Sumerians possessed new skills, such as sophisticated metalworking. If they were from somewhere else, possibly Iran or northern Mesopotamia, the Sumerians peacefully assimilated.

The Sumerians introduced incredible innovations. The growing cities needed taxes for things like building and maintaining the irrigation canals and the city walls. Everyone paid a "tax," usually of fish or grain. Yet, the administrators needed a way to keep track of the numbers. The Sumerians used a sexagesimal counting system, counting in sets of twelve and sixty. Instead of counting fingers, they counted their twelve finger joints on the four fingers of one hand. When they reached twelve, they held up one finger on the other hand and started counting again. After counting to twelve again, they held up a second finger.

Twelve joints on one hand multiplied by five fingers on the other hand came to sixty. This numerical system brought us the twelve-hour day and night, the sixty-second minute, and the sixty-minute hour. The Sumerians used little cones and balls made from clay to keep track of higher numbers before they invented writing. A small cone stood for one, a small ball represented ten, and a larger cone represented sixty.

Pictographs from Uruk, late fourth millennium [62]

By 3500 BCE, the ground-breaking Sumerians used cut reeds to draw circles (for the "ten" ball), triangles (for the "sixty" cone), and other shapes into soft clay. The clay hardened into small tablets that preserved the world's first accounting system. By 3300 BCE, the Sumerians in Uruk developed proto-cuneiform writing using simple pictographs.

Over the next several centuries, the pictographs evolved into more abstract forms, incorporating the wedge-shaped symbols characteristic of logographic cuneiform writing. Each symbol represented a word or a word part. Since the Sumerians wrote on soft clay that hardened, thousands of Sumerian tablets have survived. Cuneiform writing was later used by the Babylonians, Assyrians, and other cultures.

Sumerian cuneiform, circa 2600 BCE [63]

By 3500 BCE, the Sumerians learned that heating copper and tin alloy to high temperatures produced bronze. This revolutionized warfare and farming, since bronze is a hard metal. Plows with bronze tips cut the soil more effectively, enhancing agricultural output and contributing to population growth. Bronze armor and shields were lighter than copper yet stronger against arrows and swords.

A key element of Sumerian history and literature was the Great Flood. The *Sumerian King List* divides the history of their cities and kings into two periods: before and after the flood. The Sumerian *Eridu Genesis* and *The Epic of Gilgamesh* tell the story of the flood. In the *Eridu Genesis*[8], the gods created the dark-haired people and the animals. They handed heaven's scepter to Eridu, giving its kings authority over all the people. However, the people were noisy as they worked in the canals and fields. The gods could not sleep with the hubbub. Highly irritated, the god Enlil persuaded the other gods to destroy the people. Yet, the god Enki quietly made plans to save the humans.

At that time, Ziusudra was the king and priest of Eridu. One day, while he stood in Eridu's shrine, he heard a voice from the other side of the wall. It was Enki. "Step up to the wall and listen!" he said. "The gods have decided to destroy mankind. The command of An and Enlil cannot be revoked. A flood will sweep over the cities."

At this point in the narrative, the *Eridu Genesis* tablet is damaged, but the *Epic of Gilgamesh*[9] picks up the story as told by Utnapishtim (another name for Ziusudra). The god Ea (Enki) told Utnapishtim, "Tear down your house and build a boat! Abandon your possessions and save your family and the animals. Make them all go into the boat."

So Utnapishtim built the boat and brought his family and the animals onto it. A black cloud arose from the horizon and covered the land. A torrent of rain fell so heavily that no one could see their hand in front of their face. Water submerged the mountains and covered the people. The goddess Ishtar (Inanna) shrieked and wailed at the devastation. The rest of the gods wept with her, regretting the catastrophe.

For six days and seven nights, the storm pounded, and the flood writhed like a woman in labor. On the seventh day, all was quiet. As the

---

[8] *Eridu Genesis*, trans. Thorkild Jacobson (Livius, last updated 2020). https://www.livius.org/sources/content/oriental-varia/eridu-genesis/.

[9] *The Epic of Gilgamesh*, trans. N. K. Sandars (London: Penguin Classics, 1960).

sun came out, Utnapishtim fell to his knees, weeping. He scanned the horizon for land. Finally, he saw the tip of Mount Nimush emerging from the water. The boat lodged on the mountain, and, after seven days, Utnapishtim released a dove. It flew away but returned because it could find no place to perch. He released a swallow, and it also came back. Then he released a raven. By this time, the water had slithered off the land, and the raven did not return.

Utnapishtim came out of the boat, butchered oxen and sheep, and offered a sacrifice to the gods. Enlil was furious that some humans had survived, but Enki (Ea) intervened. Enlil sent the surviving humans to live at the mouth of the rivers (the Euphrates and Tigris—or southern Mesopotamia).

The Epic of Gilgamesh says that Utnapishtim told his story to Gilgamesh, the king of Uruk. He was still alive in Gilgamesh's day because the gods granted him immortality. Several ancient documents list Gilgamesh as a king of Uruk in the twenty-seventh century BCE, when Uruk held "kingship" or dominance over the other cities of southern Mesopotamia.

Uruk was the largest city in the world at that time, with a population exceeding fifty thousand. It had a forty-foot-high ziggurat—a rectangular sloping or stepped tower. Uruk's Anu ziggurat had the White Temple at its top. Uruk had jaw-dropping wealth because of its strategic location on the Euphrates River. Its river traffic made it a dominant trade hub, and irrigation from the river enabled the cultivation of lush farms.

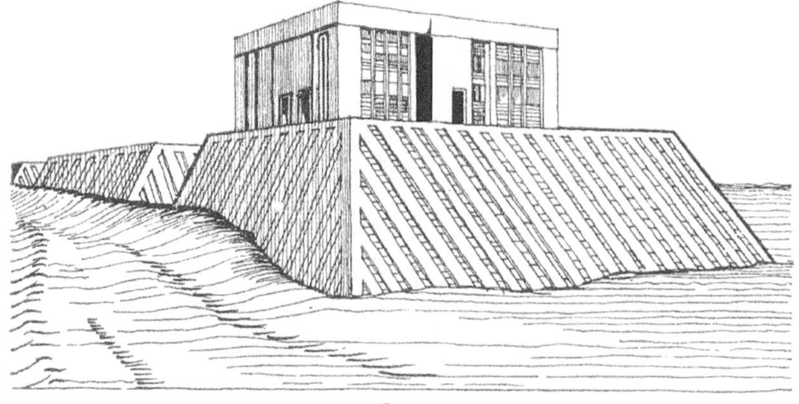

A drawing of Uruk's White Temple ziggurat "

Because writing had not been invented yet, by the sixth millennium, the Ubaid civilization used stamp seals to "sign" their names. Stamp seals were square or circular stones, approximately one inch in diameter, with a design carved into their surface. When pressed into a ball of soft clay, the clay hardened to preserve the design. Most men (and some women) had their own unique seal. The small disks of hardened clay indicated ownership of the materials they bought and sold.

Uruk took the idea of stamp seals up a notch by inventing cylinder seals around 3500 BCE. These were stone or metal cylinders, about four inches long. As with the stamp seals, each cylinder seal had a unique design, but the carving could be more complex because they were larger. The cylinder seal's owner rolled it in soft clay to leave an impression that hardened. Men and women wore cylinder seals hanging on lanyards around their necks or pinned to their clothing.

Uruk's Lady of Warka mask [65]

The "Lady of Warka" mask found in Uruk was carved from marble around 3100 BCE. It is the world's first known realistic depiction of a human face. Earlier artwork showed bizarre distortions of the face. For instance, the Ubaid "lizard-lady" statuettes, dating to around 4000 BCE, featured normal women's bodies but reptilian faces. Scholars believe the Lady of Warka mask represented Inanna, Uruk's patron goddess.

The Sumerians rebuilt Ur around 3500 BCE, and it grew to a population of around 34,000. Ur developed into an incredibly wealthy city, as seen with the fortune buried in Queen Puabi's tomb about 2600 BCE. Puabi's headdress, weighing over six pounds, had wreaths of gold leaf, beads of carnelian and lapis lazuli, and a gold comb. Her silver chariot was buried with her, along with over a hundred servants and soldiers, who were sacrificed to serve her in the afterlife.

By 2900 BCE, the weather patterns had improved, and the Sumerians rebuilt Eridu. They erected a temple called the House of Aquifer to worship Eridu's patron god, Enki, who ruled the underground water.

Over time, the Sumerians enlarged the temple until it was probably the largest Sumerian ziggurat.

Initially, Sumerian kings held the title of "ensi," which meant they held a dual role as both priest and king. As the Sumerian cities grew, the king focused more on secular affairs, such as supervising builders, farmers, fishermen, herders, and merchants. The king's title changed to "lugal" or "strongman," since he was the military's commander-in-chief and the law's chief justice. A hereditary class of priests offered sacrifices, discerned omens, and performed other religious duties.

The Sumerians worshiped many gods and goddesses. The top three gods were An, Enki, and Enlil. An (Anu) was heaven's supreme god. Enki (Ea) was the god of the earth, aquifers, and healing. He protected humans when the other gods wanted to kill them. Enlil ruled the wind and atmosphere. Inanna (Ishtar) was Uruk's patron deity and the goddess of beauty, love, sex, and war. Her twin brother, Utu, was the sun god. Enlil's son, Nanna (Sin), was the moon god.

The Sumerians thought they existed to serve the gods. Failure to appease the gods led to floods, droughts, or enemy invasions. The Sumerians prayed daily, offered incense, sang hymns, and asked for forgiveness for their sins. When they prayed, they kneeled, lay face down on the ground, or stood with their arms lifted in the air or with one hand in front of their mouth.

The world's first known wheel was a potter's wheel developed in Iran around 5200 BCE. The Sumerians adopted the potter's wheel by 3100 BCE. Then, they realized they could use it for something else— transportation! These trailblazers invented the world's first rotating axle and built the first carts. Then, they had the bright idea of using animals to pull their carts, so they developed the world's first collars for donkeys and oxen that connected to a pole, which attached to the cart. The Sumerians also invented breeching straps.

Initially, they probably used wheeled carts for hauling things. Then, they developed four-wheeled chariots pulled by four kungas (a cross between a donkey and a wild ass). The first chariots were slow and awkward, but mosaics in a wooden box called the Standard of Ur (circa 2600 BCE) show the Sumerians trampling the enemy with their kunga-drawn chariots.

The kungas pulling the front chariot mow down a victim in this Standard of Ur mosaic. [66]

By 2600 BCE, the ingenious Sumerians used multiplication, division, basic geometry, cubic roots, and square roots. By 2300 BCE, they invented a stone abacus using divisions of one, ten, sixty, six hundred, and thirty-six hundred. Instead of beads on rods, like the Chinese version, theirs had columns with tiny stones.

The Sumerians developed a calendar system around 3100 BCE consisting of twelve lunar months in a year. Each month had twenty-nine or thirty days. A new month began when the slender crescent of a new moon appeared in the sky. However, twelve lunar months were only 354 days, while the solar year was about 365 days. To fix the problem, they occasionally added an extra month.

In addition to developing the world's first writing system, the Sumerians probably wrote the world's first story, the *Epic of Gilgamesh*. We already delved into the flood story part of the epic, but its overall theme was the quest for immortality. Gilgamesh was the flawed king of Uruk, disliked by his citizens. They used a prostitute to tame a wild man named Enkidu, who lived in the wilderness, and brought him to Uruk to challenge their king.

Gilgamesh and Enkidu fought until they were worn out. They realized they were evenly matched and decided it was better to be friends than foes. They set off together on an adventure to kill the sacred Humbaba monster that guarded the cedars of Lebanon. After killing the monster, they made a raft and sailed down the Euphrates back to Uruk. However, the goddess Inanna, patron of Uruk, saw Gilgamesh bathing and was enchanted by his stunning good looks.

"Marry me!" cried Inanna. Yet, Gilgamesh was uninterested.

Inanna flew to her father, Anu, the supreme god. "I want the Bull of Heaven!"

Anu hesitated, but Inanna screamed, "If you don't give it to me, I'll unleash the zombies from the underworld on the living!"

Inanna took the Bull of Heaven to Uruk. When the bull snorted, the ground collapsed into a pit, swallowing the people. Enkidu grabbed the bull by the horns, and Gilgamesh stabbed and killed the sacred animal. However, that got them in trouble with heaven. The gods decided that one man must die for killing the two divine creatures: the Humbaba and the Bull of Heaven. Although Gilgamesh had killed both animals, the gods did not want to disrupt Uruk's kingship, so they killed Enkidu instead. Gilgamesh wept for days over his friend.

Enkidu's death reminded him that he would also die one day. Gilgamesh set off on a quest, searching for Utnapishtim, who had become immortal. Utnapishtim gave Gilgamesh tasks to become young again, but Gilgamesh failed. The king of Uruk finally realized that his mortal body would die, yet by becoming a superior king, his memory would live on forever.

In 2334 BCE, Sargon, king of Kish, united the Akkadian tribes of northern Mesopotamia. They invaded the Sumerians, taking city by city, and established the Akkadian Empire, which ruled Mesopotamia until 2154 BCE. Raids from the Gutian mountain people undid the Akkadian Empire, along with the 4.2-kiloyear BP (Before Present) aridification event, a horrific drought that turned the grassy plains into deserts.

The Sumerians survived because they used irrigation farming, while the Akkadians were primarily herders, now with no grass for their flocks. Sumer's population even doubled as Akkadian and Amorite herders migrated south. The Sumerians staged a comeback with the Third Dynasty of Ur (2112–2004 BCE). Ur was now the largest city in the world, with sixty-five thousand people. Their king, Ur-Nammu, wrote the world's first law code. Yet, in 2004 BCE, the brilliant dynasty fell to the raiding Elamites from Iran.

Imprint from a cylinder seal dedicated to Ur-Nammu [67]

Chapter 2:
The Splendor of Ancient Egypt

Ancient Egypt's magnificent civilization flourished along the life-giving waters of the Nile River. How did the Egyptians harness the Nile's resources? What can we learn from its architectural marvels, advanced knowledge, and rich cultural heritage? This chapter unwraps a complex society marked by towering pyramids, spectacular temples, a sophisticated writing system, and profound religious beliefs.

Egypt's story revolves around the Nile River, its source of life. Curiously, northern Egypt is called "Lower Egypt," and

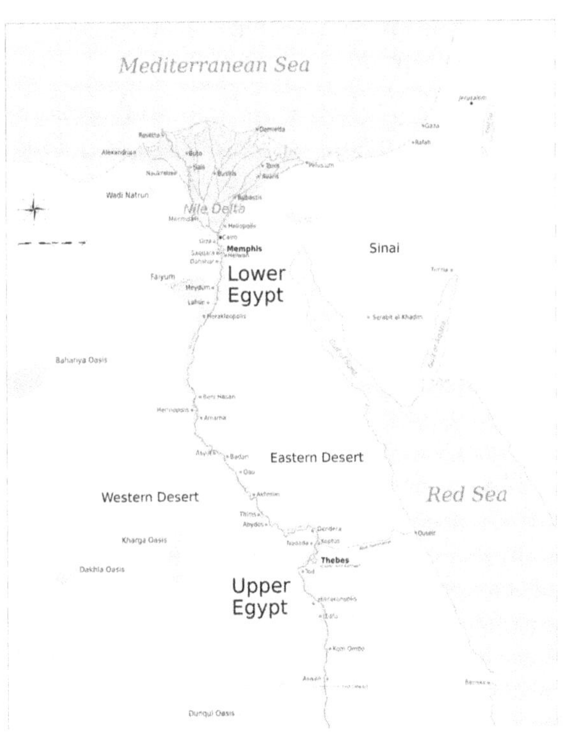

Upper and Lower Egypt [68]

southern Egypt is referred to as "Upper Egypt." Why? The Nile flows north from its southern highlands to the flat delta region in the north, where the river splits into multiple tributaries before emptying into the Mediterranean Sea.

While 92 percent of Egypt is desert, the Nile Delta is lush and green. The Nile's annual flooding deposits rich silt, which fertilizes the land. The delta had grasslands for herds and fertile soil for farming. The Nile's predictable flooding cycles also enabled agriculture along the riverbanks south of the delta. Although Egypt gets less rainfall than any other country, most years its people could depend on the Nile to irrigate their farms.

Around 3400 BCE, in the Predynastic period (4300–3100 BCE), the ancient Egyptians began building towns and cities, using sun-dried bricks. Xois was on an island in the delta region and later became one of Egypt's capitals. The town of Nekhen (Hierakonpolis) in Upper Egypt grew to at least five thousand people by 3400 BCE.

The Egyptian custom of mummifying their dead had begun by this time. At first, they buried people in the scorching desert sands, which naturally dried and preserved the bodies. By 3350 BCE, the Egyptians began using embalming agents like pine resin, plant extracts, and bitumen, a form of petroleum.

Trade began between Egypt and southern Mesopotamia in the Ubaid era. The Egyptians treasured beads made from the dazzling, deep-blue lapis lazuli stone. The Ubaid and Sumerian people acquired lapis lazuli from long-distance trade with Afghanistan, then traded it to Egypt. Through interacting with the Sumerians, the Egyptians began using cylinder seals by 3300 BCE. Their favorite stone for the seal was lapis lazuli.

People settled in Abydos, Upper Egypt, by at least 3500 BCE. The people of Abydos began writing pictographs around 3400 BCE. Some pictographs represented the object in the picture, but others represented another word that sounded like the noun in the picture. As with the ancient Sumerians, the Egyptians used pictographs for record-keeping in their early days. By 3200 BCE, the pictographs were evolving into hieroglyphics. Despite the robust trade between Egypt and Mesopotamia, Egyptian hieroglyphics were distinctive from Sumerian cuneiform.

Abydos pictographs [69]

The ability to read Egyptian hieroglyphics was lost after centuries of Roman rule over Egypt. However, scholars finally unlocked the mysterious language in the early 1800s CE after an ancient monument was unearthed that honored the coronation of a new Greek pharaoh. Alexander the Great's general, Ptolemy I, began Egypt's Ptolemaic dynasty in 305 BCE. Ptolemy's descendant, the fourteen-year-old Ptolemy V, became Egypt's pharaoh in 196 BCE. The Egyptian priests recorded the event with the Rosetta Stone, which had the same inscription written in three different languages: Greek, Egyptian hieroglyphics, and Egyptian Demotic (which emerged around 700 BCE). In 1799 CE, Napoleon's army discovered the polished black granodiorite stone. This was an exciting find because scholars could read the Greek inscription and then translate the Egyptian hieroglyphics and Demotic script from that. It unlocked Egypt's history, including its early rulers.

At the beginning of the Early Dynastic era (3100–2700 BCE), King Narmer ("Stinging Catfish") rose to power in Upper Egypt. (Egyptians did not call their rulers "pharaoh" until the New Kingdom.) King Narmer unified Upper and Lower Egypt into one kingdom, celebrating his triumph with a two-foot-high stone monument called the Narmer Palette. One side of the slab shows Narmer grasping the hair of a kneeling captive and swinging a mace with the other hand. This motif became common in Egyptian victory monuments. The other side of the stone slab has two serpopards (long-necked leopards) intertwining their necks, representing the union of southern and northern Egypt.

A drawing of the conjoined serpopards from the Narmer Palette [70]

Not only did Narmer unite Egypt, but he also expanded into the Sinai Peninsula, Gaza, and Canaan (today's Israel and Palestine). Pottery and seals with his name have been found throughout these regions. His brilliant reign ended with a deadly attack by a hippopotamus. (Even today, hippopotamuses kill twice as many people in Africa as lions.)

Four centuries later, the Old Kingdom, also known as the Age of the Pyramids, dawned (2700–2200 BCE). Egyptologists organize Egypt's ancient history into three "kingdoms" that they consider golden ages: the Old Kingdom, the Middle Kingdom, and the New Kingdom. These periods had high-powered kings who stimulated prosperity and exciting new developments. "Intermediate periods" of chaotic politics and economic downturns came between the three kingdoms.

Manetho, a third-century BCE Egyptian-Greek historian and priest, attempted to organize Egypt's long history into dynasties in which a single family, or sometimes an ethnic group, held power for a significant period. Often, two or three dynasties ruled different parts of Egypt simultaneously. Scholars squabble over when these kingdoms and dynasties began and ended, so dates in this chapter try to strike a middle ground.

King Djoser, the first king of the Old Kingdom, reunited Egypt again and built the first pyramid. His was a step pyramid, a precursor to the smooth-sided, pointy-topped pyramids typically associated with Egypt. Djoser's pyramid was an extended mastaba, a rectangular building about twenty feet high with a flat roof and sloping walls. Egyptians buried a dead person under the mastaba in a tomb at the bottom of a shaft. A second shaft led to a storage room next to the tomb for things the person needed in the afterlife, such as food, beer, games, and clothing. The Pyramid of Djoser in Saqqara had underground shafts, but instead of a single level above ground, it has six levels, each slightly smaller, rising 204 feet high.

King Djoser's pyramid in Saqqara[71]

Most of Egypt's pyramids were built during the Old Kingdom. The kings who followed Djoser employed thousands of workers and spent a fortune building higher and grander pyramids. Egypt did not have the wheel yet, so workers had to drag the massive stones on enormous sleds over the sand. Several workers went ahead of the sleds, pouring water on the sand so that the sleds would slide more easily with their heavy loads.

Around 2500 BCE, King Sneferu tried to build the world's first "true" pyramid with a pointed top and smooth sides. However, his architects did not get the foundation right, and the pyramid collapsed before it was finished, killing hundreds of workers. Sneferu tried again. His architects designed a better foundation, but they built the second pyramid at a 55-

degree angle. It was too steep, making it unstable, so the architects adjusted the angle to 43 degrees about halfway up. The pyramid did not fall, but it looked distorted, as if it were bent. His architects tried again, successfully building the entire third pyramid at a 43-degree angle.

The Bent Pyramid, Sneferu's second attempt [73]

The next pharaoh was Khufu, most likely Sneferu's son. He built the world's highest pyramid. At about 481 feet high, the Great Pyramid was the world's tallest building for nearly four thousand years until the Lincoln Cathedral was built in England. The only way for Egypt to achieve such a stunning feat was by having a strong central government. The Egyptians considered their pharaohs divine kings, intermediaries between heaven and earth. Thus, they allowed their kings to wield absolute power.

How did the Egyptians build their pyramids so well that most are still standing over four millennia later? For the Great Pyramid, they had to move 2.3 million stone blocks, each weighing about 2.5 tons. How did they pull off this massive feat without the wheel, cranes, and pulleys? How did they lift those blocks to the height of a forty-eight-story skyscraper?

NOVA's 1992 film, *This Old Pyramid*,[10] used a crew to replicate how they thought the Egyptians did it. They discovered that twelve men could

---

[10] "This Old Pyramid" Transcript, *NOVA*, PBS Airdate: February 4, 1997. https://www.pbs.org/wgbh/nova/transcripts/1915mpyramid.html.

cut 186 stones by hand in a quarry in three weeks; however, they cheated a bit and used iron tools and a winch. To build the Great Pyramid in twenty years, the builders needed 340 stones a day. The researchers estimated that with more primitive tools, it would take 1,200 men to carve 340 stones each day and get the 2.5-ton blocks to the surface.

Fortunately, stone quarries were located where the Egyptians built the pyramids at Giza. They did not have to transport the core stones of the pyramids from elsewhere. Nevertheless, it would take about twelve men to drag each stone on a sled over wet sand from the quarry to the pyramid construction site. If each team could transport two blocks a day, it would require approximately 2,000 men to move 340 massive stones to the building site each day.

Pyramids at Giza [78]

Once the gargantuan blocks arrived at the construction site, men cut each rock into the perfect shape to fit on the pyramid wall. The stone sat on a cobble with levers, allowing two workers to pivot it as two to four men carved. After that, another team of workers pushed the enormous stones up temporary ramps that ran from the ground to the top level of the pyramid. Once they completed the core, they finished the exterior of the pyramid with polished white limestone.

Despite old movies showing the Egyptians with whips in hand, forcing the Israelites to labor on the pyramids, the builders were not the Hebrews, nor were they enslaved people from central Africa. The Great Pyramid was built around 2600 BCE. According to Biblical accounts, Abraham was born in Ur about four centuries later. The Israelites did not exist yet. Native Egyptians built the pyramids, according to an analysis of bones found in the worker cemeteries at Giza. Most likely, the laborers were farmers who worked on the pyramids during the offseason when the Nile overflowed its banks and they could not do any farming.

The Great Sphinx of Giza [74]

Khufu's son Khafre built a pyramid next to the Great Pyramid that seems higher, yet this is an optical illusion. It is on higher ground. Khafre built the Great Sphinx next to his pyramid. The gigantic statue, sixty-six feet high and 240 feet long, had a lion's body and a human head. Over thousands of years, sandstorms buried the Great Sphinx up to its neck in sand. Archaeologists unearthed the rest of it in the 1800s. It was once painted in bright blue, red, and yellow.

The Egyptians built most of the pyramids in the Old Kingdom. In the Middle and New Kingdoms, they erected majestic temples. In Luxor, they built the Karnak Temple Complex to Amun-Ra, god of creation. Over twenty shrines graced the Karnak Temple Complex, one of the world's largest worship areas. The central focus was the open-air Hypostyle Hall, with columns sixty-nine feet high. The Avenue of the Sphinxes had six hundred sphinxes lining the path from the Karnak temple to the Luxor temple, almost two miles away.

 Hypostyle Hall pillars in the Karnak Temple Complex [75]

The Abu Simbel twin temples are on Lake Nassar's shores, near Egypt's modern-day border with Sudan (known as Nubia when the temples were built). The Egyptians carved the temples out of the mountainside in Rameses II's reign (New Kingdom), completing them in 1265 BCE. Four sixty-six feet high colossal statues of Rameses flank the entrance, two on each side. At the feet of these statues are smaller images of his mother, Mut-Tuy; his chief wife, Nefertari; and his eight oldest children.

Religion permeated every aspect of Egyptian life. Some gods were regional, so when Egypt united, certain gods with similar roles blended together. For instance, the supreme god Amun (Atum) was the creator, but so was Ra, the sun god. Sometimes, he was called Amun-Ra. In Egyptian mythology, before creation, the chaotic ocean of Nun existed in a state of darkness. In one version of the creation myth, a primeval goose called the Great Cackler laid an egg. Amun-Ra hatched from the egg as the sun. Amun pulled an island out of the water and spat, creating Shu, the god of the air. Next, he vomited and created Tefnut, the rain goddess. Shu and Tefnut conceived Nut, the sky goddess, and Geb, the earth god.

Tefnut, the rain goddess and mother of earth and sky [76]

The Egyptians believed that when the world was created, it was an orderly place with plenty of everything that anyone needed. However, the people rebelled against Ra, disrupting the cosmic order and bringing suffering to the world. The primary duty of the pharaoh and his people was to restore "Maat," or the cosmic order. They had to live in harmony with each other and with the gods. Their fate in the afterlife was determined by the balance and harmony they sustained while living.

The Egyptians believed that when they died, the black jackal god Anubis waited for them with his scale at the gates of the underworld. Anubis put the person's heart on one side of the scale and a feather on the other. Were their hearts as light as a feather? If the person had lived in peace and harmony, their heart would be light enough for them to enter Duat, the underworld. Ammit, the crocodile-headed goddess, ate people with heavy hearts who had been disruptive and argumentative in their lifetimes.

Ammit waits (center right) as Anubis (center left) weighs a heart. [77]

Why did the ancient Egyptians mummify their dead? They believed the body had to be preserved for the soul to continue living. The god Anubis also presided over this process.

First, the priests cut out the body's organs and put them in jars of natron salt to dry out. They covered the body with natron salt for seventy days, then applied black resin, which prevented fungal growth. The organs were returned to the body or placed in jars and buried with the body. The priests wrapped the body with linen strips before burial. The priests placed a mask, painted to resemble the person, over the linen-wrapped face and placed the body in a wooden coffin. If the dead person had been wealthy or powerful, they lowered the coffin into a stone sarcophagus with the person's image painted on it. The Egyptians understood the science of mummification so well that some mummies have survived in remarkably good condition to the present day.

The Egyptians also possessed exceptional knowledge in fields such as mathematics and medicine. The Ebers Papyrus, written around 1550 BCE, was an ancient medical guide. It featured magic spells, as Egyptians attributed ailments like migraines to evil spirits known as "demon crocodiles." However, the guide also had instructions for contraception, treating burns, and setting broken bones. The Egyptian doctors would take a person's pulse to check for a firm heartbeat and rule out blockage. The guide discussed diabetes, cancer, and dementia.

While the Sumerians and other Mesopotamian cultures were writing on clay tablets, the Egyptians developed sheets of paper-like papyrus by 2550 BCE. It was made from the pith of the papyrus reeds that grew in the water. The Egyptians developed a 365-day calendar by 3000 BCE, with three distinct seasons: the Nile flooding, winter, and harvest. They tracked the height of the Nile each year during the flood season by marking a column or measuring how high the water came up steps leading down to the river.

With limited cloud cover, the ancient Egyptians were stargazers with an exceptional understanding of astronomy. They knew the difference between stars and planets by the way planets moved through the sky. In the Old Kingdom, the Egyptians aligned their pyramids with the pole star Thuban, also known as "the Serpent," in the Draco constellation. Thuban was almost precisely due north five thousand years ago.

Ancient Egypt's rich culture and scientific understanding have left an enduring legacy that has spanned the ages.

Chapter 3: The Indus Valley

The Indus Valley Civilization, one of the world's most enigmatic cultures, was at its apex from around 2600 to 1900 BCE. It had a population of up to five million people in the villages and cities that clustered along the Indus River in present-day Pakistan, India, and Afghanistan. Its cities of Harappa and Mohenjo-daro were remarkably advanced in urban planning, architecture, and societal organization. What were the Indus Valley Civilization's sophisticated achievements? They included standardized weights and measures, elaborate drainage systems, and a yet-to-be deciphered script.

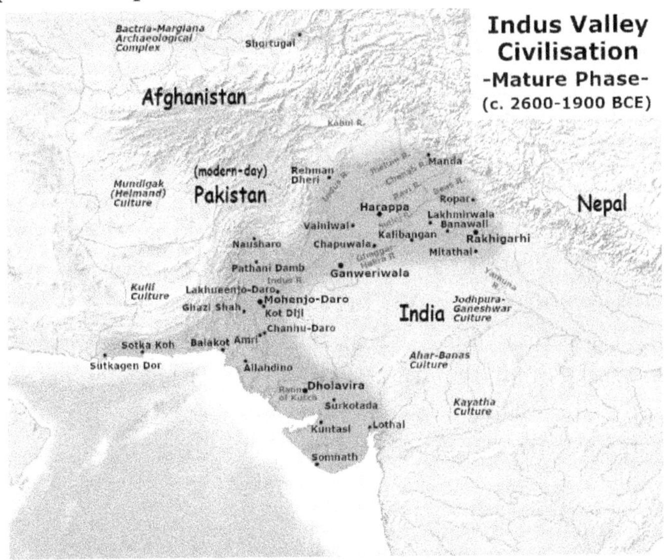

Map of the Indus Valley Civilization [78]

Several years after the British East India Company annexed the Punjab region of northwest India in 1849, they were building a railway near the village of Harappa. The builders found mounds and even partial walls of fire-baked bricks. The more the British workers dug, the more bricks they found—hundreds of thousands.

"They have always been there," the locals told them. "Sometimes we use those bricks when we need to build something."

Archaeologist James Lewis (pseudonym Charles Masson) had explored the area several decades earlier and reported on the ancient artifacts he discovered. Unaware, or uncaring, the British workers dug up the four-thousand-year-old bricks to build the track ballast for the railway line.

In the early 1900s, John Marshall, the new leader of the Archaeological Survey of India, ordered the excavation of Harappa's site. Marshall had just learned of Mohenjo-daro (Mound of the Dead), four hundred miles south of Harappa in today's Pakistan, where similar bricks and artifacts had been found, along with human bones. Both sites represented an ancient and previously unknown civilization that emerged around 3300 BCE. These discoveries revised notions of when advanced civilization originated in the Indian subcontinent.

Since that time, around one thousand sites have been uncovered, including five cities with populations of twenty to forty thousand, or even higher. The ancient people did not build these towns and cities haphazardly. They employed urban planning, meticulously following a grid pattern. Covered drains running throughout Mohenjo-daro were among the world's first sanitation systems. The cities had public baths, irrigation canals, and brick houses with multiple stories. Bricks were a standard size, and so was the width of the roads.

Curiously, the Indus Valley Civilization did not appear to have grand palaces, monuments, or elaborate tombs for its kings. Did they even have kings? The sophistication and urban planning involved in their cities suggest a strong central government. Perhaps they had a government run by a group of people, like a tribal confederation. However, a statuette from Mohenjo-daro, dating to around 2000 BCE, depicts an elegantly dressed man with neatly trimmed hair and beard and a ribbon on his head. He may have been a priest or king (or both).

A seven-inch image of a man from Mohenjo-daro [79]

Another thing missing was temples, which were abundant in ancient Mesopotamia and Egypt, as well as in India in later years. Some historians think the Indus Valley Civilization had no organized religion. However, that is not necessarily the case. The ancient Indo-Iranian religion was a precursor to the Vedic religion, which emerged in northwest India around 1500 BCE (and eventually gave birth to Hinduism). The Indo-Iranian and Vedic religions had few cult images (idols). Typically, worship took place in the open air. The rare temples were simple affairs where a sacred fire burned perpetually. Although the Indus Valley Civilization had no temples or idols, its artwork displayed mythical animals and apparent deities.

Where did the people of the Indus Valley Civilization come from? In a mountainous region of Pakistan, west of the Indus River, a Neolithic people settled Mehrgarh by 5500 BCE and possibly as early as 7000 BCE. Mehrgarh flourished concurrently with the Ubaid, Hassuna, and Samarra cultures in Mesopotamia. Like these cultures, the people of Mehrgarh were nomadic herders of sheep, goats, and cattle who eventually settled down to grow wheat and barley. Some scholars think they migrated to Pakistan from Mesopotamia.

Like the Ubaid and early Egyptians, the people of Mehrgarh had brilliant blue lapis lazuli ornaments by 5500 BCE, which meant they were trading with ancient Afghanistan, a nearby source of the precious stone. Archaeologists have discovered evidence that the Mehrgarh people had basic knowledge of dentistry. They found eleven molars that had been drilled, apparently because of decay. Evidently, the ancient "dentists" used bow drills, which were generally used for friction to create fire or bore holes into wood.

Historians divide the Indus Valley Civilization's history into three phases: Early Harappan (3300–2600 BCE), Mature Harappan (2600–1900 BCE), and Late Harappan (1900–1500 BCE). Among its earliest settlements was Kot Diji in today's Sindh province of Pakistan. Kot Diji was established around 3300 BCE across the Indus River from where Mohenjo-daro was later built. A fertile flood plain surrounded the town, which meant lush farmland and grassland for herds. Fish and wild game were plentiful.

In the Early Harappan era, the people built their houses from sun-dried mud bricks on stone foundations. They made pottery using a potter's wheel. Archaeologists got excited when they dug up a toy cart at Kot Diji from this era. The Indus Valley people were using the transportation wheel by 2600 BCE.

The Great Bath of Mohenjo-daro with a domed granary in the back [80]

The Mature Harappan period was a time when vast cities were built following a master plan with flat-roofed, multiple-story brick houses. By this time, the Indus Valley people worked with copper, bronze, and gold, but not iron (which did not begin for another millennium). They grew cotton and wove it into clothing. Each city had its own administration, but no central government united the cities.

Like the ancient Ubaid and Egyptian civilizations, the people of the Indus Valley Civilization used small, rectangular stone stamp seals to "sign" their names by 2600 BCE. The picture on a seal was usually an animal, like an elephant, rhinoceros, or tiger, with an inscription carved above it. The Indus Valley people passed a cord through a hole in the seal and wore it hanging from their necks.

Intriguingly, carvings of long-necked male unicorns appeared on tablets and over half the stamp seals from 2600 to 1900 BCE in Harappa and Mohenjo-daro. The unicorn always faces a fire-altar, like the ones that burned perpetually in Indo-Iranian and Vedic worship. The one-horned creature must have held a significant religious meaning. Carvings often showed him with stripes on his head and chest but not on the back part of his body.

A stamp seal depicting a unicorn with a fire altar under his chin, circa 2200 BCE. He may represent the god Vishnu. The script at the top of the seal has not been deciphered, but it shows three apparent fish emblems.[81]

Could he have been a two-horned animal, but his other horn did not show up in his profile? Stamp seals with hump-backed bulls and other two-horned creatures showed both horns, even in profile. Archaeologist John Marshall suggested a connection between the unicorn and the Vedic sun-god Vishnu. Another name for Vishnu was "Ekasringa," which referred to a single-horned creature that may have been a rhinoceros or a unicorn.

Unicorns sometimes appear in Bronze-Age Iranian and Mesopotamian art, looking more like a cow or antelope than a horse. Were they real animals? No one has found skeletal remains. However, the ancient Greeks said they lived in India. Ctesias, a Greek doctor who served in Persia's royal court around 405–358 BCE, said a unicorn was a type of wild ass with a twenty-eight-inch horn and a red, white, or black coat.

One Harappan stamp seal shows a tiger with feathery horns fending off an attack by a faun-like female creature. She has ox-like horns and a female body above the waist. Below her waist, she has the body and long tail of an animal. Some scholars think the bottom half is a tiger, but it has no stripes. Her tail is also thick, unlike the elegant tail of the tiger in front of her, and she appears to have cleft feet. Whether she is a goddess or a mythical figure is unclear.

Stamp seal with a faun-like female attacking a horned tiger [12]

The people of the Indus Valley Civilization traded with southern Mesopotamia. They adopted the stamp seal from the Sumerians but not the cylinder seal. They also adopted a common motif of Gilgamesh fighting wild cats, as told in the *Epic of Gilgamesh*. In the Mesopotamian version, Gilgamesh fights two lions, but in the Indus Valley version, he fights two tigers. Did the Indus Valley people know the Gilgamesh story, or were they simply copying the motif? Hopefully, a bright person will one day decode the Harappan script and reveal the civilization's mysteries.

Indus Valley "Gilgamesh" fights two tigers. Note the script at the top.[83]

Mohenjo-daro had the "Great Bath" in the Mature Harappan period. The pool was thirty-nine feet long, twenty-three feet wide, and almost eight feet deep. It was the world's first public water tank. Steps led down into the pool. A ledge above the water led from the stairs to the other end of the pool. People could walk along it without getting into the water. The floor and walls of the Great Bath were made from tightly fitted bricks held together with gypsum plaster and covered with bitumen.

A row of brick columns lined the pool on three sides, and two massive doors were at the south end. One room on the eastern side of the pool had a well to supply water. Rainwater may have also provided the pool with water. What was the purpose of the Great Bath? Was it a place for recreation? Some scholars think it was for religious purification, something like the practice of modern Hindus who bathe in the Ganges River to cleanse their souls from sin, cure illnesses, and connect with the divine.

Each neighborhood in the Indus Valley cities had a public well. Mohenjo-daro had over seven hundred public wells, and many homes had private wells. Saqiyahs and shadoofs brought the water up from underground. A shadoof uses a pole with a bucket and a counterweight. A saqiyah, still used in India, resembles a water wheel but features both a horizontal wheel and a vertical wheel. An ox or donkey turns the horizontal wheel, which has a drive shaft connected to the vertical wheel. As the vertical wheel turns, buckets on the wheel scoop up the water.

A "Punjab" or saqiyah wheel in India, 1917 [14]

In the cities, houses had a courtyard with a toilet hole. The waste was "flushed" with a bucket of water into an underground clay brick pipe that led to a brick drain that ran along the street. They also had rooftop toilets with terracotta pipes leading to the street drain. Sewage drained into a "soak pit" or cesspit. Occasionally, workers scooped out the solid waste to fertilize the fields. Liquid waste soaked into the ground. Drains running along the streets had holes leading to the street for clearing blockages.

The city of Dholavira had a sophisticated system of water storage featuring stone channels and tanks, which were among the earliest in the world. Dholavira was semi-arid and prone to droughts, so if the people could store the water from the monsoons, they could survive. At least sixteen massive reservoirs captured rainwater during the monsoon season, as well as from two streams that flowed during the rainy season but dried up for the rest of the year. The city had a rectangular step-well that was larger than the Great Bath in <u>Mohenjo-daro</u>.

The people of the Indus Valley Civilization had extraordinary technological skills. They made most of their pottery by throwing it on a potter's wheel, which leaves characteristic rings on the inside of the pot. They heated lime to use it as plaster. They used furnaces to bake bricks and fire pottery. With exceptional skill, they cut, drilled, and polished beads, which they made from a variety of stones like agate, carnelian, jasper, lapis lazuli, and steatite. With alkaline etching, they created intricate designs on the beads. The Indus Valley Civilization traded its beads, pottery, and other goods with Mesopotamia, Afghanistan, and Persia. They traveled by boat up the rivers and the Persian Gulf.

The Indus Valley Civilization began writing by at least 2800 BCE. Centuries earlier, pictographs appeared on pottery and other materials. About two thousand unearthed stamp seals have a script on them. Archaeologists also discovered inscriptions on pottery, weapons, tools, and copper plates. Altogether, about five thousand examples of the Harappan, or ancient Indus Valley, script have been found. Frustratingly, no one has unlocked its meaning. This keeps us from fully understanding the language, religion, and administrative systems of these fascinating people.

The Harappan script has between four hundred and seven hundred signs; however, only sixty-seven were used regularly. Some are seemingly obvious, such as a fish sign. However, multiple variations of a fish-like sign appear in the same row of script. Some scholars suggest a connection between the Harappan script and the Proto-Elamite script used in southwestern Iran at the same time as the Indus Valley Civilization. The Proto-Elamite script has not been translated either, but thirty-five signs are similar to the Harappan script. Proto-Elamite also has signs in common with Mesopotamian cuneiform, especially the number system.

Some archaeologists argue that the Indus Valley Civilization did not have a military. They say that the defensive walls were for flood control, not to repel invading armies. The Indus Valley Civilization had knives, spears, bows, and arrows, but these tools could have been for hunting. They had figurines and stamp seals of dancers and animals, but no artwork showing warriors. However, evidence indicates that the Indus Valley was far from a peaceful utopia. Skeletal remains of males show high rates of injury, especially to the face and skull, characteristic of battle wounds.

Some people at Harappa had leprosy and tuberculosis. They were buried outside the southeastern part of Harappa. Oddly, the men with fatal head wounds were buried at the same site. Could the men who died of head injuries have been executed or sacrificed? Were they bludgeoned to death? Otherwise, why bury the warriors with the lepers? The number of crushed skulls and victims of leprosy and tuberculosis increased toward the end of the Mature Harappan period and into its decline in the Late Harappan period. Did disease and violence close the chapter on the Indus Valley Civilization?

Climate change also played a role, as rainfall decreased and the deserts expanded. Tectonic activity was at play in that era. The large, moving plates of Earth's crust created uplift and probable earthquakes along the Makran coast, leaving coastal cities miles inland. Rivers shifted and even dried up, disrupting the robust trade on the waterways. Meanwhile, Indo-Aryan people from the Central Asian steppes were migrating in, vying for resources. The Indus Valley Civilization declined to such an extent that its people lost their knowledge of writing and hydraulic engineering. The culture had nearly disappeared by 1500 BCE.

Chapter 4: The Mysteries of the Minoans and Mycenaeans

The legendary Minoans and Mycenaeans flourished in the Bronze Age. The Minoans' sophisticated society centered on the large island of Crete, which lies in the Mediterranean Sea between North Africa and Greece's mainland. They had impressive palaces, intricate art, and extensive trade networks. As the Minoan civilization declined, the Mycenaeans developed a magnificent civilization on the Greek mainland and Crete, incorporating aspects of Minoan culture. The Mycenaeans were the immortalized heroes of Homer's *Iliad* and *Odyssey*.

The Minoans emerged from a Neolithic culture on the island of Crete around 3500 BCE. Where did the name "Minoan" come from? Greek mythology says Minos was the first king of Crete. His father was the god Zeus, and his mother was a Phoenician princess from Lebanon whom Zeus kidnapped.

About 2000 BCE, the culture suddenly became more complex, and the Minoans began building cities and palaces. This likely happened in King Minos's reign. (He was probably a real person around whom myths evolved.) Thucydides, a fifth-century BCE Greek historian, said King Minos built the first navy. The Minoans controlled the eastern Mediterranean trade, and their pottery has been found on the Iberian Peninsula (Spain and Portugal).

Just as the Minoans were starting their great leap forward, the palaces they built came crashing down. Crete had consequential seismic activity between 2000 and 1700 BCE. The island is located where the African and Eurasian tectonic plates meet and is one of the most earthquake-prone places in Europe.

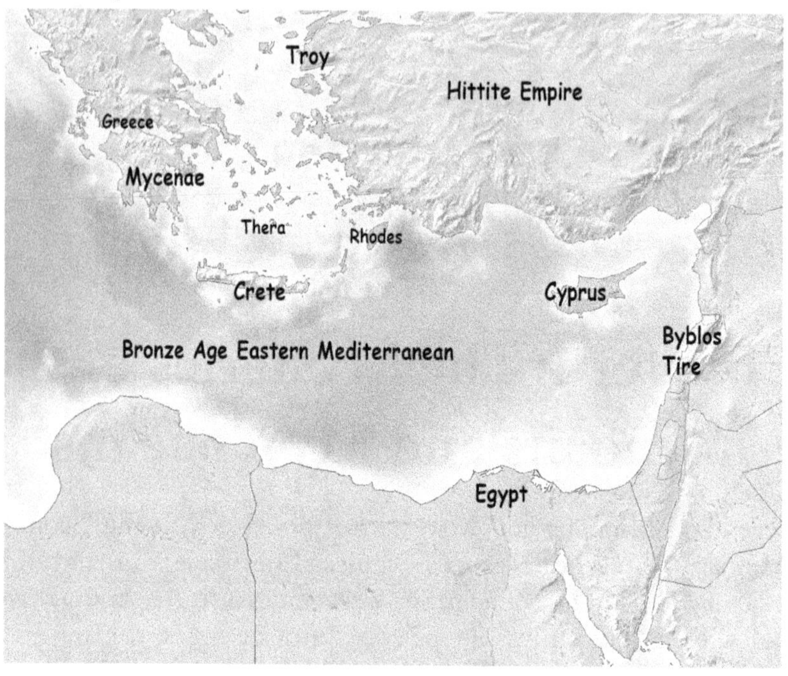

Crete's strategic location [86]

Nevertheless, the resilient Minoans rebuilt their palaces on a grander scale, showcasing advanced architecture and engineering. The palace at Knossos was four stories high, with massive colonnades. It had nearly a thousand rooms and covered an area larger than two football fields. Spectacular frescoes in bold colors decorated the walls.

The palaces served as hubs for industry, trade, and administration. Stockpiles of oil, grain, and wine were stored in the palaces, likely intended for trade or as emergency stores in the event of a famine. Workshops produced ceramics and exquisite figurines that were traded around the Mediterranean and Aegean seas.

At first, the cities on Crete were independent realms. After the Minoans rebuilt the collapsed palaces around 1700 BCE, Knossos ruled over the other cities on the island. By this time, Knossos and its nearby villages had about 100,000 people. Crete had roads connecting the major cities to each other and to the surrounding farms and villages. The Minoan civilization reached its peak between 1650 and 1450 BCE.

The Minoans possessed a sophisticated understanding of hydraulics. Aqueducts brought water to the cities and towns. Some were simple affairs, such as open ditches traveling downhill from the mountains. Others were closed, terracotta pipes. The palace at Knossos had a ten-mile aqueduct supplying water from mountain springs. The Minoans also had sewage systems for their cities, using clay pipes.

This palace at Knossos has been partially restored and painted.[86]

Crete's palaces housed libraries of clay tablets inscribed with Cretan hieroglyphs and the Linear A script. Minoans began using Cretan hieroglyphics, Europe's first written language, around 2100 BCE. No one has yet decoded this language, but its pictographs on clay tablets and stamp seals bear slight similarities to Egyptian hieroglyphics. However, Cretan hieroglyphics had only eighty-five symbols, compared to Egypt's eight hundred. This means the Cretan written language was phonetic, with the symbols standing for sounds.

Around 1800 BCE, the Minoans began using a new writing system, Linear A. They used both scripts for about a century, then abandoned the Cretan hieroglyphics. Linear A was also phonetic, with a simpler script, and more like a true alphabet. It may have been influenced by the Proto-Sinaitic script, which evolved into the Phoenician alphabet. Linear A has letters in common with the Phoenician alphabet, like the symbol that looks like our *Y* but stood for the *W* sound. Another shared symbol was a circle with a cross inside, which stood for the *T* sound in Phoenician. Scholars have been able to decipher the phonetic sounds of the Linear A symbols; however, they remain uncertain about the language that Linear A represents.

A tablet with Linear A written on it[87]

Several ancient sources say that the Minoans expanded their territory by conquering other lands. They settled the islands of Kythera, Melos, Rhodes, and Thera in the Aegean Sea. According to Thucydides, Minos annexed the Cyclades islands that lie north of Crete between Greece and Anatolia (Turkey). He also said that Minos attacked Athens, which was a small settlement at the time. The biblical book of Deuteronomy states that the Minoans (also known as the Caphtorites) invaded Gaza, destroyed the Avvites who lived there, and settled in their place (Deuteronomy 2:23). According to biblical chronology, this occurred before 1400 BCE.

Minoan ceramics were highly sought after as trade items. The Minoans crafted cups with handles that resemble today's teacups and coffee mugs. Their figurines showed men wearing loincloths and a bare-breasted goddess with a long, tiered skirt grasping a snake in each hand. The Minoans decorated their pottery with bold, black swirls and other geometric designs. They also featured images of dolphins, fish, octopuses, ibexes, and flowers.

A Minoan octopus jug from Zakros, Crete, circa 1600–1450 BCE [88]

The Minoans' striking artwork offers a glimpse into their culture, religion, and aesthetic sensibilities. The Hagia Triada sarcophagus, circa 1400 BCE, was crafted from limestone and adorned with frescoes. It depicts priests and priestesses making offerings and sacrificing bulls. Bulls were not the only sacrifice. Archaeologists have found grim evidence of child sacrifice and cannibalism. In one case, an earthquake struck, burying the priests and their sacrificial victim, an adolescent boy, under tons of rubble.

The Minoans even had a bull-vaulting ceremony. A man would take a bull by the horns and somersault over its back.

Perhaps the importance of the bull alluded to the ancient myth of Minos. The sea god Poseidon gifted Minos with a resplendent, pure white bull to underscore Minos's divine right to rule. Minos was supposed to sacrifice the bull to Poseidon, but he was so taken with the bull that he kept it and sacrificed another bull instead. Poseidon got his revenge by causing the king's wife to fall in love with the bull, which impregnated her. The baby was a hideous Minotaur, a half-bull, half-man monster who ate people. Minos kept the creature in a labyrinth but had to feed it humans. After conquering Athens, he made the people send him seven boys and seven girls as food for the Minotaur every nine years. The Athenians sent the children twice, but the third time, the semi-divine hero Theseus accompanied the youngsters and killed the monster.

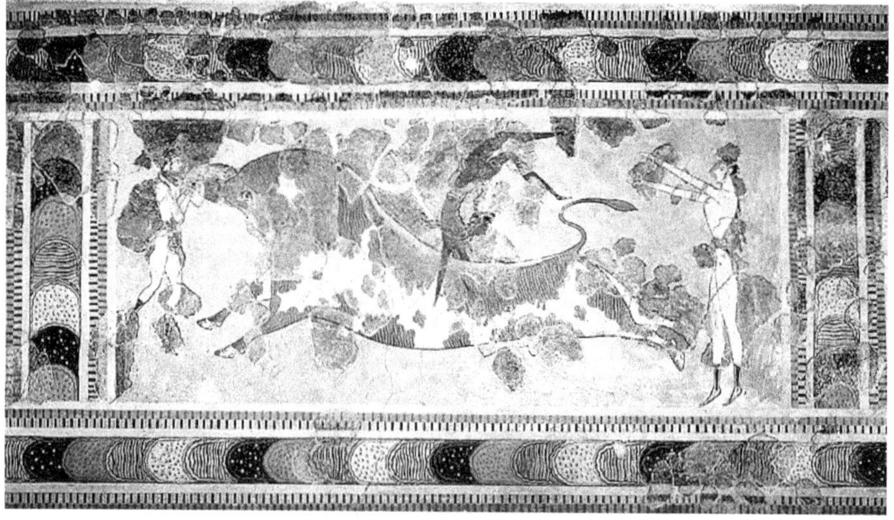

This fresco from Knossos shows a man flipping over a bull. [89]

Around 1600 BCE, a horrific volcanic eruption with a VEI-7 magnitude destroyed the island of Thera, about 120 miles north of Crete. Ten million tons of ash and rock shot up twenty miles, then buried all life on Thera. The eruption triggered earthquakes and a devastating tsunami that buried the northern part of Crete under water. Cities and ports were gone in minutes. The Minoans in southern Crete survived and struggled on in a weakened state. Losing over half its ships and ports devastated Crete's trade-based economy.

To the south, the Mycenaeans of Greece's mainland were rising in strength. They snatched up the Minoans' former sea trade and established colonies around the Aegean and eastern Mediterranean. About 1450 BCE, the Mycenaeans launched an attack on Crete, torching its palaces and temples. Although they destroyed much of Knossos, they spared its palace and renovated it for their own use. The Minoans and Mycenaeans lived together on Crete for several centuries, but the Mycenaeans became the ruling class. Crete switched from using Linear A to the Mycenaeans' Linear B script.

People had lived on the mainland of Greece since the Neolithic Age, and one early area of civilization was on the Peloponnese Peninsula. During the Neolithic Age, people in this area constructed their houses using stone blocks and cultivated crops on terraces rising up the hills. In the early Bronze Age, they built at least two coastal cities that are now submerged because of rising sea levels and earthquakes.

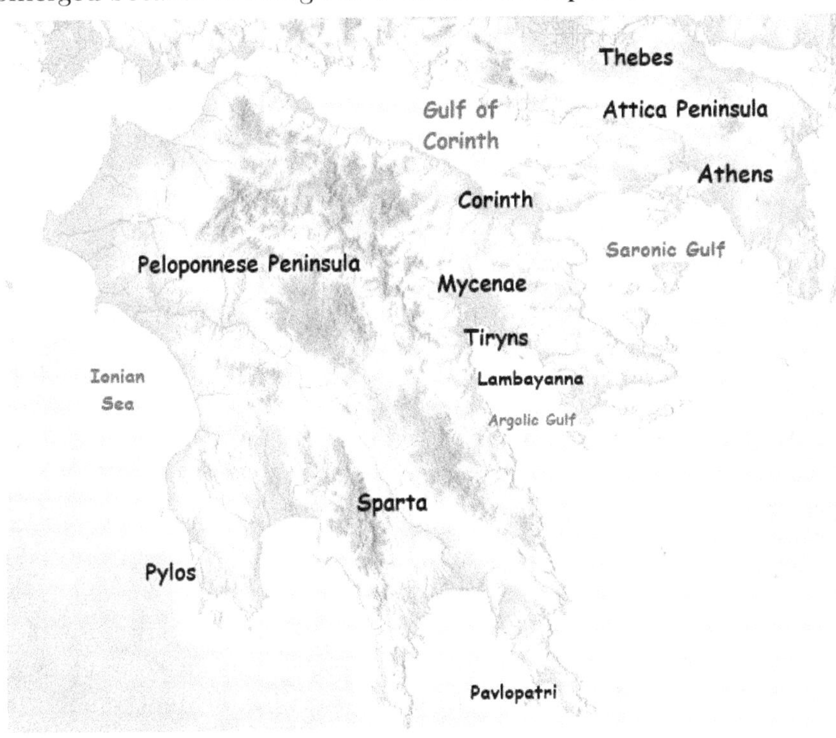

Southern Greece in the Mycenaean Civilization [90]

The Greek philosopher Plato wrote of the lost city of Atlantis, an advanced society that sank into the ocean as punishment for moral decay. Perhaps one of these cities gave rise to the legend. The cities had colossal foundations, fortified walls, two-story houses, temples, tombs, water pipes, paved roads, and towers. One sunken city is Pavlopetri, which had a population of up to two thousand people just off the island of Elafonisos. The other is Lambayanna, in the Bay of Kiladhaom.

Did the Mycenaeans build these seaside cities? It is unlikely. The Mycenaean civilization emerged around 1750 BCE, and these two cities were built approximately a thousand years before that. The Minoans were present, but they had not yet built complex cities. An earlier civilization, perhaps a precursor to the Minoans and Mycenaeans, built these cities.

However, Pavlopetri did not sink until around 1100 BCE, so it lasted through the Minoan and Mycenaean cultures. Artifacts show that the Minoans traded with Pavlopetri and that the Mycenaeans lived there. The Mycenaeans were masterful assimilators, borrowing from Minoan culture and whoever built the underwater cities. Yet, these "long-haired Achaeans," as Homer called them, took architecture, engineering, art, and military tactics to the next level.

The Peloponnesian Peninsula positioned the Mycenaeans in a strategic location for sea trade and cultural interaction with other civilizations. They traded in the Black Sea and, like the Minoans, their pottery has been found in Spain. The Mycenaeans exported linen, olives, olive oil, pottery, raisins, wine, and wool textiles. They imported copper from Cyprus, tin from the western Mediterranean (possibly even Britain), and gold and ivory from Egypt.

Highly militant, the Mycenaeans not only conquered Crete but also triumphed over southern Greece, including ancient Athens. Their brilliant engineers achieved seemingly impossible feats with bridges, defensive walls, and wastewater systems. The exploits of these overachievers were so legendary that they lived on in Classical Greek lore.

Tiryns, which overlooked the Argolic Gulf, was probably the oldest Mycenaean city, dating to the Neolithic Age. The Mycenaeans built a fortress there about 1600 BCE. By 1300 BCE, it had become a chief port with a population of approximately ten thousand people. Colossal "Cyclopean" walls surrounded Tiryns, and within these walls was a labyrinth of vaulted tunnels. What was the purpose of the tunnels? They may have been storage areas or secret hiding places if invaders overcame the city. The Mycenaeans built a palace in Tiryns around 1400 BCE; however, an earthquake collapsed it about two centuries later. Although they did not rebuild the palace, Tiryns continued to thrive. It even survived Greece's Dark Ages, a time when most cities crumpled.

Two lions guard the top of the colossal gate of Mycenae. [91]

Mycenae, north of the Saronic Gulf, was the hub of the Mycenaean civilization. It had a population of thirty thousand at its peak. This city on a cliff in the Peloponnese Peninsula had defensive walls over eighteen feet thick. With mind-blowing engineering, the Mycenaeans used enormous twenty-ton limestone boulders in the wall. The largest stones weighed over one hundred tons.

Part of the walls and the gate still stand today, after three millennia. No wonder the Greeks believed that mythical creatures like the Cyclops built the walls! How could ordinary humans lift a hundred-ton rock? However, the Mycenaeans likely used ramps and a system of rollers. Mycenae's Lion Gate, built about 1250 BCE, had a twenty-ton lintel supported by ten-foot-high boulders. Two lions stand on the lintel, hence the name.

Intriguingly, Hattusa, the capital of the Hittite Empire, also had colossal walls and a lion gate eerily similar to Mycenae's. The Hittites built their lion gate first, about a century before the one in Greece. Although the Mycenaeans may have interacted with the Hittites through trade, Hattusa was in the center of today's Turkey, nowhere near a coast. Yet, somehow, the Greeks learned of the gate and copied it.

The gate raises another question: why lions? Did Greece have lions? Yes, lions lived in the Peloponnese Peninsula until around 1000 BCE. Lions frequently appeared in Mycenaean art, usually in hunting scenes, symbolizing power and authority.

Mycenaeans typically built their cities around a hill—a custom that the Greeks continued in the Archaic and Classical periods. They built towering walls to fortify the hill, called an acropolis. This is where the Mycenaeans built their palaces and temples. The rest of the city surrounded the acropolis. Guardsmen posted on the hill could scan the surrounding terrain for hostile forces. If enemies attacked the city, the citizens dashed inside the acropolis for safety. The soldiers on the acropolis had the uphill advantage for shooting arrows and other missiles at the attackers.

Each of the major cities ruled a state that had smaller towns. Every state had an *anax*, or king, who governed that region and its industries. He was also the region's judge and commander-in-chief of the regional army. All the kings answered to a "great king," whose capital was probably Mycenae. He had a council of elders who advised him, a tradition that continued in later Greek periods.

The Mycenaeans had a hierarchical society. At the top were the king and the warrior aristocracy. The Mycenaeans buried their royals and aristocrats in "tholos" tombs, which were immense beehive structures with domes and decorative corbels built into hillsides. At the bottom of the Mycenaean society were captured people, enslaved to work in the temples and palaces. Some enslaved people could own land. Most people in Mycenaean society fell into the middle class—the craftspeople, farmers, and merchants.

The Mycenaeans adapted the Linear A script used by the Minoans into a new script known as Linear B. It used similar symbols as Linear A but added some new ones. Linear B, which has been translated, represented an ancient form of Greek that the Mycenaeans spoke. No one knows what language the Minoans spoke.

The tablet on the left and the drawing of it on the right have a list of women's names. [92]

In 1932 CE, a fourteen-year-old boy in England, Michael Ventris, attended a lecture by archaeologist Sir Arthur Evans on the Linear B script. No one had decoded it. His interest piqued. In his twenties, Ventris attempted to unlock the language through statistical analysis. He realized it was an archaic Greek dialect. Partnering with Cambridge linguist John Chadwick, he cracked the code of Linear B. Sadly, Ventris died in an automobile accident before publishing their findings. Once scholars could read the script, they realized that written Linear B was a language of record-keeping and administrative affairs. Greek literature did not emerge in written form until Homer and Hesiod began writing epic poetry after the Greek Dark Ages.

However, even record-keeping opened a window on Mycenaean culture. Lists of sacrifices offered to the gods, like spices and honey, revealed that the Mycenaeans worshipped many of the same deities as in the Archaic and Classical Greek eras that followed. The chief Mycenaean god was Poseidon, the sea deity, whom they called "Po-se-da-o." Other gods included Zeus, Dionysus, Hera, Ares, and Artemis.

Mycenaean women worshippers in a mural from the palace of Thebes[98]

Homer wrote in the *Iliad* that the Mycenaean "Great King" Agamemnon led one thousand Greek ships across the Aegean Sea to invade Troy. The Trojan prince Paris had stolen Helen, wife of King Menelaus of Sparta, who was Agamemnon's brother. Yet, the Trojan War had a practical reason. Troy (in northwestern Turkey) was strategically located on the Dardanelles Strait, linking the Aegean and Black Seas. Whoever controlled the Dardanelles controlled the lucrative Black Sea trade.

Homer wrote that after a grueling ten-year war, the Mycenaeans emerged victorious (circa 1180 BCE), and King Menelaus reclaimed his wife. Yet, the victory came at a crushing cost. In the *Odyssey,* Homer said that while the Greek kings were away for a decade, their realms destabilized. When Great King Agamemnon returned, his wife and her lover killed him. Many of Greece's mighty warriors died fighting Troy. Farms were neglected, and food was scarce.

Was Troy an actual place? Did the Trojan War really happen? Another name Homer used for Troy was "Wilusa," a city with close connections to the Hittite Empire. Homer said the Hittite name of Prince Paris was Alaksandu. The Hittite records said that Alaksandu and the people of Wilusa fought the "Ahhiyawa," possibly the Mycenaean Greeks.

In the late 1800s CE, several amateur archaeologists excavated a low hill at Hisarlik in northwestern Turkey, which they believed might be the ancient site of Troy. They unearthed nine layers, with each new city built over the older one, dating back to approximately 3000 BCE. The archaeologists bungled things and misidentified an older civilization as being Homer's Troy. Nevertheless, later excavations revealed a layer higher up that showed evidence of a prolonged siege and total destruction around 1200 BCE. Troy probably was the real city of Wilusa, and the Trojan War likely was an actual event.

Both the Mycenaean civilization and the Hittite Empire collapsed in the Bronze Age collapse (1200–900 BCE). Yet, war was not the only factor. Archaeological evidence and written records from Syria, Egypt, and the Hittite Empire reveal other horrors of the era. A mega-drought brought starvation conditions to the Eastern Mediterranean. Greek and Syrian cities fell to earthquakes. Probably displaced by war and natural disasters, the mysterious Sea Peoples raided the coastal cities and shattered the sea trade.

Most Greek cities crumbled, although people continued to live in small communities as herders, farmers, and fishers. The Greeks lost their written language for three centuries, and the stunning civilizations created by the Minoans and Mycenaeans dissolved.

Chapter 5: Ancient China — From Xia to Zhou

Gong Gong, the water god, was having a bad day. He had fought Zhurong, the fire god, and lost. On his way home, he bumped his head on Mount Buzhou. "Ai ya!" he cried, rubbing his head. Then he looked up in horror as a torrent of water poured down. Mount Buzhou was one of the four pillars supporting the sky. Gong Gong had accidentally released the floodgates of heaven.

As the floodwaters rose, King Yao hurried to his advisors, the Four Mountains. "What should I do? The water is covering the Earth!"

"Appoint your cousin, Gun, as your flood control manager," they answered.

Gun stole a divine soil called "xirang" from the gods. It continuously expanded, so he used the soil to build dams and raise the riverbanks. Despite his best efforts, the flooding continued for nine years. King Yao resigned in shame and appointed Shun as his successor. Finally, Gun's son, Yu the Engineer, diverted the water by building the "Dragon Gate," a canal through the mountains that led to the sea. At the end of his life, King Shun made the hero Yu the next ruler. Yu began the Xia dynasty and ruled for forty-five years.

Mythology shrouds ancient China's earliest dynasty, yet archaeological findings provide tantalizing clues that it existed. This chapter delves into the legendary Xia dynasty, the historically documented Shang dynasty, and the influential Zhou dynasty. How did they establish the cultural, political, and philosophical foundations of Chinese civilization that endured for thousands of years? When did the Chinese start writing and working with bronze? What was the Mandate of Heaven? How did significant philosophies like Confucianism, Taoism, and Legalism shape Chinese thought and actions?

The Xia dynasty's position in China[94]

What records do we have of the Xia, the Shang, and the Zhou dynasties? In the fifth century BCE, Confucius compiled the *Book of Documents* based on earlier works he had collected. It has speeches about the Xia, Shang, and Zhou dynasties receiving the Mandate of Heaven. The *Book of Zhou* (*Zhou Shu)* is a fourth-century BCE collection of histories of the Zhou dynasty. The *Bamboo Annals* begin with Emperor Huangdi (before the Xia Dynasty) and end in 296 BCE, when the *Annals* were buried with King Xiang of Wei in his tomb.

In the early first century BCE, Sima Qian gathered histories from older manuscripts and wrote the *Shiji,* or *Records of the Grand Historian.* It covered China's history, beginning with the legendary Yellow Emperor, who took power around 2697 BCE. Chinese lore says that the Yellow Emperor (Huangdi), an ancestor of Yu the Engineer, invented boats, wheeled carts, the compass, and writing. He also introduced the belief system of Taoism.

Archaeologists have uncovered jade treasures, bronze vessels, and ceramics that they believe date to the Xia era. The problem is that the Chinese were not writing yet, so they left no inscriptions announcing who they were. However, evidence of a prolonged and devastating flooding of the Yellow River supports the legend of a horrendous flood preceding the Xia dynasty.

In 1959 CE, archaeologists unearthed a 745-acre site in the Yiluo Basin of the Yellow River near Luoyang in Henan Province. Its palatial structures, bronze vessels, and elite burials all pointed to a social hierarchy and a central authority. At its height, its population was about twenty-four thousand. The archaeologists decided that the city, which they named Erlitou, must be the capital city of the fabled Xia. Why did they think it belonged to the Xia dynasty (2070–1600 BCE) and not the Shang dynasty that came after it? Radiocarbon dating places the time range of the city from 1860 to 1530 BCE. The Shang dynasty did not take power until around 1600 BCE, and its first capital was Bo, located 191 miles east of Erlitou.

Erlitou had China's first road network over which China's first wheeled carts traveled. It had a palace (or ceremonial hub) at its center, with adjacent workshops where craftspeople manufactured bronze items featuring turquoise and jade inlays. Although Erlitou had no fortification walls around the city, it had a thick wall surrounding the palace and workshops.

The Xia dynasty marked the beginning of China's Bronze Age. At Erlitou, archaeologists found China's first bronze weapons, tools, and ceremonial vessels, including three-legged cups and basins. The city also produced ceramics and bone tools. Its people often buried their family members under or near their houses. In one grave, archaeologists found a dragon sculpture with two thousand pieces of inlaid turquoise and jade.

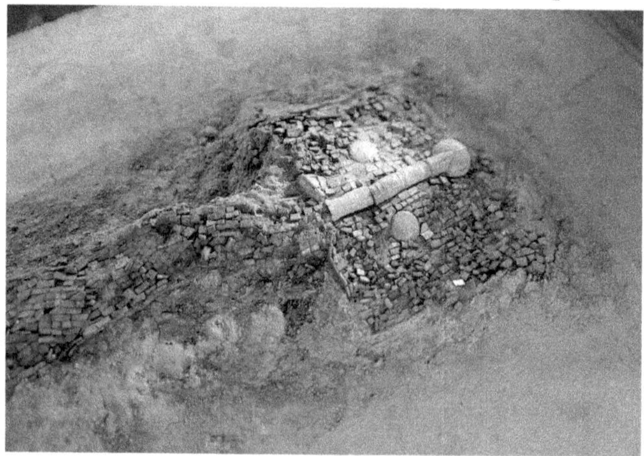

Bronze dragon with turquoise and jade inlay from Erlitou[95]

Yu the Engineer, the first king of the Xia dynasty, appointed his son, Qi, as the next ruler when he died. This broke precedent. Previously, kings chose their successors based on who they thought would do the best job. The throne did not automatically go to the king's son. Thus, by appointing his son as his successor, Yu began the first Chinese dynasty, a system in which the throne passed from father to son (or to a near relative).

Archaeologists believe that the Wangchenggang archaeological site in Henan Province is Yangcheng, the first capital of the Xia dynasty. The ancient histories say that King Yu built the city near Mount Song on the banks of the Yellow River. He introduced irrigation farming to China and built a powerful military, arming them with bronze crossbows, swords, and spears. The "Xia Calendar" is a lunar calendar that Yu or his descendants developed.

The *Shiji* lists seventeen kings of the Xia dynasty. Few details exist about their lives and reigns because no one wrote about them until centuries later.

The Shang dynasty, like the Xia dynasty, emerged in the Yellow River valley, the cradle of Chinese civilization. It covered the same area as the Xia but expanded east and south until it grew to about three times the size of the Xia dynasty.

At one time, scholars doubted the existence of the Shang dynasty, much as some still doubt the Xia dynasty. Then, the oracle bones showed up with China's earliest writing.

Chinese people have been using medicine allegedly made from dragon bones for thousands of years. In the late 1800s CE, a Chinese scholar named Wang Yirong bought some dragon-bone medicine when he was sick with malaria. Wang and his friend noticed writing scratched on the bones. They went back to the shop and bought all the bones the apothecary had. The "medicine" was not dragon bones but ancient oxen or water buffalo bones. Yet, they were valuable beyond belief, inscribed with ancient writings from thousands of years earlier.

Because the bones are organic material, scholars can carbon date them to within decades of when the animal died. Incredibly, about fifty thousand oracle bones with writing on them have survived until today, despite all the ones that were ground into "dragon-bone" medicine.

Around 1250 BCE, people began carving these inscriptions on bones (usually the shoulder bone of a water buffalo) and turtle shells. At first, they were pictographs. Later, they evolved into the symbols that eventually became Chinese written characters. Priests and fortune tellers used the oracle bones to predict the future. For instance, the king might ask, "If I attack this city, will I win the battle?" The priest wrote his question on one side of a bone. He then turned the bone over and drilled little pits on the back side of the bone. He heated a thin rod until it was red hot, then stuck it into the pits. The heat caused the bone to crack, and the priest interpreted the answer to the question based on how it cracked.

Kings were not the only people who inquired about the future this way. Anyone could consult a fortune teller who used oracle bones.

Chinese scholars have been able to interpret the ancient characters. Although it has evolved over thousands of years, the core principles of written Chinese have remained. Scholars could analyze and interpret the pictographs, ideograms (symbols that represent an idea), and phono-semantic compounds (symbols that represent a sound).

Early Shang dynasty oracle bones with pictographs. The pictographs on the top stone, with a square and a cross under it, mean "child." Today, the character is 子 (zǐ).[96]

Inscriptions from the Shang dynasty have also appeared on bronze ceremonial vessels, pottery, and jade. The people of the era wrote on bamboo and thin pieces of wood, but only a few lasted through the millennia. However, the surviving writing has enabled scholars to confirm the names of kings mentioned in histories written in later dynasties. They provide details about the Shang dynasty's military, administration, and culture.

Replica of a horse-pulled chariot. Horses and chariots came to China during the Shang dynasty.[97]

The Shang dynasty (1600–1046 BCE) began during a thunderstorm when the righteous Cheng Tang, "the perfect," overthrew the tyrannical Xia king, Jie. Cheng Tang's distant ancestor was Xie, who legend says was born after his mother swallowed an egg that a black bird dropped. Xie helped Yu (the first Xia king) control the Great Flood.

For over half a millennium, about thirty kings led the Shang dynasty. The kings also served as high priests, offering sacrifices to their ancestors and Di, the supreme god. Advisors and officials from a hereditary aristocratic class surrounded the king. The dynasty's capital city changed location several times, but Cheng Tang's capital was Shang (near today's Zhengzhou) on the Yellow River in Henan Province, about seventy miles east of Erlitou. Even when later kings chose a different political capital,

Shang persevered as the religious and ceremonial capital, where the ancestral temples remained. Shang's defensive walls were twenty-six feet high and sixty-five feet thick.

The Shang people buried their royal family in massive tombs with jade ornaments, bronze goblets, and oracle bones. They sacrificed people, probably servants, to accompany the royals in the afterlife. The tomb of Fu Hao, a military commander and priestess, was found undisturbed in 1976 CE at Yin, the Shang dynasty's last capital. Archaeologists discovered over seven hundred jade objects, dozens of bronze weapons, battle-axes, six dogs, and sixteen sacrificed humans buried with her. Her husband, King Wu Ding, had sixty-four wives, but she was one of the top three.

The people of the Xia dynasty worked with bronze, but the Shang dynasty's people did piece-mold casting of bronze ceremonial vessels. They made a clay mold with a design and poured molten bronze into it. After it cooled, they cut the clay. Some of the larger bronze pieces weighed two thousand pounds.

A bird-shaped bronze wine container, Zhou dynasty [98]

The last king of the Shang dynasty was Di Xin. He rode out to the Battle of Muye against the rebel King Wu of Zhou, a vassal state. Di Xin's soldiers defected to the Zhou side. When he saw he was in a hopeless situation, Di Xin committed suicide. King Wu made Di Xin's son, Wu Gun, a vassal king under him.

China's longest dynasty (789 years) was the Zhou dynasty (1046–256 BCE). It had two eras, the Western Zhou (1046–771 BCE) and Eastern Zhou (771–256 BCE). The Western Zhou's capital was near today's Xi'an in northern China (Shaanxi Province). A shift in political power forced the court to move over two hundred miles east to Chengzhou, near present-day Luoyang (Henan Province).

Chinese mythology says that the Zhou royalty descended from Qi, who lived during the Xia dynasty. His mother miraculously conceived him when she stepped into the footprint of Shang Di, the supreme god. She thought the strange conception was a bad omen, so she tried to abandon her baby three times. Each time, the child survived with the help of cattle, horses, and birds. Finally, she resolved to keep her baby. After Qi grew up, he taught agriculture to the people; thus, he got the title "Houji" or "Director of Grain" in the Xia dynasty.

Emperor Wu claimed that his authority to attack and conquer the Shang dynasty came from the "Mandate of Heaven." This was the idea that heaven granted the divine right to rule. If an emperor were just and wise, the mandate would remain with him, allowing him to rule for many years. The people considered their emperor the "son of heaven" and were unlikely to challenge his authority. However, if he were unreasonable, tyrannical, or unprincipled, he lost the Mandate of Heaven. Signs that he had lost the mandate included floods, famine, and other natural disasters. If he lost the mandate, people could revolt without fear of heaven's wrath. Revolts from within or invasions from without dethroned the emperor and usually established a new dynasty.

Emperors of the Western Zhou employed a decentralized government model rather than micromanaging everything. Emperor Wu appointed seventy vassal kings, usually loyal friends and family, to govern, keep order, and oversee the resources of each region. Vassal kings had to pay tribute and, if the emperor went to war, they had to provide military personnel. In exchange, the emperor gave his vassals lands and titles. The Western Zhou era became prosperous because of new agricultural methods and advanced metalworking techniques. Chinese script became widespread.

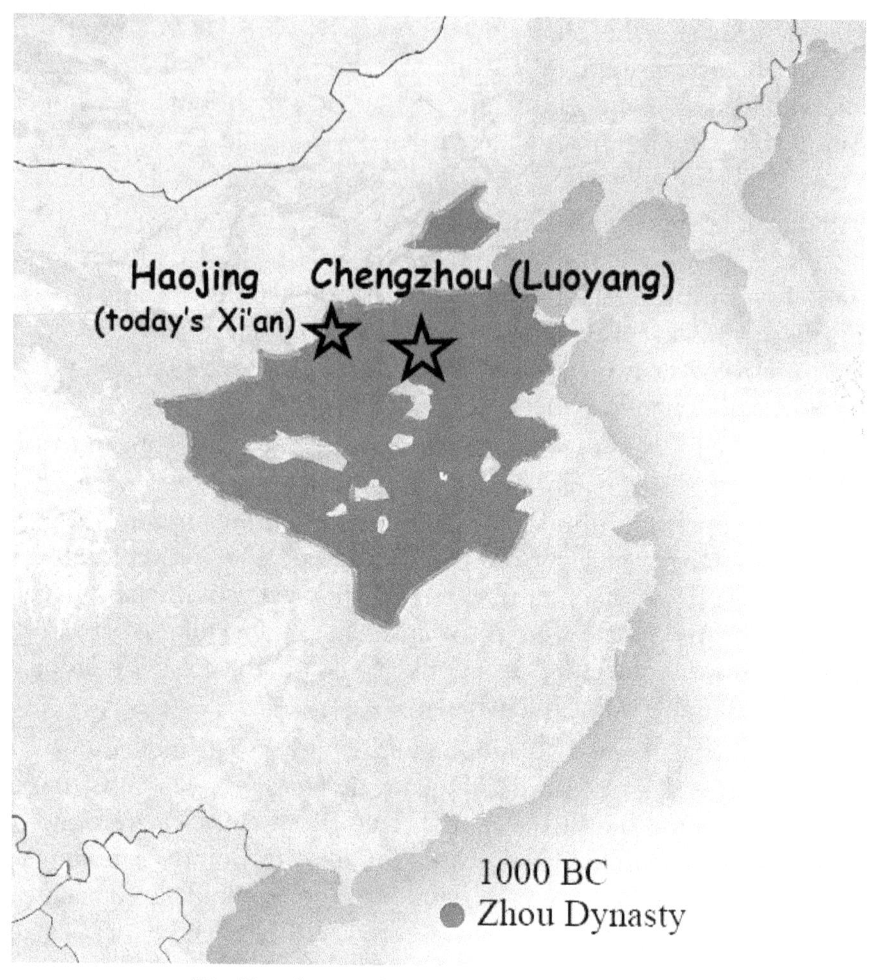

The Zhou dynasty with western and eastern capitals[99]

After three centuries, the vassal kings became increasingly powerful as the emperor's authority weakened. Politically, power shifted to the Eastern Zhou at the new capital of Chengzhou.

Despite the mayhem, the early Eastern Zhou era witnessed a cultural surge in poetry, music, and philosophy known as the Spring and Autumn period (772–476 BCE). This was when Master K'ung (Confucius) wrote (or edited) the *Spring and Autumn Annals* about the dukes of the regional state of Lu (his home province). It also tied to the history of other regions of the Zhou Empire. He used natural events, such as solar and lunar eclipses, to date his history.

Due to the philosophies Confucius and others such as Laozi (Lao Tzu) and Mozi developed during this period, it became known as the

"Hundred Schools of Thought." Confucius emphasized the importance of social harmony and taught that exceptional rulers fostered loyalty, respect, and morality. He believed everyone had a key role to play in society and should always strive to cultivate knowledge and righteous behavior. He promoted filial piety—respect, love, and obedience toward one's parents and ancestors. He had a "reverse" golden rule: "Whatever you do not wish to happen to you, do not do to others."

Laozi developed Daoism (Taoism). He believed that inaction and non-involvement in worldly things lead to oneness with Dao, the "way" that governs the universe. He thought one should live a simple life and let go of attachments. Only humble people can be wise. One should not try to force change but let events unfold naturally. One should also not resist change but embrace it, as change is inevitable.

Mozi lived in the Warring States period and taught the philosophy of Mohism. He believed a person should love everyone, regardless of whether they were family, friends, or total strangers. People should strive for what is best for everyone, not just themselves. He believed society should promote productivity by valuing labor and fostering efficiency. He hated warfare and felt that people should coexist peacefully, resolving conflicts through diplomacy.

Legalism also had roots in the Warring States era. It was almost the opposite of Confucianism, Daoism, and Mohism. Legalism taught that people are evil at their core. If left to their own devices, most people are corrupt and selfish. Thus, the government must strictly enforce laws for everyone, high and low, to keep them on the right path. People who do the right thing ought to be rewarded.

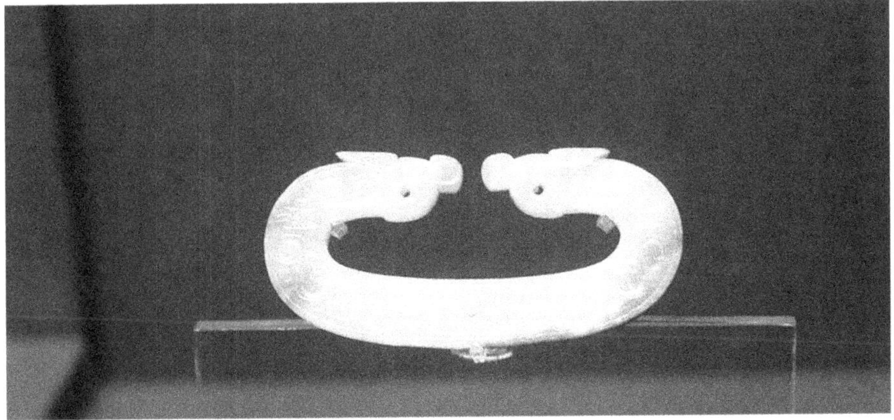

Eastern Zhou jade ornament [100]

After the Zhou dynasty relocated its capital to Luoyang, it continued a similar government model. However, the central government became weaker, while the vassal states grew stronger and more independent. As the imperial government broke down, people whispered that the Zhou dynasty had lost the Mandate of Heaven. The central government fragmented into feudal states. This led to the Warring States period (481–221 BCE), during which battles raged between the seven most powerful states, ultimately ending the Zhou dynasty. Despite turbulent times, intellectual growth and philosophical development continued unabated.

As the seven states fought each other, another threat came from the north and west. Horseback-riding nomadic tribes—including the Ordos, the Xianyun, and the Xiongnu—were crossing into China from the Russian and Mongolian steppes. The Chinese began building sections of packed earthen walls, about thirteen feet high, to keep them out. In the following Qin dynasty, Emperor Qin Shi Huang connected these sections into a unified wall.

The Xia, Shang, and Zhou dynasties left an enduring legacy in culture, government systems, philosophy, writing, technology, and many other areas. They set the stage for the unification of China under the Qin dynasty.

Chapter 6: The Rise of the Hittites and the Assyrians

A sense of foreboding gripped the Babylonians. Two recent eclipses of the moon and the sun foretold their king would die, yet none of the usual enemies posed a threat. Then, they saw dust rising in the distance. Minutes later, a guard from the northern frontier charged in.

"It's the Hittites! Hordes of them! Get into the city! Shut the gates!"

"The Hittites? They're a thousand miles away!"

The Hittite Empire *was* a thousand miles away, yet their king, Mursili I, invaded Babylon in 1595 BCE. He had no interest in ruling Babylon. He wanted their wheat. The catastrophic volcanic eruption on the island of Thera had disrupted weather patterns, causing harvests to fail. Babylon was far enough away not to be affected much, and its irrigation farming ensured a consistent wheat surplus.

Before the Babylonians knew what was happening, the Hittites swooped in and enslaved most of the people. They stole the cult image of Babylon's chief god, Marduk, stripped the temples of their treasures, and emptied their storehouses of grain.

The formidable Hittites played a pivotal role in shaping the politics and culture of the Near East. They were among the first people, if not *the* first, to invent ironworking technology. Iron weapons gave them a significant edge. When they emerged in northern Mesopotamia by 1800 BCE, no one called them "Hittites." They called themselves the "people of Nesha," a place in central Anatolia (present-day Turkey) where they lived before migrating west.

The "Hittites" of ancient Turkey were not the Hittites in the Bible. The biblical Hittites lived in Canaan before, during, and after the Hittite Empire. So, how did the people in Anatolia get the name "Hittite?" Nineteenth-century archaeologists mistakenly identified the people of the Hatti Empire as the biblical Hittites. The incorrect name stuck.

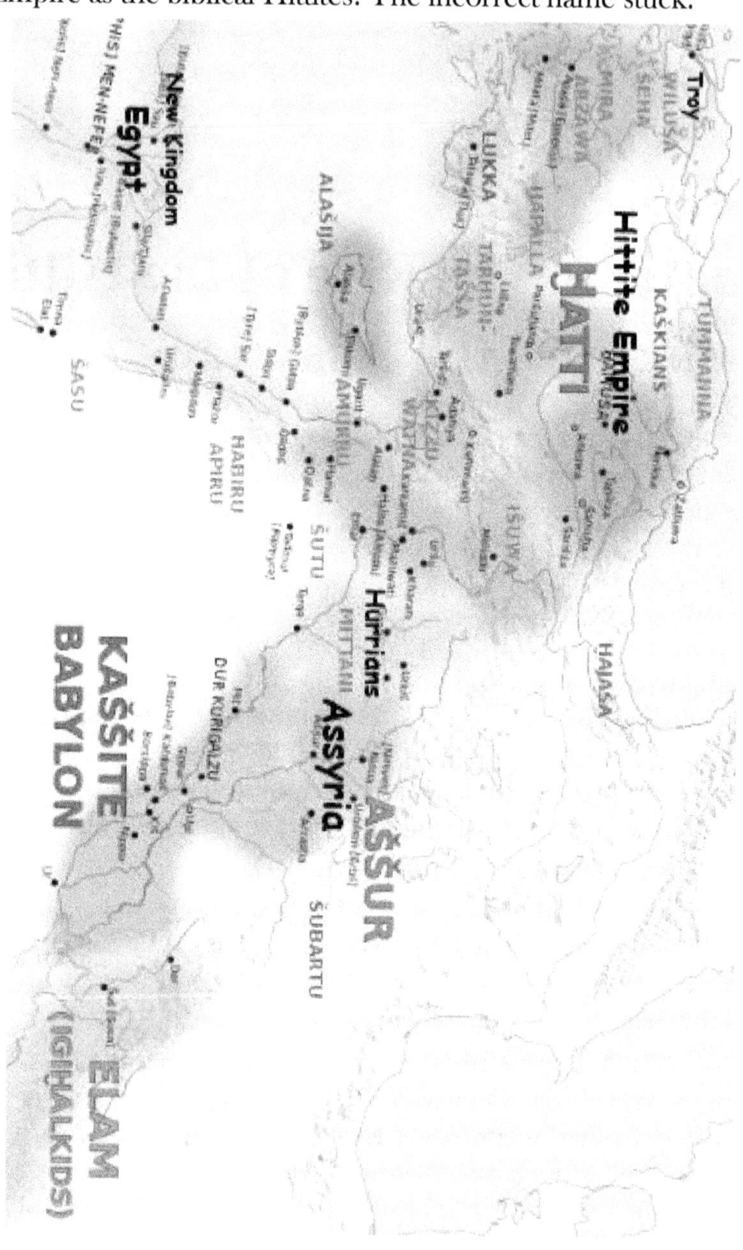

Middle East, circa 1300 BCE[101]

Where did the (non-biblical) Hittites come from? Their earliest written history places them in Kussara, in eastern Anatolia. The Hittite King Pithana conquered Kanesh (Nesha) in central Anatolia around 1780 BCE. It was a nighttime raid, and they did not kill anyone. His son, Anitta, recorded his father's exploits in the *Anitta Text,* the oldest known Hittite literature. The Hittites wrote in cuneiform, adopted from the Akkadians.

Around 1700 BCE, King Anitta invaded Hattusa in central Anatolia, the capital of the Hattian people. The Hittites burned the city, then left it abandoned. Fifty years later, Anitta's descendant, Hattusili I, rebuilt Hattusa and made it the new Hittite capital. It had colossal stone walls and a lion gate facing southwest—the one the Mycenaean Greeks copied. Two sphinxes guarded Hattusa's southern gate. Hattusa's archive held ten thousand tablets, shining a light on Hittite history.

Hattusa Sphinx Gate [109]

The Hurrians of the Mitanni kingdom were neighbors of the Hittites. They lived at the Hittites' southeastern border, west of the Assyrians. The Hittites translated and recorded Hurrian mythology, as well as other writings. One book the Hittites translated was a guide to training chariot horses. (The Hurrians perfected lightweight war chariots with spoked wheels.)

The Hittites had thousands of gods, but their chief deity was Tarhunt, the god of thunder, who ruled the heavens and the mountains. He was in perpetual conflict with Illuyanka, the serpent. Another important deity was Tarhunt's wife, Arinna (Wurušemu), the sun goddess.

The Hittite king Šuppiluliuma I shattered the friendship with the Hurrians by launching a surprise attack. He conquered part of the Mitanni kingdom in 1344 BCE and made the Hurrian king a vassal under his rule.

At this time, Egypt controlled the Mediterranean coastline up to Syria. When Egypt's teenage pharaoh, Tutankhamun, unexpectedly died without an heir, his advisor, Ay, tried to usurp the throne. Part of his plan was coercing King Tut's widow, Ankhesenamun, to marry him. The widow snorted at the thought of marrying a non-royal. Instead, she reached out to Šuppiluliuma I, asking him to send one of his sons to marry her.

Tarhum (Tarhunt), the Hittite god of thunder [108]

The Hittite king's jaw dropped when he read her letter. Whoever heard of a woman arranging her own marriage? Yet, he liked the idea of a son on Egypt's throne. He sent his son, Zannanza, to marry Ankhesenamun. Ay heard he was coming and killed the young Hittite prince. Enraged, Šuppiluliuma attacked Egyptian territory in Syria and

Canaan—a fatal move. The Egyptian military was sick with either tularemia (rabbit fever) or the bubonic plague. The disease killed Šuppiluliuma I, his son Arnuwanda II, and much of the Hittite military.

In this era, the Hurrians, Hittites, Assyrians, Babylonians, and Egyptians were what modern scholars call the "Great Powers" of the Middle East. They occasionally fought each other, but they also arranged marriages between their royal families. They wrote letters back and forth, calling each other "brother."

Although fierce warriors, the Hittite kings were also skilled negotiators. The Hittites' Treaty of Kadesh with Egypt was one of the earliest peace treaties, showcasing the Hittites' sophisticated approach to law and diplomacy.

The famous Battle of Kadesh set the stage for this treaty. In 1274 BCE, Egypt's high-powered pharaoh, Ramesses II, charged north, determined to regain the territory lost to the Hittites. His target was Kadesh, a city in Syria that Egypt had ruled for 150 years. Now, the Hittites had it. As he neared Kadesh, Ramesses noticed two shepherds sitting in the shade.

"Do you know where the Hittites and their King Muwatalli are?"

"Far away!" the shepherds grinned. "Muwatalli was quivering in fear when he heard you were coming. He ran away to Aleppo."

Ramesses was so eager to capture Kadesh that he rushed off with only his advance unit of five thousand men and five hundred chariots, leaving the other three-quarters of his army far behind. Little did he know the shepherds were Muwatalli's misinformation agents. They tricked Ramesses into riding into a trap. The Hittite army was waiting for Ramesses in Kadesh with 37,000 men and 3,000 chariots.

Most of the Hittites had iron spearheads and swords, far stronger than the bronze weapons the elite Egyptian warriors carried. Most Egyptian soldiers carried copper swords and spearheads, which were brittle and difficult to sharpen.

As Ramesses approached Kadesh, he paled when he saw the Hittites pouring out from behind a nearby mountain. He looked over his shoulder. Some of his men were wading across the Orontes River, while others were struggling up the hill toward the city. Vastly outnumbered, the Egyptian troops scattered as the Hittites charged. The Hittites encircled Ramesses with their chariots, cutting him off from his men.

However, the Egyptian chariots were easier to maneuver. Ramesses charged the Hittites, over and over, until he broke through their line.

Sweat pouring from his brow, Ramesses grinned when he saw more of his men arriving. They pinned the Hittites between the other Egyptian units, then forced them into the river. Some escaped to safety on the other side, while others drowned.

Ramesses II's propaganda painting shows him pushing the Hittites into the Orontes River. [104]

Both sides declared victory. Ramesses II crowed, "We pushed the Hittites into the river!"

Hattusili III, Muwatalli's brother and the next Hittite king, called him out: "You failed to take Kadesh! Wasn't that the point?"

Hattusili and Ramesses mended fences and agreed to the "Eternal Peace Treaty," in which each promised not to attack or take the other's land.

Two years after the Battle of Kadesh, the Assyrian king Shalmaneser I launched an assault against the Hittites and Hurrians. He bragged about capturing tens of thousands and gouging out their eyes. The Hittites struggled through the next six decades and fell during the Bronze Age collapse. Drought led to food shortages. An earthquake storm rocked the region between 1225 and 1175 BCE. Internal strife, invasion by the Sea Peoples, and battles with Assyria led to the Hittites' downfall. However, their groundbreaking technology in iron manufacturing survived and changed the course of history.

The Assyrians of northern Mesopotamia built a spine-chilling reputation. Their advanced military technology and strategies, coupled with abject cruelty, struck terror among their foes.

But what were the origins of the Assyrians? How did they rise to power?

Semitic herders migrated into northern Iraq during the Sumerian era. Nineveh, built by the Hassuna civilization during the Neolithic Age, was already thriving on the eastern banks of the Tigris River. Most early Assyrians were nomadic herders, and their first seventeen chieftains lived in tents.

A man named Aššur (Ashur) built a city by the same name around 2600 BCE on the Tigris River's western banks. The chief Assyrian god also had the name Ashur. (They probably elevated their ancestor to god status.) Besides worshiping Ashur, the Assyrians erected temples to the goddess Ishtar and Adad, the Amorite rain god.

Ashur, the Assyrian founder and patron god [105]

Around 2025 BCE, Puzur-Ashur I launched the Old Assyrian Empire. Powerful kings expanded Assyrian territory into former Akkadian and Sumerian lands.

In 1808 BCE, King Šamši-Adad I of Terqa (in Syria) conquered Assyria. He claimed he had the right. "My ancestors were Assyrian chieftains!" Assyria became a true empire as it swept parts of Anatolia, Syria, Lebanon, and Canaan under its rule. Assyrian supremacy fell only six decades later. Mari (in Syria) and Eshnunna (in central Iraq) snatched all the lands Šamši-Adad I had annexed.

The Adaside dynasty began about 1700 BCE, launching Assyria into an era of strength and prosperity. In the 1400s BCE, Egypt's pharaoh Thutmose III conquered the coastline up to Syria. He then crossed the Euphrates and took the Mitanni kingdom. The Hurrians and Hittites fought together against the Egyptians. However, the Assyrians allied with Egypt, a deadly mistake. The furious Hurrian-Hittite forces launched a surprise attack on Assyria in 1430 BCE, wiping out the Old Assyrian Empire.

For thirty-eight years, the Assyrians paid tribute to the Hurrians while quietly rebuilding their strength. They smiled when the Hurrian-Hittite coalition frayed. Finally, in 1392 BCE, the Assyrian king Eriba-Adad I broke free from the Hurrians. The Middle Assyrian Empire launched, more dynamic than ever. Within decades, it snatched part of the Mitanni kingdom when a revolt rocked the Hurrians.

The Assyrian king Arik-den-ili (1317–1306 BCE) subdued the nomadic Aramean and Sutean tribes west of the Euphrates. He built the great ziggurat in Ashur. His son, Adad-nirari I, charged south, taking Babylonia's northern territory. He captured the Hurrian king, forcing him to swear loyalty. When the Hittite king Mursili I heard, he wrote an irate letter: "So, you have become a 'Great King,' have you? But why do you still talk about 'brotherhood?'"[11]

Shalmaneser I, who obliterated the Mitanni kingdom, began the Assyrian custom of population relocation. The Assyrians moved entire cities of rebellious conquered people to other provinces and resettled the cities with people from elsewhere. In the Neo-Assyrian period, Sargon II conquered northern Israel and deported over twenty-seven thousand Jews to Assyria. He resettled the Israeli towns with conquered people from Babylonia and Syria.

The Assyrian king Tukulti-Ninurta smashed the Hittites in 1245 BCE, enslaving twenty-eight thousand, bragging, "I filled the caves and ravines of the mountains with their corpses. I made heaps of their corpses like (grain) piles beside their gates. Their cities I destroyed, ravaged, and turned into ruin hills."[12]

---

[11] Harry A. Hoffner, Jr., *Letters from the Hittite Kingdom: Writings from the Ancient World* (Atlanta: Society of Biblical Literature, 2009), 322–4.

[12] *The Great Inscription of Tukulti-Ninurta I,* trans. Yigal Bloch (Omnika). https://omnika.org/texts/626

A royal lion hunt in a relief in Nineveh [106]

Not only did Assyria survive the Bronze Age collapse, but King Tiglath-Pileser I (1114–1076 BCE) conquered the Phoenician cities of Tyre, Sidon, Berytus (Beirut), and Byblos. He rebuilt Assyria's temples and offered human sacrifices to the gods. Tiglath-Pileser bragged of killing fourteen elephants and nearly a thousand lions, both of which lived in the Middle East in those days.

The rulers after Tiglath-Pileser lost the lands he had conquered. Assyria shrank to its original homeland, and the Middle Assyrian Empire ended in 1055 BCE.

The Neo-Assyrian Empire leaped into action in 911 BCE with Adad-nirari II. It expanded into the largest empire the world had yet seen. The Assyrians' virtually unbeatable military machine, renowned for its brutality, struck fear across the Middle East.

Adad-nirari marched into Anatolia, petrifying the Neo-Hittites, who were disrupting Assyrian trade routes. Who were the Neo-Hittites? Some were the Luwian people who had lived in the Hittite Empire before it fell. Scholars

The Neo-Hittite King Suppiluliuma [107]

believe they shared the same mother tongue as the Hittites.

Next, Adad-nirari swept into Babylonia, plundering the city's incredible wealth and using it to rebuild Assyria's military with the latest iron weapons and siege technology. Their deadly siege engines enabled them to get through or over the thick walls of the cities they attacked. Some siege engines had iron battering rams. Others were tall towers on wheels that the Assyrians used to launch arrows into the city. They could also throw up portable ladders from their wheeled towers and climb into the city.

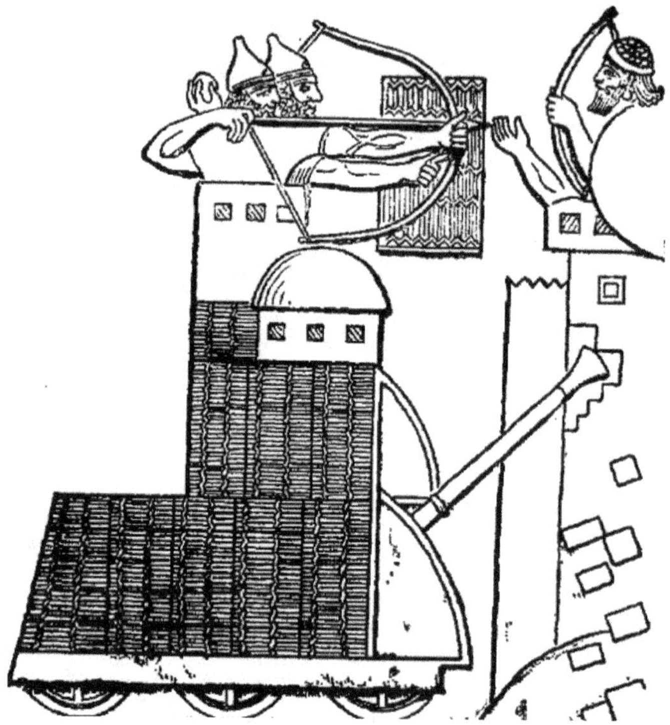

This wheeled siege engine in a drawing of an Assyrian relief has both a battering ram and a tower from which to shoot arrows into the city. [108]

Assyrian engineers also dug underneath the city walls, causing them to fall down. Another tactic was diverting irrigation canals to flood the city.

The Assyrians peeled the skin off of captured soldiers or impaled them on stakes in view of horrified onlookers from the walls. These shock and terror tactics often impelled cities to surrender immediately when the Assyrians attacked, rather than suffer such atrocities.

Tukulti-Ninurta II (890–884 BCE) subdued the Medes and Persians of ancient Iran. They had to pay tribute of horses, camels, copper, gold, and iron to Assyria. Controlling the Medes and Persians also meant access to the Great Khorasan Road, which ran from Babylon into Central Asia. It was part of the Silk Road to China, bringing unimaginable riches in trade.

Ashurnasirpal II (883–859 BCE), the son of Tukulti-Ninurta, savagely conquered parts of Anatolia and Syria. He bragged about cutting the heads off eight hundred soldiers and burning the teen boys. He impaled five hundred soldiers and built a pile of heads at the city gate. His son, Shalmaneser III (859–824 BCE), defeated Babylon, an epic win that gave the Assyrians control of all Mesopotamia. Yet, a coalition of nations gathered to fight him.

On the Kurkh Monoliths, Shalmaneser III described the 853 BCE Battle of Qarqar. It was the largest battle in Middle Eastern history to that point. In the inscription, Shalmaneser said he was making his annual tour of his conquered lands. When he reached Hamath in west-central Syria, pandemonium broke out. The Luwian people resisted, so he trashed their palaces and city.

As he left Hamath, a massive coalition confronted him. King Ahab of Israel, King Hadadezer of Damascus, and King Irhuleni of Hamath were waiting for him. With them were the Arabians, Jordanians, Lebanese, and Neo-Hittites. He said that 52,000 infantry, 3,900 chariots, 1,900 cavalry, and 1,000 men on camels covered the plain.

Of course, Shalmaneser claimed victory on his monument, saying he killed 14,000 men, while none of the other kings lost their lives or thrones. No doubt, he consolidated his control over Syria and Israel. Several years later, the Assyrian Black Obelisk pillar pictured King Jehu of Israel presenting tribute to Shalmaneser.

King Jehu of Israel bows before Shalmaneser III on the Black Obelisk carving [109]

Through its sophisticated administration, advanced siege technology, and nearly invincible military, the Neo-Assyrian Empire reached its greatest extent around 670 BCE, following King Esarhaddon's conquest of

Egypt. It stretched from the Zagros Mountains in the east to Egypt in the southwest and Anatolia in the north.

The Neo-Assyrian king Ashurbanipal (668–627 BCE) built the sensational Library of Ashurbanipal in Nineveh. It was not the world's first library, but it was the first to systematically organize a mind-boggling collection of tablets from around the known world. The library preserved not only Assyrian works but also the history and literature of the Sumerians, Akkadians, Babylonians, and other ancient civilizations. It was a repository of Mesopotamian literature, science, and history.

Sadly, the majestic library, which housed approximately thirty thousand tablets, stood for only about three decades before the Medes and Babylonians sacked and burned Nineveh. However, thousands of the clay tablets survived, buried under the rubble, and were uncovered by archaeologists Sir Austen Henry Layard and Hormuzd Rassam in the 1850s CE.

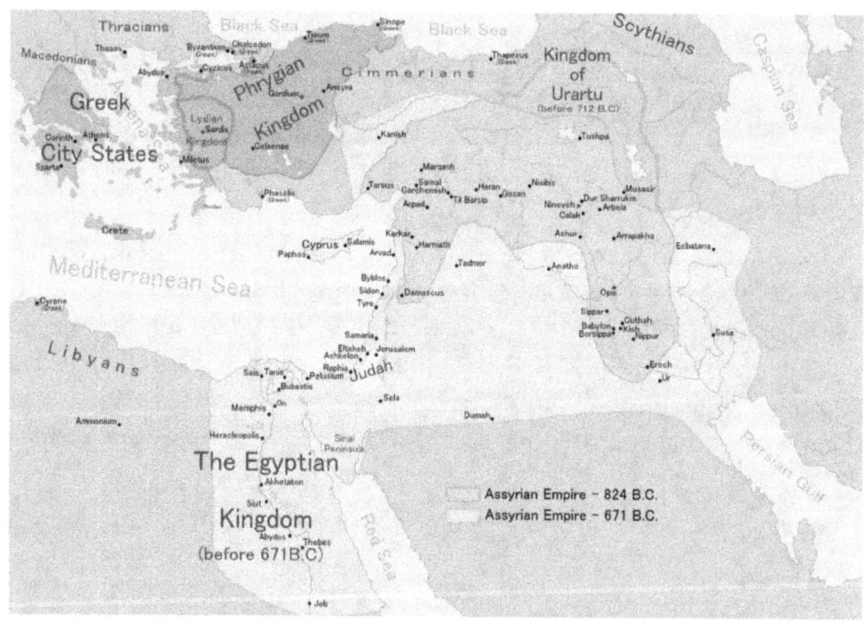

The Neo-Assyrian Empire at its height in 671 BCE [110]

Conquering and creating the world's largest empire was one thing. Maintaining it proved impossible, especially after a catastrophic drought and a military revolt exacerbated the situation. In 612 BCE, the Babylonians, Medes, Persians, Chaldeans, Scythians, and Cimmerians plotted their revenge against the Assyrians' vicious inhumanity. Their sheer numbers were staggering.

After the capital of Nineveh fell, the Medes killed King Sinsharishkun. The royal family fled to Harran in Anatolia and desperately messaged the Egyptian pharaoh Necho for help. He marched north, but King Josiah of Judah stood in his way. Necho killed Josiah, but the delay allowed the Babylonians and Medes to break into Harran. Necho arrived too late to save the Assyrians. Then, to his horror, the Babylonian crown prince Nebuchadnezzar II wiped out the Egyptian army.

Chapter 7: The Persian Empire

When Cyrus the Great took the reins, ancient Persia's unassuming realm suddenly mushroomed into the globe's first mega-empire, covering a vast swath of Central and West Asia. Under Darius the Great, it spread over an area of two million square miles in Asia, Africa, and Europe.

This chapter covers the Achaemenid Empire, the first of the three Persian empires. Where did this name come from? Cyrus the Great and Darius I claimed an eighth-century Persian chieftain named Achaemenes as their ancestor.

Where did it all begin? Persia emerged as a small kingdom where today's Fars province lies in southwestern Iran. "Soft lands breed soft people," Cyrus the Great once said. His homeland was certainly not soft. It lay on the rugged Iranian Plateau, bordered by the jagged Zagros Mountains and the desolate Lut and Kavir salt deserts. The name "Iran" originates from "Aryan," which means "free and noble" in the Indo-Iranian language of Cyrus's ancestors, who once inhabited the regions of today's Afghanistan, Turkmenistan, and Uzbekistan. Around 1500 BCE, the Aryan migration spread these Indo-Iranian tribes south and west. One group arrived in northern Iran about 1100 BCE and established the Median Kingdom. Another group speaking "Old Persian" arrived in southwestern Iran, where the ancient Elamites lived.

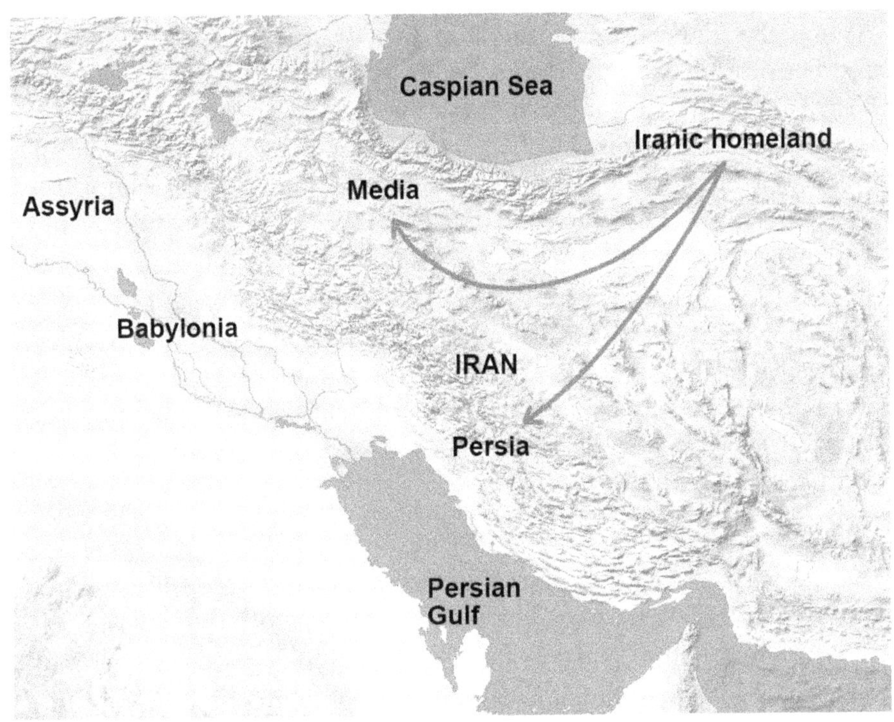

Indo-Iranic Migration of Medes and Persians [iii]

The Persians lived alongside the Elamites, adopting their cuneiform script. Iran was a part of the Neo-Assyrian Empire at that time. The Assyrian King Shalmaneser III wrote on the "Black Obelisk" in 836 BCE that he received tribute from twenty-seven Persian kings (probably tribal chieftains). The Persians were renowned for the horses they bred, so Assyrian kings demanded horses as tribute payments.

When the Medes and Persians resisted the Assyrians, the Assyrian king Tiglath-Pileser III (745–727 BCE) deported 65,000 Medes to Syria and imported Phoenicians and Syrians to northern Iran. He did not relocate the Persians, but he cut off the thumbs of the men's right hands so they could not wield weapons.

Like most Indo-Iranian tribes, the early Persians rarely created cult images. They offered sacrifices to their ancestors and worshiped outdoors in their nomadic days. Later, they built simple temples with perpetual fires burning. They sacrificed horses and worshipped the gods of the Vedic religion, prevalent among the Indo-Iranian people. Early Persian religious rituals included drinking haoma, derived from the soma plant, to receive enlightenment and draw closer to the divine. They also poured out haoma as an offering to the gods.

When the Persians first migrated into Iran, they were independent clans. Teispes (Cyrus's great-grandfather), the founder of the Achaemenid dynasty, united the Persian clans. Darius the Great claimed that he also descended from Teispes, but from a different line than Cyrus. Teispes's son, Cyrus I (grandfather of Cyrus the Great), joined the coalition forces that wiped out the Assyrians. At that time, the Medes were the strongest tribe in ancient Iran, and the Persians were their vassals.

Cyrus I made a treaty with the Median King Astyages, and Cyrus's son, Cambyses, married Astyages's daughter, Mandane. The young couple had a baby, Cyrus II (Cyrus the Great), around 600 BCE. However, King Astyages had a nightmare that Cyrus would capsize his kingdom. Highly agitated, Astyages called his astrologers.

"What should I do?" he asked.

"You must kill the baby!" they insisted.

Astyages invited his daughter to visit him so that he could see his new grandson. However, he gave his general Harpagus these orders: "When Mandane isn't looking, grab the baby and kill him!"

Harpagus snatched the infant, but instead of killing him, he gave him to Mithradates, the cowherd, whose newborn son had just died. King Astyages found out that his grandson was still alive when Cyrus was ten years old.

"The omen has passed! The boy is no longer a danger to you," his astrologers assured him.

Astyages sent Cyrus back to Persia to live with his birth parents. Yet, he often invited his grandson to visit him. When Cyrus became a teenager, Astyages taught him the art of war and made him one of his generals. Around 559 BCE, Cyrus's father died, and he became king of Persia. As a vassal king under his grandfather, Cyrus paid tribute and provided soldiers for the Median army. However, the warm relationship between Cyrus and his Median grandfather soured. His grandfather was forcing the Persian farmers into slave labor.

The Median general Harpagus, who had saved Cyrus as a baby, messaged him. "March out with your men against your grandfather. My troops will abandon him and join you," he told Cyrus.

Harpagus hated Astyages because the king had killed Harpagus's son when he discovered Harpagus had spared the infant Cyrus.

The Median soldiers handed King Astyages over to Cyrus, who spared his life. Cyrus became the ruler of the massive Median Empire, stretching from the Arabian Sea to the Black Sea. But Cyrus was only getting started. Cyrus's next target was Sardis, the capital of Lydia in western Anatolia. Its king, the wealthy Croesus, had captured a Median city in Cappadocia and enslaved its people. Croesus turned pale as 196,000 Medes and Persians approached, the ground shaking under their horses' hooves.

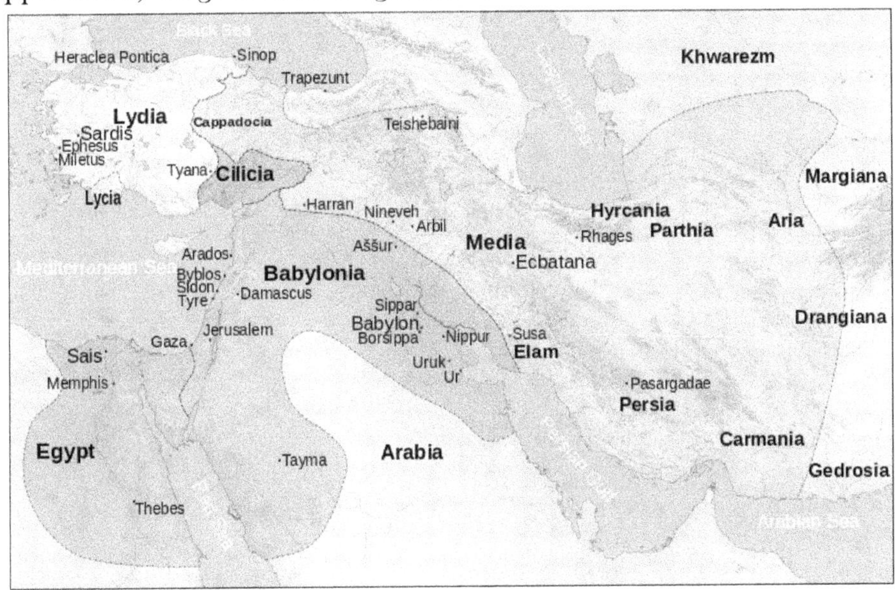

The Median Empire at its height [112]

"I still have twice as many men!" Croesus muttered to himself.

General Harpagus came to Cyrus's aid once again, telling him, "Put your three hundred camels on your front line!"

They were pack animals, not war camels. Yet, Croesus's warhorses had never encountered camels—or smelled their musky odor. They reared up and raced off. The Lydians dashed inside the city walls, yet Cyrus deployed his siege towers, from which his archers released fiery arrows into the city. Sardis fell in two weeks.

Cyrus attempted to execute Croesus by burning; however, a timely rainstorm extinguished the fire. Croesus dusted himself off and dryly remarked, "Tell your men to stop ransacking the city."

"Why?"

"It's your city now! Why let them ruin it?"

Cyrus laughed and appointed Croesus as his advisor. General Harpagus and the Median army then conquered Ionia, a region of ancient Greek colonies on Anatolia's west coast. The mainland Greeks gasped when they heard how swiftly Ionia fell. Harpagus let the Ionians continue to self-rule, except they had to provide military men for Cyrus's war machine and pay tribute.

Alternating Persian soldiers in long gowns and Median warriors in short tunics and boots, from a bas relief at the Persepolis Apadana [118]

Meanwhile, Cyrus charged east to present-day Uzbekistan to conquer the Sogdians. With that accomplished, he headed to the Phoenician cities on Lebanon's coast. Tyre, Sidon, Byblos, and Tripoli pragmatically surrendered immediately. Cyrus only required them to pay a portion of 350 talents of silver annually (Syria, Judah, and Cyprus paid the rest.) Cyrus needed a navy for his long-term goals, and the Phoenicians were exceptional shipbuilders and sailors.

When Cyrus became king of the Medes and Persians, King Nabonidus of Babylon had been sulking in the desert for a decade. He was not meant to rule. Nabonidus was a descendant of the Assyrian king Ashurbanipal. After Harran fell, Nebuchadnezzar II brought the child Nabonidus and his mother back with him to Babylon, where Nabonidus served as a courtier. His son, Belshazzar, had staged a palace coup and put him on the throne.

Nabonidus was more interested in religion than running an empire. When the Babylonians resisted his religious reforms, Nabonidus left Belshazzar as his regent and abandoned Babylon. However, news of Tyre surrendering to Cyrus stirred Nabonidus. It had taken Nebuchadnezzar II thirteen years to conquer Tyre. Nabonidus could not let the Persians have it! He hurried back to Babylon.

When Nabonidus heard Cyrus was marching toward Babylon's northern border, he marched to meet him, leaving Belshazzar in charge of Babylon. Nebuchadnezzar had built a wall stretching from the Tigris to the Euphrates River to keep the Medes out of Babylon. The cities of Opis (on the Tigris) and Sippar (on the Euphrates) were at each end of the wall. Nabonidus stationed himself at Sippar.

Cyrus and his general, Gubaru the Mede, approached Opis in late September 539 BCE when the rivers were at their lowest. The Medes and Persians overcame the Babylonian forces stationed at Opis. Then, the Persian engineers diverted the Tigris into irrigation canals, lowering the river level until it was knee deep. Once his army crossed the river, Cyrus sent Gubaru and half his men south to Babylon.

Cyrus led the rest of his army to Sippar, which surrendered without a fight. Shocked, King Nabonidus slipped out of Sippar and raced toward Babylon, which was celebrating a festival honoring Sin, the moon god. The Babylonians had no idea Cyrus had bypassed the barrier wall by wading across the river. General Gubaru reached Babylon in the dead of night. The Babylonians were drunkenly dancing in the streets, unaware of the danger that loomed. Belshazzar, the regent, was hosting a dinner for a thousand nobles, drinking from the silver and gold goblets that Nebuchadnezzar II had pilfered from Jerusalem's temple.

The biblical book of Daniel says that Belshazzar suddenly looked up in horror to see disembodied fingers writing on the wall. He called for his astrologers, but no one could read the writing. Then, the queen (Nabonidus's wife) strode into the banquet hall. "Call for Daniel," she said. "He will give you the interpretation. He has insight, intelligence, and wisdom like that of the gods."

Nebuchadnezzar II had brought some royal boys from Jerusalem, including Daniel, when he conquered the city. Now an old man, Daniel, entered the banquet hall and said, "The writing on the wall says, 'MENE, MENE, TEKEL, PARSIN.' It means you have been weighed on the scales and found lacking. Your kingdom is given over to the Medes and Persians" (Daniel 5).

As Daniel spoke, General Gubaru's army arrived on the other side of the Euphrates River from Babylon. Once again, his engineers diverted the river into the irrigation canals, and the military waded across. Xenophon, a fourth-century Greek historian, wrote that the Medes swept through the city to the king's palace, where Belshazzar stood in the banquet hall, his scimitar in his hand. They killed Belshazzar and all the nobles. Nabonidus was captured when he arrived two days later. However, Cyrus spared his life and sent him to govern the province of Carmania in Persia.

One of Cyrus's first acts was to undo the population-relocation policy of the Assyrians and Babylonians. All the Syrians, Medes, Jews, and other deported people could return to their homelands. Cyrus continued conquering until his mega-empire stretched from Afghanistan to the Mediterranean Sea. The Royal Road spanned fifteen hundred miles from Susa in Persia to Sardis, enabling the empire's efficient postal system to deliver a message from one end of the empire to the other in one week.

The Cyrus Cylinder, a summary of his reign[114]

Cyrus ruled with tolerance and respect for the religions of conquered peoples. He honored the Babylonian chief god Marduk and rebuilt the Jewish temple in Jerusalem. He also allowed local governments a high level of autonomy. His policies led to a thriving economy, loyalty, and stability. On the "Cyrus Cylinder," he inscribed his genealogy and how he captured Babylon, restored temples, corrected injustices, and released deported people to return home.

Cyrus permitted most conquered kings and governors to retain their positions as long as they remained loyal. He preserved the social order and customs of conquered lands. Cyrus appointed twenty-six satraps (governors) to rule the "satrapies" (provinces) of the empire. The satraps collected taxes, judged court cases, and maintained the road system. The empire introduced a uniform monetary system and standardized weights and measures. Cyrus's royal inspector, called the "King's Eye," helped him spy out corruption or brewing rebellions. His legal system had standardized laws and required evidence to convict a person. Even a woman could be a witness in court, something unheard of in ancient times.

An illustration of the Apadana in Persepolis[115]

Cyrus the Great chose Persepolis, surrounded by the Zagros Mountains of Persia, as his ceremonial capital. He planned the city, but Darius the Great initiated the building project. Other kings continued building. Magnificent sixty-five-foot columns supported the roof of the luxurious king's hall, called the Apadana. At the eastern and northern ends, staircases featured bas-reliefs of various ethnicities from the empire bringing tribute, including a hippopotamus from Egypt.

After all his glorious triumphs, a woman named Tomyris killed Cyrus. She ruled over the Massagetae, a branch of the Scythes, another Indo-Iranian group. They were launching raids on Persia's northern borders. Cyrus thought he could tame the troublemakers by marrying their queen, but Tomyris rejected his overtures. In the ensuing bloodbath, she killed the seventy-year-old king in 530 BCE.

Cyrus's son, Cambyses, assumed the throne and conquered North Africa and Cyprus. While he was organizing Egypt's administration, word came of an uprising in Persia. While rushing home, he accidentally stabbed himself in the thigh. The wound developed gangrene, and he died of septic shock in 522 BCE. At least, that was the story Darius, his lance bearer, told everyone. Since Cambyses had no children, the next in line to the throne was his brother, Bardiya. However, Bardiya died mysteriously at about the same time. No descendants of Cyrus were left.

At that point, Darius, the lance bearer, claimed royal blood,

Bas relief of Darius I[116]

announcing that he was also a descendant of Achaemenes, Cyrus's ancestor. Many were skeptical, but Darius furiously eliminated anyone who questioned his right to be "king of kings." Although likely a pretender to the throne, he took the Persian Empire to glorious new heights, the largest empire yet seen.

Darius the Great expanded into northern India's Punjab region, then subdued the Scythes who had killed Cyrus. He built a pontoon bridge over the Bosphorus Strait, which separates Asia from Europe, and crossed over to subdue Thrace (present-day Bulgaria) and Macedonia. Thrace was to be his staging area for conquering Greece.

A brilliant relief of a unicorn in the Apadana that Darius the Great built in Susa [117]

In 499 BCE, the tyrant Histiaeus of Miletus spurred the Greeks of Ionia to rise in rebellion, allied with Athens and Eretria in southern Greece. However, their infighting and Darius's larger navy, commanded by General Mardonius, proved the Ionian Greeks' undoing. In 492, the Persians headed to Greece to punish Athens and Eretria. They were supposed to march through Thrace and into Greece, but their plans went awry. First, the Byrgi tribe attacked the land army. Although the Persians won, they were too weakened to battle the Greeks, leading to their retreat to Persia. Meanwhile, a diabolical storm sank three hundred vessels and killed twenty thousand men in the Persian navy headed to Greece.

Two years later, Darius organized a new army and navy to take on Greece. He had already sent ambassadors to Greece, ordering them to surrender to Persia or face his wrath. All the Greek city-states accepted Darius's demands, except Athens and its neighbor, Eretria.

"It's always the Athenians!" Darius fumed. "They and the Eritreans sent ships to aid the Ionian revolt. They will pay the price!"

Darius launched six hundred triremes (battleships) toward Greece. When the people of Eretria saw the Persian ships approaching on the horizon, most of them fled to Mount Olympus. However, two defectors opened the city gates. The Persians grabbed all the treasures they could carry, burned the city's temples, and enslaved anyone still in the city. Then, they sailed to Athens.

General Datis of Persia fights the Greek Kallimachos in a drawing of the 460 BCE Painted Portico in Athens. [118]

Instead of waiting for the Persians to lay siege to their city, the Athenians marched across the peninsula to fight the Persians at Marathon. What the Persians did not know was that Marathon had mud pits that could swallow a person alive. It was also swampy, with mountain ridges reaching the sea. The Persians could not use their cavalry on the terrain.

The Greeks lined up on the side of a mountain. As the Persians approached, they ran full speed down the incline and crashed into the Persian forces before the Persian archers could shoot many arrows. The Persian soldiers broke through the Greek middle line, but the Greeks on the flanks encircled them. Panicked, the Persians turned and made a mad dash for the beach, some falling into the mud pits, never to be seen again. The Persians lost 6,400 men, but the Greeks only lost 203.

Darius seethed at the ignominious loss, vowing he would get revenge. Yet, his unexpected death meant that his son, Xerxes, inherited the throne and the quest for vengeance against Greece: "I will not rest until I have burned Athens to the ground!"

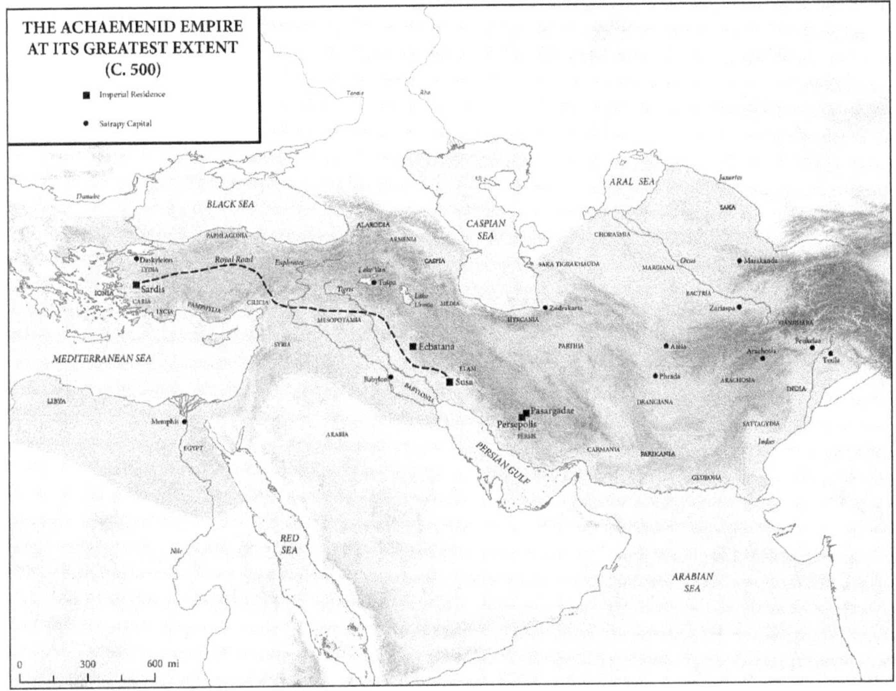

Achaemenid Empire under Darius I. The Royal Road stretched from Susa to Sardis.[119]

Chapter 8: The Golden Age of Classical Greece

Extraordinary developments in philosophy, politics, art, and science marked Greece's Classical period (499–323 BCE). The pinnacle of this vibrant era was the Golden Age (480–423 BCE). In these glory days, dynamic city-states experimented with democracy. Thriving intellectual pursuits and towering figures, such as Socrates, Plato, and Aristotle, left their imprint on Western civilization.

Greece's Golden Age launched when the Greeks scored a major victory against Persia in 480 BCE. The Persian king of kings, Xerxes I, marched out with his million-man army, planning to cross the Dardanelles Strait into Europe using a pontoon bridge. Xerxes's engineers lashed 674 shallow boats together over the one-mile span, then built planking over them. However, a violent squall blew the bridge to pieces. Xerxes erupted in fury. He beheaded his engineers and even punished the water—three hundred lashes!

Finally, a new team of engineers reassembled the bridge, and the million-man army crossed over into Europe while the Persian navy sailed along the coast. Did Xerxes's army really have a million men? The Greek historian Herodotus, who lived in the Persian Empire at the time, insisted there were 2.5 million. Ctesias, a physician to Persian royalty about eight decades later, stated that Persia had 800,000 soldiers, along with support personnel. Still, the logistical challenges of managing and feeding a million men moving through enemy territory strain credibility.

As Xerxes marched into Greece, the northern and central Greek city-states offered no resistance. The Athenians in southern Greece knew they were Xerxes's target and were relieved when Sparta allied with them. Usually, the two cities were rivals.

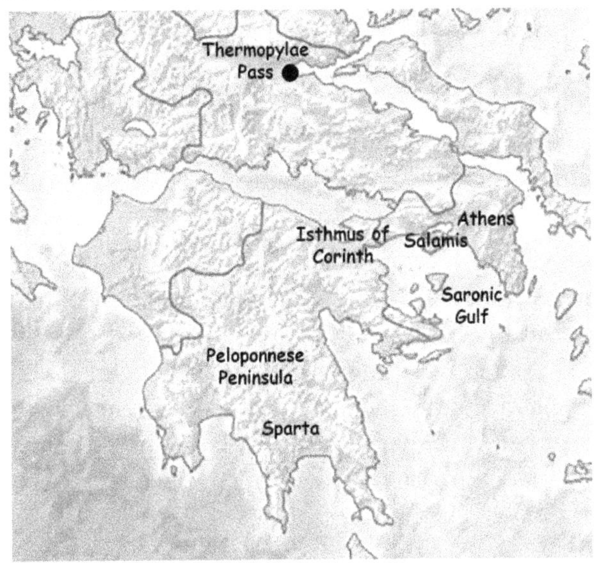

Southern Greece [190]

To reach southern Greece, the Persians had to march through the narrow Thermopylae pass between the Malian Gulf and Mount Kallidromo. A crumbling ancient wall ran from the gulf to the mountain. That is where seven thousand men from Sparta and Thebes awaited them, led by Sparta's King Leonidas. They had been repairing the defensive wall. Could they hold off Xerxes's massive army?

The Greeks stood shoulder to shoulder in the classic Greek phalanx formation. Their shields overlapped slightly, forming a defensive wall. The men behind the front line held their shields over their heads, creating a protective ceiling from arrows. Each man on the front line held an eight-foot spear, pointing toward the enemy.

Xerxes unleashed his ten thousand "Immortals," Persia's deadliest forces, against the Greeks. Yet the Spartans, renowned for their rigid discipline, stood firm for two days. If a soldier fell, the one behind him stepped into his place. The Persian archers shot volleys of arrows that darkened the sky, but they bounced off the Greeks' shield "ceiling."

On the third day, a Greek shepherd, hoping for a reward from Xerxes, showed the Persians a narrow path over the mountain. A contingent of

Immortals climbed the path and went down the other side, to the rear of the Greeks. King Leonidas ordered a unit to attack the Persians approaching their rear. He instructed most of the soldiers to withdraw to southern Greece to protect the Peloponnesian Peninsula.

King Leonidas and 1,400 men held off the Persians while the rest of the men escaped. Eventually, more Immortals crossed the shepherds' pass and attacked the Greeks from behind. Hundreds of thousands of Persians pressed in from the front, killing every Greek left in the pass, including Leonidas. Their sacrifice permitted a future victory for Greece.

Meanwhile, the Persian navy, with 1,200 ships, sailed down the Aegean Sea toward Athens. A fierce storm sank one-third of the fleet off northern Greece's coast of Magnesia. The Athenian and Corinthian navies were waiting for them at the Straits of Artemisium. For three days, the Greeks prevented the Persians from sailing into the Euboean Gulf and down the Straits of Euboea. Some Persian ships headed south on the open sea, where another storm sank two hundred ships. The Greeks cheered at the news that storms had sunk half of the Persian fleet.

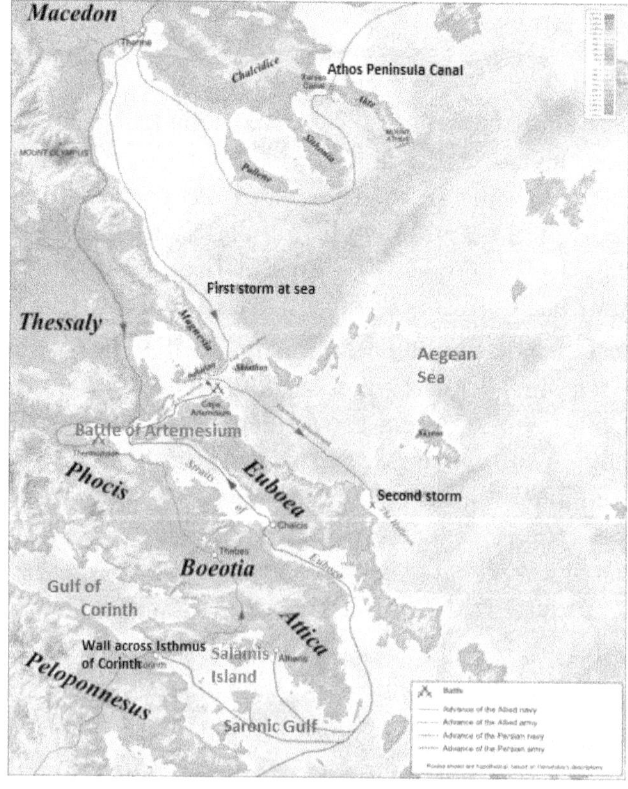

Progress of Xerxes' navy [131]

Athens' navy raced to the Saronic Gulf, desperate to get there before the Persian ships. They evacuated Athens' population to the island of Salamis in the Saronic Gulf. Fleets from Sparta, Corinth, and Macedonia gathered at Salamis. Meanwhile, Xerxes's army approached the Peloponnese Peninsula. The delay at Thermopylae enabled the Spartans, Corinthians, and other Greeks on the Peloponnese Peninsula to finish rebuilding a four-mile ancient wall on the Isthmus of Corinth, blocking entry to the peninsula.

Xerxes marched to Athens first, eager to settle old scores. He entered the ancient city unhindered and killed the few people left. The Persians ransacked Athens and reduced its elegant temples on the Acropolis to ashes. Xerxes then led his men toward the Peloponnese Peninsula to get revenge on Sparta. However, the rebuilt, heavily guarded wall blocked the Isthmus of Corinth. Xerxes muttered curses as he laid siege to the wall.

Meanwhile, the leaders of Athens, Corinth, and Sparta held a war council at Salamis. They worried about Xerxes getting through the wall. He would devastate Sparta, Corinth, and the other cities on the peninsula.

"Let's distract Xerxes! Bring him here—to Salamis!" said Athens's naval commander, Themistocles, leaning forward eagerly. "He only has about six hundred ships left. Our Athenian navy just proved ourselves against his navy at Artemisium—and they had almost twice the ships! He doesn't know your navies are here. Together, we can beat him!"

The others frowned. "If we lure him here, we're endangering our women and children. We brought them to Salamis for safety."

"They will be safe," Themistocles insisted. "The Persians are better fighters on the open sea, but we've proved our superiority in tight places. We'll ambush him in the straits between Salamis and the mainland!"

The plan was daring and terrifying. Yet, the Greeks agreed to it. First, they needed to lure Xerxes's navy to Salamis. Themistocles messaged Xerxes, telling him he was clandestinely on the Persian side: "The rest of the Greeks are panicking. They're arguing among themselves, almost coming to blows. The Spartans are sailing home to protect their city. Send your fleet here to Salamis. We'll join our navies and conquer Greece together!"

Xerxes eagerly sent his navy to the Saronic Gulf. He ordered his men to carry his portable throne to the top of a mountain overlooking the gulf, where he could watch the battle. All the Greek ships, except fifty Corinthian vessels, hid behind Georgios Island. When the Persian navy arrived, they only saw the Corinthian ships, which turned and fled into the strait between Salamis and the mainland. The Persians chased them right into the trap.

The Persians heard an eerie sound wafting over the water. It was men singing a hymn to Apollo! Then they saw them. Hundreds of Greek battleships sailed around the bend of the island, blocking the Persian fleet in the strait. The Greeks struck the trapped Persian vessels over and over with their battering rams. Dead bodies and ship wreckage covered the water. Watching the carnage from the mountain above, Xerxes turned white. The war on Greece was over, for now. The Greeks had sunk his navy, and he was running out of food and supplies for his army.

Sea Battle of Salamis[122]

The battles against the Persian Empire united the southern Greek city-states against a common foe, fostering a sense of shared Hellenic identity.

Collectively, they were on the offensive against Persia. Collaboration had been the key to winning the war. If they wanted to end the Persian threat permanently, they needed to continue working as a team.

The victory at Salamis encouraged several Greek city-states in Ionia to rebel, assisted by the Spartans and Athenians. In a spectacular victory, the Greeks seized control of the Aegean Sea. However, the Spartans predicted the Persians would try to retake Ionia. "The Ionian Greeks should move to mainland Greece!" they suggested.

The Ionians responded angrily, "We've lived here for centuries! We're not leaving!"

The Athenians agreed. "Our ancestors established these colonies. We can't let the Persians have them! We will form a league to protect the Aegean Sea."

Thus, 330 Greek cities surrounding the Aegean Sea formed the Delian League in 478 BCE, with Cimon, a hero of the Battle of Salamis, as its naval commander. The cities in the league donated ships, crews, or funding to keep the Persians out of the Aegean. When the Persians rebuilt their navy and attacked Pamphylia, Cimon sank two hundred Persian warships. The Persians dared not enter the Aegean for the next fifteen years. The Delian League also ejected the pirates from the Aegean.

In 460 BCE, Egypt rebelled against Persia. Pericles, a rising star in Athens, led 250 ships of the Delian League to help the Egyptians gain independence. It was a disaster for the Greeks, who lost twenty thousand men and most of their ships.

Initially, the Delian League's treasury was at the sacred island of Delos in the Aegean. Pericles expressed concern that the Persians might raid the small island and take it. He moved the treasury to Athens, ostensibly for safekeeping. So, when the Greeks sent in their dues for the Delian League, instead of going to a neutral island, the money went to Athens. Pericles was not just using the money to support the league. He was rebuilding Athens with the funds. The rest of the Greek cities were unhappy, yet when they tried to withdraw from the League, Pericles harshly punished them.

Pericles [128]

In 451 BCE, Cimon sailed two hundred ships to seize Cyprus from the Persians. Cimon was killed, but the Greeks won. The war with Persia ended with the Callias Peace Treaty. Persia promised not to enter the Aegean Sea or try to retake Ionia. The Greeks gave Cyprus back to Persia and pledged not to attack North Africa or Anatolia. The Callias Peace Treaty lasted for thirty years.

Greece was still not at peace. Athens and Sparta had resumed their former animosity. Sparta led the Peloponnesian League, a rival of the Delian League. The First Peloponnesian War erupted in 460 BCE, pitting Athens against Corinth, Sparta, and other cities on the Peloponnese Peninsula. Athens had an impressive navy, but its army was no match for the Peloponnese forces. Sparta attacked Boeotia, north of Athens, and won the Battle of Tanagra. Athens sailed around the Peloponnese, attacking the coastal cities. Eventually, the First Peloponnesian War ended with the Thirty Years' Peace treaty in 445 BCE.

Only fourteen years passed before Sparta instigated the Second Peloponnesian War (431–404 BCE) by raiding the farms around Athens. Pericles knew the Spartans were trying to lure the Athenians into a land battle. Instead of fighting, he brought the rural people inside Athens and arranged for grain shipments from Egypt to feed everyone. He then established a naval blockade, cutting off sea trade to the Peloponnese.

However, the grain shipments brought rats, which spread a plague to the overcrowded city of Athens. The disease began with headaches, fever, and eye inflammation, then progressed to coughing, vomiting, violent diarrhea, and skin lesions. Tissue death caused people's fingers and toes to turn black and fall off. One-third of the city died, including Pericles. On the bright side, the Spartans evacuated the area, terrified of the plague. Ironically, the Athenian blockade kept ships from Egypt away from the Peloponnese; thus, the plague did not spread there.

Eventually, the plague burned out, and Athens resumed raiding the Peloponnese ports while building forts on the peninsula. Sparta bombarded the Athenian fort at Pylos; however, the Athenians surprised everyone by thrashing the Spartans. Their epic win filled them with confidence. They *could* win a land battle! When the Spartans commandeered Athens' silver mines in Thrace, Athens fought them in the heated Battle of Amphipolis. Sparta technically won but returned the silver mines to Athens in exchange for hostages.

While the Greek wars raged, its philosophers debated knowledge, reality, and truth. Socrates used a question-and-answer format to help his students navigate complex issues. Socrates explained he did not have all the answers, calling it "simple ignorance." Yet, "double ignorance" — someone who knows nothing but thinks he knows everything—was worse. A person like this was a "double fool." People lacking self-reflection and critical thinking skills were useless. "The unexamined life is not worth living!" Socrates insisted.

The leaders of Athens believed Socrates was instilling dangerous ideas in his students' minds. He faced trial for corrupting Athens's youth and for introducing "new spiritual things." Socrates criticized the Greek gods: "They lie, steal, and cheat on their spouses! How can we humans be moral if our gods are not?" However, Socrates was not an atheist. He believed in a good, wise, and perfect divine being. He spoke of a "daimonion," a guiding voice that warned him against certain actions. The court convicted Socrates on both counts and ordered him to die by drinking hemlock.

Socrates' forced suicide [194]

Plato was a student and close companion of Socrates. He preserved Socrates' teachings through his *Dialogues,* a collection of texts in which Socrates discusses philosophy. Plato established the Academy around 387 BCE, where scholars met to debate and listen to lectures on philosophy, mathematics, astronomy, and politics.

In his "Theory of Forms," Plato explained that our understanding of reality is only a reflection of what is real. He compared it to living in a cave where people cannot see the sun, only the shadows on the cave walls. Most people fail to realize that the shadows are reflections of actual reality. What if someone got out of the cave? Plato explained what would happen:

> "He will be able to see the sun, and not mere reflections of him and he will contemplate him as he is. He will then argue that this is he who gives the seasons and the years and is the guardian of all that is in the visible world, and in a certain way the cause of all things."[13]

Hippias, who debated with Plato in his *Dialogues,* was a philosopher who could discuss a wide range of topics, including astronomy, history, and mathematics. He discovered the geometric quadratrix, the intersection of a rotating line and a line moving parallel to itself. Hippias would attend the Olympic Games and invite people to choose any topic, then give a speech on that topic without advance preparation. Hippias

---

[13] Plato, *The Republic,* Book VII, trans. Benjamin Jowett (Daniel C. Stevenson, Web Atomics). http://classics.mit.edu/Plato/republic.9.viii.html.

complained that the concept of right and wrong was in constant flux as society changed. He argued that an unchanging "natural law" has always existed. Good is always good. Evil is always evil.

Plato's student Aristotle believed that an eternal, unchanging "unmoved mover" existing outside of time and space set the universe in motion. Aristotle taught the principle of deduction: if a premise is true, a conclusion based on that premise is also correct. For instance, a cat is a mammal (premise); thus, all lions are mammals (deduction). By contrast, induction makes a presumption based on observed fact. It may or may not be true. For example, one could see geese flying overhead (observed fact) and make the induction that all geese fly south for the winter.

Hippocrates, the "Father of Medicine," was from the island of Kos. At that time, people thought disease was a punishment from the gods. However, Hippocrates believed that lifestyle, diet, and environmental factors caused disease. He introduced clinical diagnosis, such as checking a patient's pain level, temperature, pulse, and range of motion. He also analyzed a patient's urine and bowel movements to determine their illness.

Before and during Greece's Golden Age, its city-states had a variety of government systems. A few had kings (Sparta had two at a time), some had a council, some had early forms of democracy, and some had a tyrant who came to power by popular support or through force and ruled with absolute power. A few cities experimented with several political systems. General Pericles reformed Athens's constitution and governmental structure to "the rule of the many instead of the few." He wanted Athens to be a model of democracy. Pericles pressed for equal justice for everyone and for all classes to serve in government. He paid working-class citizens for jury duty so they could afford to take time off from work.

Athens's Erechtheion temple with Caryatid pillars [185]

After Xerxes burned the Acropolis in Athens in 480 BCE, Pericles rebuilt its walls and temples. The Parthenon, a temple to Athena, had a thirty-eight-foot statue of the goddess covered with gold sheet, with an ivory face and arms. A second breathtaking temple to Athena was the Erechtheion. It has caryatid pillars in the shape of beautiful young women, each one different.

Greece's sculptures in its Golden Age displayed emotion and lively movement. The *Hermes of Praxiteles* sculpture in the Temple of Hera at Olympia portrays the baby Dionysus in Hermes's arms. Hermes stands with his weight on one leg in the "contrapposto" pose popular in Greece's Classical period.

Greece's Golden Age left a lasting legacy of democracy, philosophy, art, and science that continues to influence contemporary thought, governance, and culture.

Hermes holding Dionysius. [196]

Chapter 9: Ancient Rome

This final chapter unfolds the formative stages of ancient Rome, beginning with its foundational story of Romulus and Remus, where myth and history intertwine. What influence did the Etruscans have on ancient Roman culture, governance, and architecture? Why did the Romans abandon their monarchy for a republic? What triggered early struggles between the social classes—the patricians and plebeians? How did Rome's initial territorial expansions and legal developments like the Twelve Tables play out? Let's examine how these foundational elements laid the groundwork for Rome's future dominance.

The legend of Romulus, the founder of Rome, begins with his ancestor Aeneas, a member of Troy's royal family. When the Greeks destroyed Troy (circa 1200 BCE), Aeneas escaped with his son and father. Along with other Trojan survivors, Aeneas experienced hair-raising adventures and adversities but finally settled in central Italy. Aeneas married Lavinia, the daughter of King Latinus of the Latin tribe.

Twelve generations later, his descendant Numitor was king of the Latin-Trojan coalition. Numitor's brother Amulius staged a coup, sent Numitor into exile, and forced Numitor's daughter, Rhea Silvia, to become a Vestal Virgin (he did not want her to have children). However, Rhea Silvia conceived twins during an eclipse, from being raped by the god Mars, she said. Furious, Amulius locked her in a tower and told his guard to drown the babies in the river.

But the guard did not have the heart to kill the boys. Instead, he put their basket in the river and let it float downstream. A wolf found the basket that had washed ashore with the crying twins. Her pups had died, so she suckled the boys from her swollen teats. Later, a shepherd found the babies and took them home to his wife to raise.

Romulus and Remus with the wolf in this statue from Brussels's Maison de la Louve [127]

When the twins grew up, they encountered their grandfather, Numitor, who was in exile. When the shepherd told Numitor how he found the infant boys by the river, Numitor realized they were his long-lost grandsons. The teens killed Amulius and restored their grandfather to his throne. Then, they set off to build their own city by the Tiber River, in the land of seven hills where their basket had landed when they were infants.

However, the young men quarreled over which hill to build on and which of them should be king. In the heat of the moment, Romulus killed his brother. He instantly regretted the fratricide, dissolving into tears. However, with his small band of men, he set to work building Rome and invited people in the surrounding areas to come live in his city. "Everyone will be a citizen, regardless of social status," he said. "Yes, even if you are a former slave, you can be a citizen in my city."

Rome's expansion efforts began at its inception. Romulus attracted several thousand young men to his new city, but they needed wives. The neighboring cities were unwilling to arrange marriages with this unknown upstart and his motley crew. So, Romulus devised a plan to abduct women for his people to marry. He threw a religious festival and invited the neighboring Sabines to come. He served strong wine to the Sabine men.

When the Sabine men fell over drunk, the Romans stole their young women.

Once they sobered up, the Sabines demanded their women back, but Romulus refused to give them up. The men from the two Sabine cities who had attended the festival attacked Rome but failed to retrieve their women. So, they traveled around the Sabine lands, recruiting support. This took months, and during this time, many of the Sabine women had become pregnant.

When the two armies lined up to face each other, the women ran into the gap between the Romans and the Sabines. They turned toward the Romans and said, "Husbands! Stop fighting against our fathers and brothers!"

Then, they swirled around toward the Sabines and pleaded, "Fathers! We are pregnant with your grandchildren! Will you leave them fatherless? Please, don't fight because of us!"

The men on both sides wept at the women's pleas and put away their swords and spears. They formed a united Roman-Sabine kingdom led by co-rulers: Romulus and King Tatius of the Sabines. Five years later, an unknown assailant killed Tatius, leaving Romulus as the sole king of both lands.

Early Rome was home to diverse ethnicities, including Trojans, Latins, Greeks, Etruscans, and Sabines. The Etruscans were a neighboring civilization in central Italy. Although some Etruscans joined Romulus's new city, most Etruscans were Rome's adversaries, and war between them occasionally flared up. Rome conquered the Etruscans and the other tribes of central Italy by 264 BCE.

Rome's fifth king, Lucius Tarquinius Priscus, was the son of a Corinthian Greek and an Etruscan woman. He moved to Rome, where his pleasant and helpful personality made him a favorite of King Marcius. Rome did not have hereditary kings yet, so when Marcius died, the senators elected Tarquinius as king around 616 BCE. An impressive military commander, he expanded Rome's territory in central Europe, taking control of Latin, Etruscan, and Sabine territories.

Lucius Tarquinius Priscus built the Circus Maximus stadium for gladiator games (adopted from the Etruscans) and chariot races using Etruscan engineering techniques, including the arch and the tunnel vault. For waste removal, he built the Cloaca Maxima, one of Europe's first advanced sewer systems.

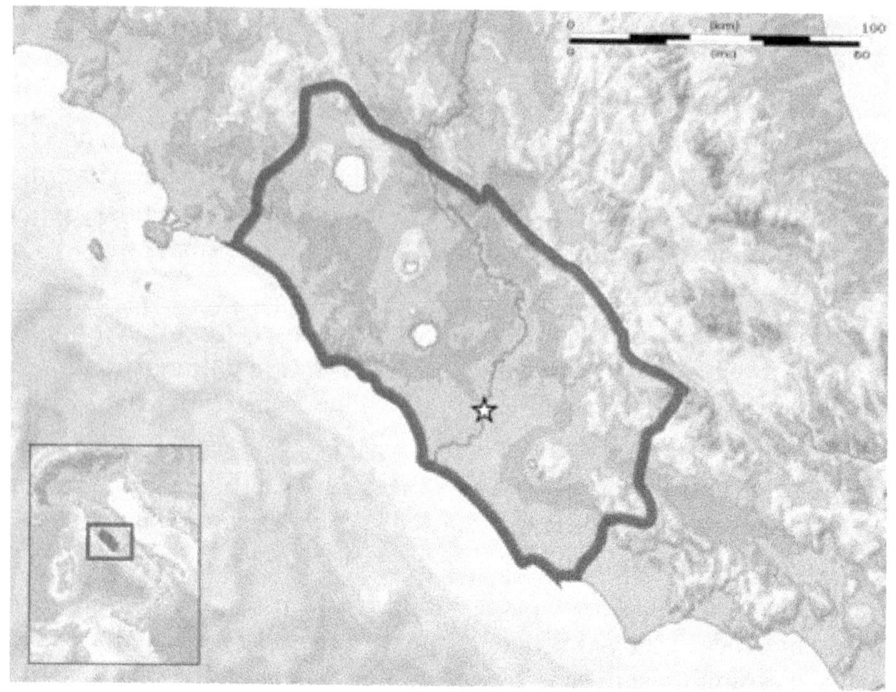

Rome's territory in its late monarchy [198]

Rome adapted the Etruscan alphabet into the Latin alphabet, the prototype for the alphabet used in most European countries today. The Etruscan alphabet descended from the Greek alphabet, which was based on the Phoenician alphabet. Rome also adopted Etruscan methods of foreseeing the future, such as haruspicy—examining animal intestines—and interpreting thunder and lightning.

Lucius Tarquinius Priscus had an enslaved woman, the widow of a Latin prince he killed in battle. He thought her son (and probably his), Servius Tullius, was brighter and had better omens than his legitimate sons, so he named Tullius as his heir. Meanwhile, the two sons of the former king Marcius, seething that they had been passed over for the throne, arranged for Tarquinius's murder. After Tarquinius's brutal end, his wife Queen Tanaquil manipulated events so that Servius Tullius became the regent for her two sons until they were old enough to rule.

However, Tullius never gave up the throne. He took Rome's first census, which counted about 80,000 citizens. He was a revolutionary, giving the working-class plebeians the right to vote and suggesting that the Romans free their slaves—even grant them citizenship. Tullius was a hero to Rome's working people but a threat to the aristocratic patricians, the ruling class. Queen Tanaquil's son Tarquin plotted with the senators to overthrow Tullius. The conspirators murdered Tullius, and the Senate elected Tarquin as Rome's next king.

Within weeks, the senators realized they had made an abysmal mistake. King Tarquin the Proud was a villainous ruler, assassinating or exiling anyone who dared question him. He suppressed the Senate's power, and his killing spree even included his family members.

His son, Sextus Tarquinius, was equally evil. Tarquin's relative, Collatinus, had a beautiful wife named Lucretia. When Sextus tried to seduce Lucretia, she spurned his advances, so he raped her. Lucretia's husband and father were fighting in the army, but she messaged them to come home and bring two witnesses.

One witness was Brutus, the nephew of King Tarquin. He hated his uncle, who had killed his brother and father. Lucretia told the men what had happened and then pleaded, "Swear to me! Promise you will avenge what Sextus had done!"

Then, she pulled a knife from her robe and stabbed herself in the chest. Her father and husband screamed, collapsing in grief. But Brutus yanked the knife from her body and held it high. Drops of blood fell to the floor as he cried, "I swear! I will avenge Lucretia! Who is with me?"

The Oath of Brutus, by François-Joseph Navez [129]

All the men in the room held their daggers in the air and swore, "We will rid Rome of its kings!

They carried Lucretia's bloodstained body to the Forum. "Look what Sextus Tarquinius has done to a virtuous wife and daughter!" they told the senators.

The senators gathered, horrified. An uproar arose from the growing crowd. In a fury, they vowed to overthrow the royal family: "We will end this reign of terror! No more tyranny! No more kings!"

In 509 BCE, Rome's senators voted to abolish the monarchy and establish a republic—a new form of government. "Instead of a king, we'll elect two consuls to rule together for a one-year term," they determined.

Brutus and Collatinus, Lucretia's husband, were Rome's first two consuls. The king and his sons fled Rome, desperately trying to get the Etruscans and Latins to support them in retaking the city. Tarquin still had supporters inside Rome, even the two sons of Brutus and his brothers-in-law. In a gruesome ritual, the conspirators killed a man and, touching his intestines, swore they would restore King Tarquin to his throne. A servant saw the grisly scene and reported it. Agonized, Brutus had no choice but to order his sons' execution.

In the new Roman Republic, the two elected consuls also served as commanders-in-chief of the military. Why two? If the Republic was at war, and it usually was, one man could lead the military while the other took care of administrative duties. If one man was too extreme, the other consul could veto his decisions. After his one-year term, a consul usually had to wait ten years before being reelected.

The Centuriate Assembly, made up of the military, voted for the consuls and other head leaders. One hundred soldiers formed a century, which got one vote in the elections. The consuls appointed the senators. In Rome's monarchy, the senators' chief function was to elect and advise the king. In the Republic, they passed new laws and controlled the budget. As the Republic rapidly grew, the Senate also focused on foreign policy.

To balance the military Centuriate Assembly, Rome later added an Assembly of Tribes, which represented geographical regions. It made laws, judged serious crimes, and elected certain magistrates. These included consuls, military commanders, and other top leadership positions, all serving one-year terms.

As the Romans thoughtfully developed their new Republic, they implemented checks and balances to keep one man or one group from having too much power or abusing power. These included elections, separation of powers, term limits, vetoes, impeachments, and quorum requirements. In the event of a crisis, the Senate could appoint a dictator for a term of up to six months. A dictator could make swift decisions without having to wait for the usual checks and balances. However, once the crisis was over, the dictator's term ended.

In the "Conflict of the Orders," beginning around 500 BCE, the plebeians—farmers, craftspeople, construction workers, and shopkeepers— struggled for political power. Rome's aristocratic landowners (patricians) held all the power in Rome's early days. They were the consuls, the senators, and the magistrates. As time passed, the plebeians demanded a voice in the government.

Initially, the patricians disregarded the pleas of the working-class people. The upper classes wanted to maintain the status quo. However, the plebeians had a secret weapon: *Secessio plebis*, or plebeian withdrawal. The patricians relied on the plebeians to farm, fight in the military, sell goods in the shops, and construct temples and amphitheaters. So, the plebeians all went on strike. They closed their shops, left their farms and building sites, and even abandoned the military outposts, heading to the countryside for a vacation.

The plebeian soldiers went on strike. [180]

It worked. The patricians could not function without the support of the plebeians. They were ready to come to the table and discuss the plebeians' grievances, which sounded something like this: "You pass new laws but don't inform us! Then, you arrest us for breaking a law we had no idea existed. You're also forcing us off the land on which we have been tenant farmers for centuries. You're bringing in all these prisoners-of-war as slaves and replacing us. Where are we supposed to live? When we cannot find work in the towns, you beat us and imprison us because we can't pay our debts!"

Rome established the Plebeian Assembly in 494 BCE, which could propose laws to the Senate and veto laws supported by the patricians. It addressed inequalities and grievances and eventually became a key political force. The Plebeian Assembly elected tribunes who protected the plebeians from the patricians' abuse of power.

In 450 BCE, twelve bronze tablets displaying the Law of the Twelve Tables were erected in the Forum in response to plebeian demands for written laws. This was Rome's first codified law system, a standard code for everyone. It put into writing early unwritten laws responding to legal questions such as family law, property issues, personal injury, and impiety.

Temple of Hera in Campania, Italy, built circa 460 BCE[181]

The Law of the Twelve Tables even addressed Rome's exceptional road system. Rome was constantly building roads during its Republic era as it conquered new territories, creating a network of roads led from all points in Italy to Rome. Rome financed the construction of these roads, but the law stipulated that the provinces had to maintain the roads that passed through their territory and that the roads had to be at least eight feet wide.

Before Rome's founding, Romulus's ancestors, the Latins and Trojans, had formed the Latin League, comprising about thirty cities, to defend themselves against mutual enemies. The league considered the Etruscans its greatest threat. Rome joined the Latin League in its early days, and the union persevered through Rome's monarchy period. When Rome became a Republic, it renewed its alliance with the cities in the league. In the *Foedus Cassianum*, the members vowed to fight together against common enemies, with an equal split of the spoils of war. Roman generals would lead their coalition armies. The Latin League was an almost unstoppable power.

In 458 BCE, the Aequi mountain tribe, located east of Rome, launched an attack on Rome's territories. Rome rose to the occasion and subdued the Aequi, but they attacked again months later. Rome decided it was time to put a temporary dictator into action. Cincinnatus, a former public servant, had retired to his farm in the countryside, but he was the one the Senate recommended. Although nominated for a six-month term, he trounced the Aequi in just over two weeks, resigned his dictatorship, and went back to his farm.

Ten years later, the Aequi allied with the Volsci people south of Rome. The coalition outnumbered Rome's army in the 446 BCE Battle of Corbio. The Romans split their army and circled around to the flanks of the Volsci-Aequi forces. Although the Romans won the battle, they lost six thousand men. Over the next sixty years, allied with the Latin League, the Romans finally subdued the Volski and Aequi, trounced the Etruscans, and blocked the Celtic invasion from the north.

Still, the Romans and Latins quarreled. In 338 BCE, Rome dissolved the Latin League and absorbed all the Latin cities into its Republic.

Once it controlled central Italy, Rome focused on the south. Centuries earlier, the Greeks had established colonies in southern Italy. In 280 BCE, Roman ships sailed into the Gulf of Taranto in southern Italy, and the Greeks promptly sank five of them. Rome declared war, and the Greeks asked King Pyrrhus of Epirus in northern Greece to help them. Pyrrhus had dreams of building an empire. This might be his chance!

Pyrrhus lacked resources, but he had wealthy relatives ruling Egypt, Macedonia, and the Middle East. He borrowed funds, military men, cavalry, and war elephants and sailed to Italy. Pyrrhus defeated the Romans in his first two battles but lost so many men that they were "pyrrhic victories," costing him more than what he won. He lost the third battle and sailed home in 275 BCE. Rome swallowed all of southern Italy, and by 270 BCE, it controlled the entire Italian peninsula.

Conclusion

What did these ancient civilizations have in common, and what set them apart? How did they contribute to human progress? When faced with challenges, how did their responses shape their trajectories and legacies?

One commonality was learning to write. The Sumerians used simple pictographs by 3500 BCE, which developed into cuneiform symbols. Other civilizations adapted cuneiform, including the Hittites, Assyrians, and Persians. The Indus Valley Civilization's script shared similarities with Proto-Elamite, a script that evolved from Uruk's cuneiform. The Egyptians developed pictographs that evolved into hieroglyphics and influenced the early Greek scripts, which impacted the Roman alphabet. Around 1250 BCE, people in China's Shang dynasty began carving inscriptions on bones and shells. These characters influenced other East Asian scripts and evolved over the millennia into the modern Chinese writing system.

These civilizations all originated as herders or farmers who began building cities and evolved into complex societies with social hierarchies, extensive trade networks, and advanced technologies. They interacted with other civilizations and shared innovations. They were all warlike, determined to take more territory and expand their empires. The interconnectedness of these societies through trade, warfare, and cultural exchange illustrates early globalization.

Although their development followed a standard trajectory, their cultures were diverse. For instance, Sumerian cuneiform, Egyptian hieroglyphics, the Greek alphabet, and Chinese characters were all distinct writing systems. These civilizations had different religious systems, unique art forms, and varied philosophies. When conquering other lands, the Assyrians used shock and terror to subdue conquered people. Cyrus the Great took a more enlightened approach, using diplomacy and religious tolerance.

A common threat to these ancient civilizations was environmental changes, which either spelled disaster or inspired innovation and adaptation. The Sumerian culture burst on the scene after flooding destroyed the Ubaid city of Ur, and Eridu fell to drought and sandstorms. The Sumerians successfully rebuilt these cities, which continued to thrive for centuries, thanks to improved weather conditions and advanced technology for flood management and irrigation. Egypt's innovative farming techniques took advantage of the annual Nile flooding. The Hittite Empire and the Mycenaean civilization perished during the Bronze Age collapse, undone by a mega-drought, earthquakes, war, and disrupted sea trade. Climate change, like drought and desertification, also triggered the Indus Valley civilization's fall. Earthquakes that shifted rivers disrupted farming and river trade. However, in China, astute flood control helped Yu the engineer save the day and become the first emperor of the Xia dynasty.

Whether short or long-lived, these ancient civilizations contributed to our modern structures and ideologies. The Roman Republic was the foundation for modern democracy. Classical Greek philosophy shaped Roman politics and continues to influence our thinking today. The Persian Empire pioneered an administrative system that influenced the Roman Empire and today's governmental systems.

Through innovations in writing, technology, art, architecture, governance, and philosophy, these civilizations continue to impact us today.

Here's another book by Enthralling History that you might like

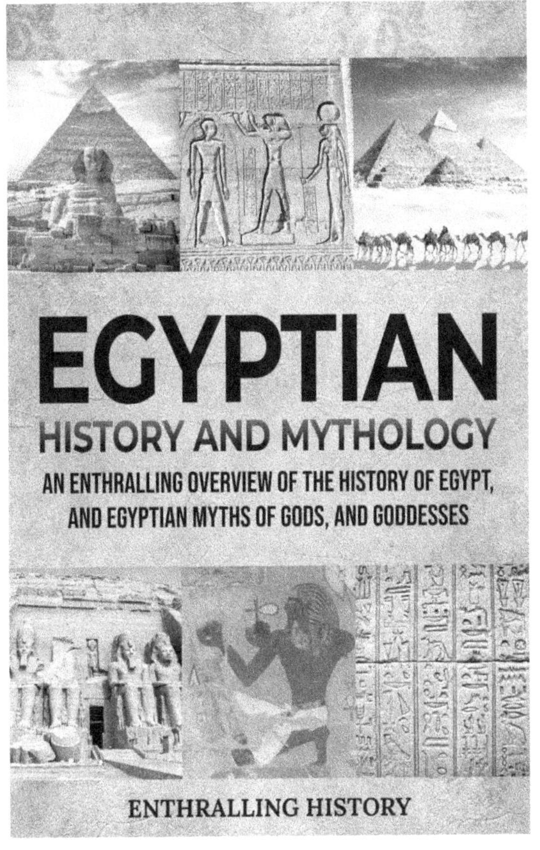

Free limited time bonus

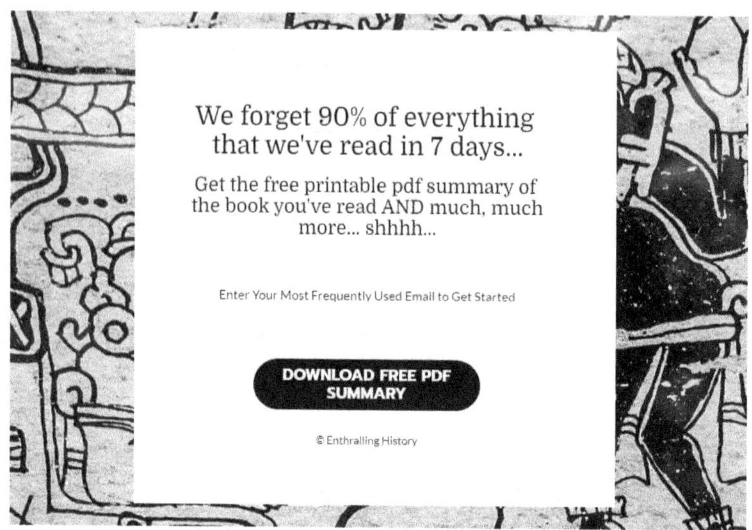

Stop for a moment. We have a free bonus set up for you. The problem is this: we forget 90% of everything that we read after 7 days. Crazy fact, right? Here's the solution: we've created a printable, 1-page pdf summary for this book that you're reading now. All you have to do to get your free pdf summary is to go to the following website:

https://livetolearn.lpages.co/enthrallinghistory/

Or, Scan the QR code!

Once you do, it will be intuitive. Enjoy, and thank you!

Bibliography

Part 1: History of Empires

Barchiesi, Alessandro and Walter Scheidel. *The Oxford Handbook of Roman Studies*. Oxford University Press, 2010.

Beate, Dignas and Engelbert Winter. *Rome and Persia in Late Antiquity. Neighbours and Rivals*. Cambridge University Press, 2007.

Bevan, E. R. *The House of Ptolemy*. Methuen Publishing, 1927. https://penelope.uchicago.edu/Thayer/E/Gazetteer/Places/Africa/Egypt/_Texts/BEVHOP/6*.html.

Boatwright, Mary T., Daniel J. Gargola, Noel Lenski, Richard J. A. Talbert. *The Romans: From Village to Empire: A History of Rome from Earliest Times to the End of the Western Empire*. Oxford University Press, November 22, 2011.

Clements, Jonathan. *The First Emperor of China*. Sutton Publishing, 2007.

Coe, Michael D., Javier Urcid, Rex Koontz. *Mexico: From the Olmecs to the Aztecs*. Thames & Hudson, September 17, 2019.

Cooper, Jerrold S. and Wolfgang Heimpel. "The Sumerian Sargon Legend." *Journal of the American Oriental Society* 103, no. 1 (1983): 67–82. https://doi.org/10.2307/601860.

Dalziel, Nigel and John Mackenzie. *The Penguin Historical Atlas of the British Empire*. Penguin Books, 2006.

Davidson, Ian. *The French Revolution*. Pegasus Books, 2017.

De la Bedoyere, Guy. *The Fall of Egypt and the Rise of Rome: A History of the Ptolemies*. Yale University Press, 2024.

Dio, Cassius. *Roman History*. Translated by H. B. Foster. Published in Vol. I of the Loeb Classical Library edition, Macmillan Publishers, 1914. https://penelope.uchicago.edu/Thayer/E/Roman/Texts/Cassius_Dio/1*.html.

Duncan, Michael. *The Storm Before the Storm: The Beginning of the End of the Roman Republic.* Public Affairs, 2017.

Elzey, Wayne. "A Hill on a Land Surrounded by Water: An Aztec Story of Origin and Destiny." *History of Religions,* 31, no. 2 (1991):105-49. http://www.jstor.org/stable/1063021.

Eppihimer, Melissa. "Assembling King and State: The Statues of Manishtushu and the Consolidation of Akkadian Kingship." In *American Journal of Archaeology* 114, no. 3 (2010): 365-80. http://www.jstor.org/stable/25684286.

Fenby, Jonathan. *The Dragon Throne: China's Emperors from the Qin to the Manchu.* Quercus Publishing, Ltd., 2015.

Ferguson, Niall. *Empire: How Britain Made the Modern World.* Penguin Books, 2018.

Foster, Benjamin R. *The Age of Agade: Inventing Empire in Ancient Mesopotamia.* Routledge, 2016.

Gardiner, Sir Alan. *Egypt of the Pharaohs.* Oxford: University Press, 1979.

Grayson, A. K. "The Empire of Sargon of Akkad." *Archiv Für Orientforschung* 25 (1974): 56-64. http://www.jstor.org/stable/41636304.

Hassig, Ross. *Time, History, and Belief in Aztec and Colonial Mexico.* University of Texas Press, 2001.

History and Mythology of the Aztecs: The Codex Chimalpopoca. Translated by John Bierhorst. The University of Arizona Press, 1992.

Hölbl, Günther. *A History of the Ptolemaic Empire.* Translated by Tina Saavedra. Routledge, 2000.

James, Lawrence. *The Rise and Fall of the British Empire.* St. Martin's Press, 1997.

Kenez, Peter. *A History of the Soviet Union from the Beginning to Its Legacy.* Cambridge University Press, 2016.

Lewis, Mark Edward. *The Early Chinese Empires: Qin and Han.* Harvard University Press, 2007.

Livy. *The Rise of Rome: Books One to Five.* Oxford: Oxford University Press, July 1, 2009.

Manning, J. G. *Land and Power in Ptolemaic Egypt.* Cambridge University Press, 2007.

Martin, Thomas R. *Ancient Rome: From Romulus to Justinian.* Yale University Press, September 10, 2013.

McLynn, Frank. *Genghis Khan: His Conquests, His Empire, His Legacy.* Da Capo Press, 2015.

McMeekin, Sean. *The Russian Revolution.* Basic Books, 2017.

Morton, Nicholas. *The Mongol Storm: Making and Breaking Empires in the Medieval Near East.* Basic Books, 2022.

Plutarch. *Fall of the Roman Republic.* London: Penguin Classics, April 25, 2006. https://archive.org/stream/FallOfTheRomanRepublicPlutarch.rOpts/Fall%20Of TheRomanRepublic%20Plutarch.r-opts_djvu.txt.

Pollock, Susan. *Ancient Mesopotamia.* Cambridge University Press, 1999.

Popkin, Jeremy D. *A New World Begins: A History of the French Revolution.* Basic Books, 2019.

Sargon and Ur-Zababa. *The Electronic Text Corpus of Sumerian Literature.* Oxford: Faculty of Oriental Studies, University of Oxford, 2006. https://etcsl.orinst.ox.ac.uk/cgi-bin/etcsl.cgi?text=t.2.1.4#.

Schama, Simon. *Citizens: A Chronicle of the French Revolution.* Vintage Books, 1990.

Sheridan, Paul. "The Sacred Chickens of Rome." *Anecdotes from Antiquity.* November 8, 2015. http://www.anecdotesfromantiquity.net/the-sacred-chickens-of-rome/.

Siani-Davies, Mary. "Ptolemy XII Auletes and the Romans." *Historia: Zeitschrift Für Alte Geschichte* 46, no. 3 (1997): 306–40. http://www.jstor.org/stable/4436474.

Sima Qian, *Shiji, Records of the Grand Scribe.* China Knowledge: An Encyclopaedia on Chinese History and Literature. Accessed March 13, 2025. http://www.chinaknowledge.de/Literature/Historiography/shiji.html.

Sumerian King List. Translated by Jean-Vincent Scheil, Stephen Langdon, and Thorkild Jacobsen. Livius. Accessed March 13, 2025. https://www.livius.org/sources/content/anet/266-the-sumerian-king-list/#Translation

The Legend of Sargon of Akkadê, c. 2300 BCE. Fordham University, Internet Ancient History Sourcebook. Accessed March 13, 2025. https://sourcebooks.fordham.edu/ancient/2300sargon1.asp.

The Secret History of the Mongols. Translated by Christopher Atwood. Penguin Classics, 2023.

Townsend, Richard F. *The Aztecs* (3rd, revised ed.). Thames & Hudson, 2009.

Weatherford, Jack. *Genghis Khan and the Making of the Modern World.* Broadway Books, 2004.

Westenholz, Joan Goodnick. *Legends of the Kings of Akkade: The Texts.* Eisenbrauns, 1997.

Zubok, Vladislav M. *Collapse: The Fall of the Soviet Union.* Yale University Press, 2022.

Part 2: Ancient Civilizations

Africanus, Sextus Julius. "The king lists of Africanus." Peter Lundström, 2011. Accessed May 19, 2025. https://pharaoh.se/africanus-king-list.

Barchiesi, Alessandro, and Walter Scheidel. *The Oxford Handbook of Roman Studies.* Oxford University Press, 2010.

Beate, Dignas, and Engelbert Winter. *Rome and Persia in Late Antiquity. Neighbours and Rivals.* Cambridge University Press, 2007.

Bertman, Stephen. *Handbook to Life in Ancient Mesopotamia.* Oxford University Press, 2005.

Boatwright, Mary T., Daniel J. Gargola, Noel Lenski, Richard J. A. Talbert. *The Romans: From Village to Empire: A History of Rome from Earliest Times to the End of the Western Empire.* Oxford University Press, November 22, 2011.

Brosius, Maria. *A History of Ancient Persia: The Achaemenid Empire.* Wiley Blackwell, 2020.

Castleden, Rodney. *The Knossos Labyrinth: A New View of the 'Palace of Minos' at Knossos.* Routledge, 2012.

Clements, Jonathan. *The First Emperor of China.* Sutton Publishing, 2007.

Clogg, Richard. *A Concise History of Greece.* Cambridge University Press, 2021.

Dalley, Stephanie. *Myths from Mesopotamia: Creation, the Flood, Gilgamesh, and Others.* Oxford University Press, 2008.

Dio, Cassius. *Roman History.* Translated by H. B. Foster. Published in Vol. I of the Loeb Classical Library edition, Macmillan Publishers, 1914. https://penelope.uchicago.edu/Thayer/E/Roman/Texts/Cassius_Dio/1*.html.

Dunand, Françoise, and Christiane Zivie-Coche. *Gods and Men in Egypt: 3000 BCE to 395 CE.* Translated by David Lorton. Cornell University Press, 2004.

Enuma Elish: The Seven Tablets of Creation. Translated by Leonard William King, 1902. https://www.sacred-texts.com/ane/stc/index.htm.

Eridu Genesis. Translated by Thorkild Jacobson. Livius, last updated 2020. https://www.livius.org/sources/content/oriental-varia/eridu-genesis/

Fenby, Jonathan. *The Dragon Throne: China's Emperors from the Qin to the Manchu.* Quercus Publishing, Ltd., 2015.

Gardiner, Sir Alan. *Egypt of the Pharaohs.* University Press, 1979.

"Gilgamesh and Aga." *The Electronic Text Corpus of Sumerian Literature,* Faculty of Oriental Studies, University of Oxford, 2000. https://etcsl.orinst.ox.ac.uk/section1/tr1811.htm.

Grayson, Albert Kirk. *Assyrian Rulers of the Early First Millennium BC: I (1114-859 BC).* University of Toronto Press, 2002. https://ia804706.us.archive.org/26/items/AssyrianRulersOfTheEarlyFirstMillenni

umBc11114-859Bc/A.Kirk_Grayson_Assyrian_Rulers_of__Early_First_MBookFi.org.pdf.

Grayson, A. K. *Assyrian Rulers of the Early First Millennium BC II (858-745 BC)*. University of Toronto Press, 1996.

Hoffner, Harry A. *Letters from the Hittite Kingdom: Writings from the Ancient World.*" Society of Biblical Literature, 2009.

Kelder, Jorrit M. (2010). *The Kingdom of Mycenae: A Great Kingdom in the Late Bronze Age Aegean.* CDL Press, 2010.

Kenoyer, Jonathan Mark. *Ancient Cities of the Indus Valley Civilization.* Oxford University Press, 1998.

Kuhrt, Amélie. *The Persian Empire: A Corpus of Sources from the Achaemenid Period.* Routledge, 2007.

Lazaridis, I, A. Mittnik, N. Patterson, S. Mallick, N. Rohland, S. Pfrengle, A. Furtwängler, et al. "Genetic Origins of the Minoans and Mycenaeans." *Nature* 548 (August 10, 2017): 214-18. https://doi.org/10.1038/nature23310.

Lewis, Mark Edward. *The Early Chinese Empires: Qin and Han.* Harvard University Press, 2007.

Livy. *The Rise of Rome: Books One to Five.* Oxford University Press, July 1, 2009.

Lupack, Susan. "Mycenaean Religion." *The Oxford Handbook of the Bronze Age Aegean,* edited by Eric H. Cline, 2012. https://doi.org/10.1093/oxfordhb/9780199873609.013.0020.

Martin, Thomas R. *Ancient Rome: From Romulus to Justinian.* Yale University Press, September 10, 2013.

Matyszak, Philip. *The Rise of the Hellenistic Kingdoms, 336–250 BC.* Pen & Sword Military, 2019.

Parpola, Asko. *The Roots of Hinduism: The Early Aryans and the Indus Civilization.* Oxford University Press, 2015.

Pinch, Geraldine. *Egyptian Mythology: A Guide to the Gods, Goddesses, and Traditions of Ancient Egypt.* Oxford University Press, 2002.

Plato. *The Republic.* Translated by Benjamin Jowett. Daniel C. Stevenson, Web Atomics. Accessed June 28, 2025. http://classics.mit.edu/Plato/republic.9.viii.html.

Pollock, Susan. *Ancient Mesopotamia.* Cambridge University Press, 1999.

Pomeroy, Sarah B., Stanley M. Burstein, Walter Donlan, Jennifer Tolbert Roberts, David W. Tandy, and Georgia Tsouvala. *Ancient Greece: Politics, Society, and Culture.* Oxford University Press, 2020.

Possehl, Gregory L. *The Indus Civilization: A Contemporary Perspective.* AltaMira Press, 2002.

Raulwing, Peter. *The Kikkuli Text. Hittite Training Instructions for Chariot Horses in the Second*
Half of the 2nd Millennium B.C. and Their Interdisciplinary Context. The Long Riders Guild Academic Foundation, 2009. http://www.lrgaf.org/Peter_Raulwing_The_Kikkuli_Text_MasterFile_Dec_2009.pdf.

Rhodes, P. J. *Athenian Democracy* (Edinburgh Readings on the Ancient World). Oxford University Press, 2004.

Sima Qian, *Shiji, Records of the Grand Scribe.* Ulrich Theobold, 2010. http://www.chinaknowledge.de/Literature/Historiography/shiji.html.

Sumerian King List. Translated by Jean-Vincent Scheil, Stephen Langdon, and Thorkild Jacobsen. Livius, last updated 2020. https://www.livius.org/sources/content/anet/266-the-sumerian-king-list/#Translation.

The Epic of Gilgamesh. Translated by N. K. Sandars. Penguin Classics, 1960.

The Great Inscription of Tukulti-Ninurta I. Translated by Yigal Bloch, 2017. https://omnika.org/texts/626.

"This Old Pyramid" Transcript. *NOVA.* PBS Airdate: February 4, 1997. https://www.pbs.org/wgbh/nova/transcripts/1915mpyramid.html.

Waters, Matt. *Ancient Persia: A Concise History of the Achaemenid Empire, 550-330 BCE.* Cambridge University Press, 2014.

Weatherford, Jack. *Genghis Khan and the Making of the Modern World.* Broadway Books, 2004.

Xenophon. *Cyropaedia: The Education of Cyrus.* Translated by Henry Graham Dakyns. Project Gutenberg, last updated 2011. https://www.gutenberg.org/files/2085/2085-h/2085-h.htm.

Zarghamee, Reza. *Discovering Cyrus: The Persian Conqueror Astride the Ancient World.* Mage Publishers, 2018.

Image Sources

1 Photo modified: names of modern-day countries and seas added. Credit: Karl Musser, CC BY-SA 2.5 <https://creativecommons.org/licenses/by-sa/2.5>, via Wikimedia Commons; https://commons.wikimedia.org/wiki/File:Tigr-euph.png

2 https://commons.wikimedia.org/wiki/File:Ur_chariot.jpg

3 https://commons.wikimedia.org/wiki/File:Tableta_con_trillo.png

4 Photo Modified: zoomed in. Source: Metropolitan Museum of Art, CC0, via Wikimedia Commons; https://commons.wikimedia.org/wiki/File:Cylinder_seal,ca._18th%E2%80%9317th_century_B.C._Babylonian.jpg

5 https://commons.wikimedia.org/wiki/File:Sargon_of_Akkad_(1936).jpg

6 Map zoomed-in, labels of seas and regions added. Source: Enyavar, CC BY-SA 4.0 <https://creativecommons.org/licenses/by-sa/4.0>, via Wikimedia Commons https://commons.wikimedia.org/wiki/File:Alter_Orient_2500BC.svg#/media/File:Ancient_Near_East_2300BC.svg

7 Jans, G. / Bretschneider, J. 1998: "Wagon and Chariot Representations in the Early Dynastic Glyptic," BY-SA 4.0 <https://creativecommons.org/licenses/by-sa/4.0>, via Wikimedia Commons: https://commons.wikimedia.org/wiki/File:Beydar-1.png

8 Rama, CC BY-SA 2.0 FR <https://creativecommons.org/licenses/by-sa/2.0/fr/deed.en>, via Wikimedia Commons: https://commons.wikimedia.org/wiki/File:Naram-Sin.jpg

9 https://commons.wikimedia.org/wiki/File:QinShiHuang19century.jpg

10 https://commons.wikimedia.org/wiki/File:CheLieShangYang.JPG

11 Philg88, CC BY-SA 3.0 <https://creativecommons.org/licenses/by-sa/3.0>, via Wikimedia Commons: https://commons.wikimedia.org/wiki/File:EN-WarringStatesAll260BCE.jpg

12 Photo zoomed in; Source: Tris T7, CC BY-SA 4.0
<https://creativecommons.org/licenses/by-sa/4.0>, via Wikimedia Commons:
https://commons.wikimedia.org/wiki/File:Qin_Shi_Huang_Emperor_by_Trisorn_Tri
boon_70.jpg

13 Luca Casartelli, CC BY-SA 2.0 <https://creativecommons.org/licenses/by-sa/2.0>, via
Wikimedia Commons: https://commons.wikimedia.org/wiki/File:Great_Wall_of_
China_in_Beijing_(21006986438).jpg

14 https://commons.wikimedia.org/wiki/File:La_expedici%C3%B3n_de_Xu_
Fu,_por_Utagawa_Kuniyoshi.jpg

15 User:airunp, Public domain, via Wikimedia Commons:
https://commons.wikimedia.org/wiki/File:Xian_guerreros_terracota_detalle.JPG

16 https://commons.wikimedia.org/wiki/File:Cesare_Maccari._Appius_
Claudius_Caecus_in_senate.jpg

17 Mathiasrex, CC BY-SA 3.0 <http://creativecommons.org/licenses/by-sa/3.0/>, via
Wikimedia Commons; https://commons.wikimedia.org/wiki/File:Romtrireme.jpg

18 Mary Harrsch, CC BY-SA 4.0 <https://creativecommons.org/licenses/by-sa/4.0>, via
Wikimedia Commons: https://commons.wikimedia.org/wiki/File:The_First_
Triumvirate_of_the_Roman_Republic_720X480.jpg

19 Labels added. Source: Shuaaa2, CC BY 4.0
<https://creativecommons.org/licenses/by/4.0>, via Wikimedia Commons:
https://commons.wikimedia.org/wiki/File:Roman_Republic_-_50_BC.png

20 https://commons.wikimedia.org/wiki/File:Venus_and_Cupid_from_the_
House_of_Marcus_Fabius_Rufus_at_Pompeii,_most_likely_a_depiction_of_Cleopat
ra_VII_(2).jpg

21 Stephencdickson, CC BY-SA 4.0 <https://creativecommons.org/licenses/by-sa/4.0>,
via Wikimedia Commons: https://commons.wikimedia.org/wiki/File:
Augustus_Caesar.png

22 Igor Merit Santos, CC BY-SA 4.0 <https://creativecommons.org/licenses/by-sa/4.0>,
via Wikimedia Commons: https://commons.wikimedia.org/wiki/File:
The_Great_Library_of_Alexandria,_O._Von_Corven,_19th_century.jpg

23 Ptolemaic Kingdom III-II century BC - ru.svg: Kaidor (talk · contribs)derivative work:
rowanwindwhistler (talk)derivative work: Amphipolis, CC BY-SA 4.0
<https://creativecommons.org/licenses/by-sa/4.0>, via Wikimedia Commons:
https://commons.wikimedia.org/wiki/File:Ptolemaic_Kingdom_III-II_century_BC_-
_en.svg

24 Scan by NYPL, CC BY-SA 4.0 <https://creativecommons.org/licenses/by-sa/4.0>, via
Wikimedia Commons: https://commons.wikimedia.org/wiki/File:Ptolemy
_(II)_Philadelphos.jpg

25 Burger, Ludwig, CC BY-SA 2.5 <https://creativecommons.org/licenses/by-sa/2.5>, via
Wikimedia Commons: https://commons.wikimedia.org/wiki/File:Coin_of_
Ptolemy_V.,_Epiphanes_(1878)_-_TIMEA.jpg

26 Jean-Léon Gérôme, oil on canvas, 1866., CC BY-SA 4.0
<https://creativecommons.org/licenses/by-sa/4.0>, via Wikimedia Commons:
https://commons.wikimedia.org/wiki/File:Cleopatra_Before_Caesar.png

27 Daderot, CC0, via Wikimedia Commons:
https://commons.wikimedia.org/wiki/File:Cleopatra_VII_statue_fragment,_69-
30_BC_-_Royal_Ontario_Museum_-_DSC09761.JPG

28 https://commons.wikimedia.org/wiki/File:Roman_Wall_painting_from_the_
House_of_Giuseppe_II,_Pompeii,_1st_century_AD,_death_of_Sophonisba,_but_m
ore_likely_Cleopatra_VII_of_Egypt_consuming_poison.jpg

29 https://commons.wikimedia.org/wiki/File:DiezAlbumsArmedRiders_I.jpg

30 Photo zoomed in. Mongol region circled. Source: Talessman at English Wikipedia,
CC BY 3.0 <https://creativecommons.org/licenses/by/3.0>, via Wikimedia
Commons: https://commons.wikimedia.org/wiki/File:Asia_1200ad.jpg

31 https://commons.wikimedia.org/wiki/File:YuanEmperorAlbumGenghisPortrait.jpg

32 https://commons.wikimedia.org/wiki/File:Tem%C3%BCjin_proclaimed_
as_Genghis_Khan_in_1206_Jami%27_al-tawarikh_manuscript.jpg

33 Canuckguy and many others, CC BY-SA 4.0
<https://creativecommons.org/licenses/by-sa/4.0>, via Wikimedia Commons
https://upload.wikimedia.org/wikipedia/commons/thumb/9/9b/Great_Mongol_Empir
e_map.svg/3100px-Great_Mongol_Empire_map.svg.png

34 https://commons.wikimedia.org/wiki/File:HulaguAndDokuzKathun.JPG

35 https://commons.wikimedia.org/wiki/File:ToltecaChichimeca_Chicomostoc.jpg

36 British Museum, CC BY-SA 4.0 <https://creativecommons.org/licenses/by-sa/4.0>, via
Wikimedia Commons; https://commons.wikimedia.org/wiki/File:Double_headed_
turquoise_serpentAztecbritish_museum.jpg

37 https://commons.wikimedia.org/wiki/File:Boturini_Codex_(folio_4).JPG

38 https://commons.wikimedia.org/wiki/File:Escudo_de_la_
Rep%C3%BAblica_Central_Mexicana.svg

39 https://commons.wikimedia.org/wiki/File:El_templo_mayor_en_Tenochtitlan.png

40 Map zoomed in. Source: File:Lago de Texcoco-posclásico.png: YavidaxiuFile:Valley
of Mexico c.1519-fr.svg: historicair 13:51, 11 September 2007 (UTC)derivative work:
Sémhur, CC BY-SA 4.0 <https://creativecommons.org/licenses/by-sa/4.0>, via
Wikimedia Commons: https://commons.wikimedia.org/wiki/File:
Basin_of_Mexico_1519_map-en.svg

41 Manuel de Corselas, CC BY-SA 3.0 <https://creativecommons.org/licenses/by-sa/3.0>,
via Wikimedia Commons: https://commons.wikimedia.org/wiki/File:
M%C3%A1scara_de_Tezcatlipoca._British_Museum._MPLC_01.jpg

42 en:User:Ancheta Wis, CC BY-SA 2.5 <https://creativecommons.org/licenses/by-
sa/2.5>, via Wikimedia Commons; https://commons.wikimedia.org/wiki/File:
Aztec_Sun_Stone_Replica_cropped.jpg

43 Ramirez72, Andersmusician, Vadac, CC BY-SA 2.5
<https://creativecommons.org/licenses/by-sa/2.5>, via Wikimedia Commons:
https://commons.wikimedia.org/wiki/File:British_Empire.png

44 https://commons.wikimedia.org/wiki/File:Portrait_of_East_India_
Company_official.jpg

45 https://commons.wikimedia.org/wiki/File:Sepoy_Mutiny_1857.png

46 https://commons.wikimedia.org/wiki/File:Dore_London.jpg

47 https://commons.wikimedia.org/wiki/File:Amy_Carmichael_with_children2.jpg

48 https://commons.wikimedia.org/wiki/File:Mahatma-Gandhi,_studio,_1931.jpg

49 https://commons.wikimedia.org/wiki/File:Queen_Elizabeth_II_on_her_
Coronation_Day_(cropped_2).jpg

50 https://commons.wikimedia.org/wiki/File:Marie-Antoinette,_1775_-
_Mus%C3%A9e_Antoine_L%C3%A9cuyer.jpg

51 https://commons.wikimedia.org/wiki/File:Chateau_Versailles_Galerie_des_Glaces.jpg

52 https://commons.wikimedia.org/wiki/File:Anonyme_-
_Prise_de_la_Bastille,_le_14_juillet_1789_(P804)_-_P804_-
_Mus%C3%A9e_Carnavalet.jpg

53 https://commons.wikimedia.org/wiki/File:Guillotine_(PSF).png

54 https://commons.wikimedia.org/wiki/File:Russian_poster_WWI_009.jpg

55 https://commons.wikimedia.org/wiki/File:Lenin-last-underground,_1917.jpg

56 https://commons.wikimedia.org/wiki/File:Revoluci%C3%B3n-marzo-rusia--
russianbolshevik00rossuoft.png

57 Steve Knight from Halstead, United Kingdom, CC BY 2.0
<https://creativecommons.org/licenses/by/2.0>, via Wikimedia Commons:
https://commons.wikimedia.org/wiki/File:Long_Live_the_USSR!_Blueprint_for_the_
Brotherhood_of_all_Working_Classes_of_all_the_World%27s_Nationalities!_1935_
(51724375511).jpg

58 Mos.ru, CC BY 4.0 <https://creativecommons.org/licenses/by/4.0>, via Wikimedia
Commons: https://commons.wikimedia.org/wiki/File:Laika_in_1957.jpg

59 Labels of today's countries and seas added for context. Karl Musser, CC BY-SA 2.5
<https://creativecommons.org/licenses/by-sa/2.5>, via Wikimedia Commons;
https://commons.wikimedia.org/wiki/File:Tigr-euph.png

60 ALFGRN CC BY-SA 2.0 <https://creativecommons.org/licenses/by-sa/2.0>, via
Wikimedia Commons; https://commons.wikimedia.org
/w/index.php?curid=78172134

61 Umma, CC BY-SA 3.0 <http://creativecommons.org/licenses/by-sa/3.0/>, via
Wikimedia Commons; https://commons.wikimedia.org/wiki/File:Sumer_map.jpg

62 Louvre Museum, CC BY 3.0 <https://creativecommons.org/licenses/by/3.0>, via
Wikimedia Commons: https://commons.wikimedia.org/wiki/File:

P1150884_Louvre_Uruk_III_tablette_%C3%A9criture_pr%C3%A9cun%C3%A9ifor
me_AO19936_rwk.jpg

63 https://commons.wikimedia.org/wiki/File:Sumerian_26th_c_Adab.jpg

64 https://commons.wikimedia.org/wiki/File:The_White_Temple_%27E_at_
Uruk,_3500-3000_BCE.jpg

65 Osama Shukir Muhammed Amin FRCP(Glasg), CC BY-SA 4.0
<https://creativecommons.org/licenses/by-sa/4.0>, via Wikimedia Commons:
https://commons.wikimedia.org/wiki/File:Warka_mask_(cropped).jpg

66 LeastCommonAncestor, CC BY-SA 3.0 <https://creativecommons.org/licenses/by-
sa/3.0>, via Wikimedia Commons:
https://commons.wikimedia.org/wiki/File:Standard_of_Ur_-_War_-
_Detail_Bottom_Left.jpg

67 https://commons.wikimedia.org/wiki/File:Seal_dedicated_to_Ur-
Nammu_(III_Dynasty_Ur)_(Ancient_Seals_of_the_Near_East,_No._6)_(1940).jpg

68 Map zoomed in. Jeff Dahl, CC BY-SA 4.0 <https://creativecommons.org/licenses/by-
sa/4.0>, via Wikimedia Commons:
https://commons.wikimedia.org/wiki/File:Ancient_Egypt_map-en.svg

69 https://commons.wikimedia.org/wiki/File:Design_of_the_Abydos_
token_glyphs_dated_to_3400-3200_BCE.jpg

70 Quibell,1898, pl. 13, CC BY-SA 4.0 <https://creativecommons.org/licenses/by-
sa/4.0>, via Wikimedia Commons:
https://commons.wikimedia.org/wiki/File:Narmer_Palette_verso.svg

71 Charles J. Sharp, CC BY-SA 3.0 <https://creativecommons.org/licenses/by-sa/3.0>, via
Wikimedia Commons:
https://commons.wikimedia.org/wiki/File:Saqqara_pyramid_ver_2.jpg

72 Photo zoomed in. lienyuan lee, CC BY 3.0
<https://creativecommons.org/licenses/by/3.0>, via Wikimedia Commons:
https://commons.wikimedia.org/wiki/File:Bent_Pyramid_%E6%9B%B2%E6%8A%98
%E9%87%91%E5%AD%97%E5%A1%94_-_panoramio.jpg

73 Walkerssk, CC0, via Wikimedia Commons:
https://commons.wikimedia.org/wiki/File:Pyramids_in_Giza_-_Egypt.jpg

74 Petar Milošević, CC BY-SA 4.0 <https://creativecommons.org/licenses/by-sa/4.0>, via
Wikimedia Commons: https://commons.wikimedia.org/wiki/File:Great_
Sphinx_of_Giza_(%D8%A3%D8%A8%D9%88_%D8%A7%D9%84%D9%87%D9%
88%D9%84).jpg

75 Diego Delso, CC BY-SA 4.0 <https://creativecommons.org/licenses/by-sa/4.0>, via
Wikimedia Commons: https://commons.wikimedia.org/wiki/
File:Templo_de_Karnak,_Luxor,_Egipto,_2022-04-03,_DD_170-172_HDR.jpg

76 Eternal Space, CC BY-SA 4.0 <https://creativecommons.org/licenses/by-sa/4.0>, via
Wikimedia Commons: https://commons.wikimedia.org/wiki/File:
Tefnut_(Goddess).png

77 https://commons.wikimedia.org/wiki/File:BD_Hunefer_cropped_1.jpg

78 Photo zoomed in; labels added. Avantiputra7, CC BY-SA 3.0 <https://creativecommons.org/licenses/by-sa/3.0>, via Wikimedia Commons: https://commons.wikimedia.org/wiki/File:Indus_Valley_Civilization,_Mature_Phase_(2600-1900_BCE).png

79 Mamoon Mengal, CC BY-SA 1.0 <https://creativecommons.org/licenses/by-sa/1.0>, via Wikimedia Commons: https://commons.wikimedia.org/wiki/File:Mohenjo-daro_Priesterk%C3%B6nig.jpeg

80 Saqib Qayyum, CC BY-SA 3.0 <https://creativecommons.org/licenses/by-sa/3.0>, via Wikimedia Commons: https://commons.wikimedia.org/wiki/File:Mohenjo-daro.jpg

81 Matsyameena, CC BY-SA 4.0 <https://creativecommons.org/licenses/by-sa/4.0>, via Wikimedia Commons: https://commons.wikimedia.org/wiki/File:Intaglio_seal_(H97-3433-7617-01)_Indus_Fish_symbol_.png

82 Gary Todd, CC0, via Wikimedia Commons: Commons: https://commons.wikimedia.org/wiki/File:Harappa_Indus_Valley_seal_with_fighting_scene.jpg

83 Ismoon (talk) 18:40, 21 February 2012 (UTC), CC0, via Wikimedia Commons: https://commons.wikimedia.org/wiki/File:Figure_between_two_tigers._Mold_of_Seal,_Indus_valley_civilization.jpg

84 Geoff Soper, CC BY-SA 4.0 <https://creativecommons.org/licenses/by-sa/4.0>, via Wikimedia Commons: https://commons.wikimedia.org/wiki/File:A_Punjab_Wheel,_India_c1919.jpg

85 Map zoomed in, labels added. Edited by w:nl:hanhil, Public domain, via Wikimedia Commons: https://commons.wikimedia.org/wiki/File:Levantine_Sea.jpg

86 cavorite https://www.flickr.com/photos/cavorite/, CC BY-SA 2.0 <https://creativecommons.org/licenses/by-sa/2.0>, via Wikimedia Commons: https://commons.wikimedia.org/wiki/File:Palace_of_Knossos.jpg

87 Mary Harrsch, CC BY-SA 4.0 <https://creativecommons.org/licenses/by-sa/4.0>, via Wikimedia Commons: Commons: https://commons.wikimedia.org/wiki/File:Linear_A_tablet_Clay_from_Chania.jpg

88 Zde, CC BY-SA 4.0 <https://creativecommons.org/licenses/by-sa/4.0>, via Wikimedia Commons: https://commons.wikimedia.org/wiki/File:Marine_Style,_Zakros,_1600-1450_BC,_AMH,_145043.jpg

89 https://commons.wikimedia.org/wiki/File:Knossos_Bull-Leaping_Fresco.jpg

90 Labels added. Ulamm 23:14, 20 January 2008 (UTC), CC BY-SA 3.0 <https://creativecommons.org/licenses/by-sa/3.0>, via Wikimedia Commons: https://commons.wikimedia.org/wiki/File:Peloponnisos-b2.png

91 William Neuheisel from DC, US, CC BY 2.0 <https://creativecommons.org/licenses/by/2.0>, via Wikimedia Commons: https://commons.wikimedia.org/wiki/File:Lions_Gate_at_Mycenae_(5228010382).jpg

92 Zde, CC BY-SA 4.0 <https://creativecommons.org/licenses/by-sa/4.0>, via Wikimedia Commons: https://commons.wikimedia.org/wiki/File: Linear_B_tablet,_AM_of_Mycenae,_201726.jpg

93 User:George E. Koronaios, CC BY-SA 4.0 <https://creativecommons.org/licenses/by-sa/4.0>, via Wikimedia Commons: https://commons.wikimedia.org/wiki/File:Mural_composition_from_the_Palace_of_ Thebes_(14th-13th_c._B.C.)_at_the_Archaeological_Museum_of_ Thebes_on_10_April_2019_(cropped).jpg

94 w:en:User:Gurdjieff (Lamassu Design), CC BY-SA 3.0 <https://creativecommons.org/licenses/by-sa/3.0>, via Wikimedia Commons: https://commons.wikimedia.org/wiki/File:Xia_dynasty.svg

95 僧盐, CC BY-SA 4.0 <https://creativecommons.org/licenses/by-sa/4.0>, via Wikimedia Commons: https://commons.wikimedia.org/wiki/File:%E7% BB%BF%E6%9D%BE%E7%9F%B3%E9%BE%99%E5%BD%A2%E5%99%A88.jpg

96 BabelStone, CC BY-SA 3.0 <https://creativecommons.org/licenses/by-sa/3.0>, via Wikimedia Commons: https://commons.wikimedia.org/wiki/File:Oracle_bones_at_Pitt_Rivers_Museum.jpg

97 Gary Todd, CC0, via Wikimedia Commons: https://commons.wikimedia.org/wiki/File:Shang_Chariot_Replica.jpg

98 Mary Harrsch, CC BY-SA 4.0 <https://creativecommons.org/licenses/by-sa/4.0>, via Wikimedia Commons: https://commons.wikimedia.org/wiki/File:Bronze_Bird- Shaped_Wine_Container_(Niao_Zun)_Shang_dynasty_12th- 11th_century_BCE_China.jpg

99 Labels added. Territories_of_Dynasties_in_China.gif: Ian Kiu, CC BY-SA 3.0 <http://creativecommons.org/licenses/by-sa/3.0/>, via Wikimedia Commons; https://commons.wikimedia.org/wiki/File:Zhou_dynasty_1000_BC.png

100 Photo zoomed in. Gary Lee Todd, Ph.D., CC0, via Wikimedia Commons: https://commons.wikimedia.org/wiki/File:Eastern_Zhou_Jade_Ornament_04.jpg

101 Map zoomed in, labels added. Enyavar, CC BY-SA 4.0 <https://creativecommons.org/licenses/by-sa/4.0>, via Wikimedia Commons: https://commons.wikimedia.org/wiki/File:Ancient_Near_East_1300BC.svg

102 Bernard Gagnon, CC BY-SA 3.0 <https://creativecommons.org/licenses/by-sa/3.0>, via Wikimedia Commons: https://commons.wikimedia.org/wiki/File: Sphinx_Gate,_Hattusa_01.jpg

103 https://commons.wikimedia.org/wiki/File:Weather_God.jpg

104 https://commons.wikimedia.org/wiki/File:Modern_loose_ interpretation_at_the_The_Pharaonic_Village_in_Cairo_of_a_Battle_scene_from_th e_Great_Kadesh_reliefs_of_Ramses_II_on_the_Walls_of_the_Ramesseum.jpg

105 https://commons.wikimedia.org/wiki/File:Ashur_symbol_Nimrud.png

106 Lawson G. Stone, CC BY-SA 4.0 <https://creativecommons.org/licenses/by-sa/4.0>, via Wikimedia Commons; https://commons.wikimedia.org/wiki/File:Assyrian_King_Kills_a_Lion.jpg

107 Dosseman, CC BY-SA 4.0 <https://creativecommons.org/licenses/by-sa/4.0>, via Wikimedia Commons; https://commons.wikimedia.org/wiki/File: Antakya_Archaeological_Museum_Statue_of_Suppiluliuma_sept_2019_5792.jpg

108 https://commons.wikimedia.org/wiki/File:C%2BB-Siege-Fig3-AssyrianSiegeTower.PNG

109 User Chaldean on en.wikipedia, CC BY-SA 3.0 <http://creativecommons.org/licenses/by-sa/3.0/>, via Wikimedia Commons; https://commons.wikimedia.org/wiki/File:ShalmaneserIII.jpg

110 Map zoomed in. Nigyou, CC BY-SA 3.0 <https://creativecommons.org/licenses/by-sa/3.0>, via Wikimedia Commons: https://commons.wikimedia.org/wiki/File:Neo-Assyrian_map_824-671_BC.png

111 Photo zoomed in, labels added. Natural Earth, CC BY-SA 4.0 <https://creativecommons.org/licenses/by-sa/4.0>, via Wikimedia Commons; https://commons.wikimedia.org/wiki/File:Colorful_shaded_map_of_Middle_East.jpg

112 Original: User:SzajciEnglish: User: WillemBK, CC BY-SA 3.0 <https://creativecommons.org/licenses/by-sa/3.0>, via Wikimedia Commons https://commons.wikimedia.org/wiki/File:Median_Empire-en.svg:

113 Aneta Ribarska, CC BY-SA 3.0 <https://creativecommons.org/licenses/by-sa/3.0>, via Wikimedia Commons https://commons.wikimedia.org/wiki/File: Persepolis_carvings.JPG

114 Cyrus the Great, CC BY-SA 4.0 <https://creativecommons.org/licenses/by-sa/4.0>, via Wikimedia Commons: https://commons.wikimedia.org/wiki/File:At_the_British_Museum_2024_235.jpg

115 https://commons.wikimedia.org/wiki/File:Persepolis_Reconstruction_Apadana_Chipiez.jpg

116 Frank-Haf, CC BY-SA 4.0 <https://creativecommons.org/licenses/by-sa/4.0>, via Wikimedia Commons; https://commons.wikimedia.org/wiki/File:Darius_the_Great.jpg

117 Mohammad.m.nazari, CC BY-SA 4.0 <https://creativecommons.org/licenses/by-sa/4.0>, via Wikimedia Commons; https://commons.wikimedia.org/wiki/File: Unicorn_in_Apadana,_Shush,_Iran--2017-10.jpg

118 https://commons.wikimedia.org/wiki/File:Datis_fighting_Kallimachos_at_the_Battle_of_Marathon_in_the_Stoa_Poikile_(reconstitution).jpg

119 Original creator: MossmapsCorrections according to Oxford Atlas of World History 2002, The Times Atlas of World History (1989), Philip's Atlas of World History (1999) by पाटलिपुत्र, CC BY-SA 4.0 <https://creativecommons.org/licenses/by-sa/4.0>, via Wikimedia Commons: https://commons.wikimedia.org/wiki/File:

Achaemenid_Empire_at_its_greatest_extent_according_to_Oxford_Atlas_of_World
_History_2002.jpg

120 Photo zoomed in, labels added. Greece_location_map.svg: Lencer / derivative work:
Uwe Dedering, CC BY-SA 3.0 <https://creativecommons.org/licenses/by-sa/3.0>, via
Wikimedia Commons: https://commons.wikimedia.org/wiki/File:
Greece_relief_location_map.jpg

121 Photo modified: labels added. Aegean_Sea_map_bathymetry-fr.svg: Eric Gaba (Sting
- fr:Sting)derivative work: MinisterForBadTimes, CC BY-SA 3.0
<https://creativecommons.org/licenses/by-sa/3.0>, via Wikimedia Commons;
https://commons.wikimedia.org/wiki/File:Thermopylae_%26_Artemisium_campaign
_map.png

122 https://commons.wikimedia.org/wiki/File:Ship_dashed_
against_ship,_till_the_Persian_Army_dead_strewed_the_deep_like_flowers.jpg

123 Vatican Museums, CC BY 3.0 <https://creativecommons.org/licenses/by/3.0>, via
Wikimedia Commons: https://commons.wikimedia.org/wiki/File:Pericles_Pio-
Clementino_Inv269_n4.jpg

124 Jacques-Louis David, CC0, via Wikimedia Commons;
https://commons.wikimedia.org/wiki/File:The_Death_of_Socrates_MET_DT40.jpg

125 lensnmatter, CC BY 2.0 https://creativecommons.org/licenses/by/2.0>, via
Wikimedia Commons: https://commons.wikimedia.org/wiki/File:
Caryatids_of_Erechtheion_(20419658495).jpg

126 Photo zoomed in. Paolo Villa, CC BY-SA 4.0
<https://creativecommons.org/licenses/by-sa/4.0>, via Wikimedia Commons;
https://commons.wikimedia.org/wiki/File:02_2020_Grecia_photo_Paolo_Villa_FO19
0025_(Museo_archeologico_di_Olimpia_-
_Statua_Ermes_con_Dioniso_Bambino_scolpita_da_Prassitele,_Arte_pre_Ellenistica
,_dettaglio_superiore).jpg

127 Photo zoomed in. Trougnouf, CC BY 4.0
<https://creativecommons.org/licenses/by/4.0>, via Wikimedia Commons:
https://commons.wikimedia.org/wiki/File:Maison_de_la_Louve_(DSC_0377).jpg

128 © Sémhur / Wikimedia Commons:
https://commons.wikimedia.org/wiki/File:Late_Roman_kingdom_map-blank.svg

129 https://commons.wikimedia.org/wiki/File:Fran%C3%A7ois-Joseph_Navez001.jpg

130 https://commons.wikimedia.org/wiki/File:Secessio_plebis.JPG

131 Norbert Nagel, CC BY-SA 3.0 <https://creativecommons.org/licenses/by-sa/3.0>, via
Wikimedia Commons: https://commons.wikimedia.org/wiki/File:Hera_temple_II_-
Paestum-_Poseidonia_-_July_13th_2013_-_04.jpg

www.ingramcontent.com/pod-product-compliance
Lightning Source LLC
Chambersburg PA
CBHW050751150726
48196CB00004B/424